Growing Child®

Contributors:

Phil Bach, O.D., Ph.D.

Miriam Bender, Ph.D.

Joseph Braga, Ed.D.

Laurie Braga, Ph.D.

George Early, Ph.D.

Carol R. Gestwicki, M.S.

Liam Grimley, Ph.D.

Robert Hannemann, M.D., F.A.A.P.

Sylvia Kottler, M.S.

Bill Peterson, Ph.D.

© 2012 Growing Child, Inc.

P.O. Box 2505

W. Lafayette, IN 47902

ISBN: 0-9729649-2-4

800-927-7289

www.growingchild.com

In 1971 a group of people sat around a lunch table at Purdue University to discuss the beginning of *Growing Child*. This group of developmental professionals--who became our first contributors--helped my son overcome learning disabilities which could have been addressed much earlier had my wife and I been better-informed parents.

The purpose of *Growing Child* was then and still is to provide parents with a child development newsletter that is timed to the age of their child. We wanted to help parents provide the right kind of stimulation at the right time in the child's development; to alert parents to the typical pattern of development; and to encourage parents to consult with their physician when they had questions about their child's development.

As parents, we hope that each of our children will grow up to be a good citizen, a loving spouse, a cherished friend, a friendly neighbor. Most importantly, when the time comes, we hope our children will be ready for school. But parents don't always know what they can do to help achieve these goals, and many times, no one tells them.

Having a child is one of life's most special events, and this occurs with greater ease, comfort and joy when parents assume their roles with knowledge. No one is at their best when they are living in a state of fear or uncertainty, when they are apprehensive about the well being of their child. When parents know what to expect and have reasonable expectations about their child's development, they can enjoy being a parent.

The chapters of this book are the same as the monthly newsletter issues that our subscribers receive. The best way to use this book is to mark your calendar to read the issue that is appropriate for your child's age each month.

Not every child will follow the same development exactly, but they will be close. While it will be tempting to read ahead and to try and accelerate a child's rate of development, this is not always in the best interests of the child and can lead to frustration for both child and parent.

As grandparents, one of our bits of advice to parents is to enjoy being a parent. Don't be in a hurry to make your children into adults and rob them of the joy of mud and dandelions. The time to put away teddy bears and dolls will come all too soon.

There are many ways to raise a child but the key ingredient is your unconditional love. Children need to feel that they are safe and loved. Hannah Kahn said, "Child, give me your hand that I may walk in the light of your faith in me."

We hope you will learn from *Growing Child* articles the importance of unstoppable curiosity, enthusiasm for learning, and realistic goals for your child. Enjoy the light.

Dennis Dunn, Publisher
Nancy Kleckner, Editor

> Don't be in a hurry to make your children into adults and rob them of the joy of mud and dandelions. The time to put away teddy bears and dolls will come all too soon.

Index

The Family Table

The title of this article would lead you to believe it will be about food, but it isn't. It is about family communications and how the family table is the meeting place for families.

The family table is where children learn to talk, learn to behave, take turns, be polite, not interrupt when someone else is speaking, how to share, and when you have guests, how to entertain. These are all good lessons for life.

There is a body of research to support the conclusion that families who have a family table and eat there together on a regular basis have children who do better in school and are less likely to smoke, drink or take drugs.

One study shows that eating meals with their family was a stronger predictor of academic success than whether they lived with one or both parents.

Families may not have money, education or a spouse but they do have it in their power to eat with their kids.

I recently attended a meeting where the subject was the family table. What a surprise it was to learn that there are a number of families that do not have a table on which they eat.

Instead they eat in front of the television, with family members eating at different times.

For other families, their meals featured different formats but many had several things in common. They talked, shared joys, achievements and disappointments. Each person—children included—was expected to participate and contribute.

At one family table, if the child had nothing to say, he was expected to go to the encyclopedia and bring back a point of interest.

In time, the children came to the table prepared. Their bit of information added to the conversation.

Another family used a paper tablecloth and wrote messages to each other on the paper—a starting point for an entertaining evening's discussion.

These are the habits our children will take with them and most likely merge with other traditions as they marry, have children, and eat together around their family table.

Mealtime was so important at my aunt's house that the doorbell and the telephone went unanswered.

Today this would mean no TV, cell phones or other distractions during mealtime. The family dinner is an eyeball-to-eyeball, ear-to-ear, heart-to-heart event.

It used to be said: "Children should be seen and not heard." Not anymore. I read somewhere that laughter is the best dinnertime music, and the atmosphere at your table should be that laughter is welcome.

Everyone at the table should feel free to talk, to contribute to the conversation, and encouraged to listen. This is also a good time to pass on those family traditions and stories from your childhood.

When the meal is over and the table cleared, use it for games and puzzles. This is your chance to be a role model for your children. Let them learn from you.

Each child wants to share his or her days with the most important people in their lives—their parents—other relatives, and adults. They want to be seen and to be heard. They want to be rewarded for their success by sharing their experiences with their family.

Begin having conversation and dinner together around your family table. Give your children the gift of growing up as a child in a family that cares.

Dennis D. Dunn, Publisher

For more information on Family Mealtime visit the Purdue University Center for Families' Promoting Family Meals Project: www.cfs.purdue.edu/CFF/promotingfamilymeals

FREE BONUS

Here's how to make this book work for you:

❶ Go to www.GrowingChild.com/bonus

❷ Complete the subscription form.

❸ On your child's monthly birth date, as a reminder, you will receive the Growing Child newsletter, timed to his/her age. (It will be the same or updated copy of the issue in your book.)

❹ This Free Bonus goes from the current age of your child until he or she is a senior in high school. You may also add other children to this subscription at no cost.

❺ Plus: You will also receive each month the Growing Parent newsletter and essays about "Grandma Says" (twice a month). These publications are brief and easy to read. See samples at www.GrowingChild.com/bonus.

GUARANTEE: All of our newsletter are free of commercial bias with our no-advertisement policy; all addresses are used only to administer subscriptions, and are not disclosed to other individuals or organizataions. You may cancel any subscription at any time if it does not meet your needs.

To purchase other books or send a Growing Child gift, go to: www.GrowingChild.com

NOTE: To make certain you continue to receive our e-mail, please add: service@GrowingChild.com and GrandmaSays@GrowingChild.com to your address book or safe sender list.

How Young Children Think

Our understanding of how young children think has been greatly enhanced by the work of a Swiss scientist named Jean Piaget.

While Piaget was working in France administering intelligence tests to young children, he became intrigued with the wrong answers these children gave. He noticed certain similarities in the incorrect answers of the children.

He found that young children think differently from older children. This led him to study the different stages of children's cognitive development.

Adults who develop some understanding of how young children think will become aware that a young child's thinking is different, rather than concluding that his thinking is wrong. As a result, these adults can relate to a young child in more appropriate ways.

An example will help clarify what we mean. Let's suppose Aunt Millie gives her four-year-old nephew, Joe, an expensive gift.

She also gives Joe's brother, Billy, three little presents which together cost less than Joe's one gift. But Joe is very upset because, as he says, "Billy got more presents than I did."

An adult who is aware that a young child's thinking is different could have avoided this painful experience.

She would have known that at four years of age, Joe is more concerned with concrete details—how many presents he got—than with the more abstract concept of overall cost of the presents.

Another example of how a four-year-

old child thinks differently from adults is transductive reasoning. An example would be the child who says: "It can't be afternoon yet because I haven't taken my afternoon nap."

In the child's mind, the connection between "nap" and "afternoon" is such that you can't have one without the other. (An adult, of course, also exhibits this type of illogical thinking when he says: "I must wear my lucky hat whenever I go to the game," as though there is some permanent connection between the hat and winning the game.)

Knowledge about these differences in children's thinking can help an adult relate better to a young child.

It can also help parents to better understand their youngster's behavior and to develop more effective strategies for teaching their young child.

Between the ages of two and six years, the child, in Piaget's theoretical framework, goes through the pre-operational period.

During this period the child gradually changes from one who learns primarily by doing to one who can function at a conceptual and symbolic level. He is increasingly able to represent events internally— to think about them in his mind.

He is also less dependent upon trial-and-error actions for direction of his behavior.

Words come to represent objects. The emergence of language increases the power of thought. However, the child's thinking is still strongly influenced by his perceptions.

His thinking remains centered in himself. Piaget described it as "egocentric" thinking.

The child doesn't question his own thinking even when confronted with contradictory evidence. His thinking, from his point of view, is always quite logical and correct.

This self-centered thinking will gradually decrease during years six and seven when the child begins to communicate his thoughts more to his peers and to listen to their communication.

The pre-operational child is capable of representational or symbolic thinking. For example, the word "broom" now mentally represents the object he uses to clean the floor.

Likewise, the action of riding on the broom can represent in his mind riding a horse. The child can now use symbols— words, images, or actions—to represent or stand for something else.

Using symbols, the pre-operational child can also mentally rehearse in his mind what he is planning to do.

continued on page 296

The Importance of Play

continued from page 295

It is generally through play that a four-year-old child learns about the world around her and then assimilates what she has learned into her concept of reality.

We will first discuss some of the forms of play in which a four-year-old engages and then consider some of the effects of play on her development.

At this age, children enjoy three different forms of play, namely, physical, manipulative, and symbolic play.

Physical play refers to activities that involve use of the muscles. These activities, in which there is an emphasis on action, would include running, hopping, jumping, climbing, throwing, sliding, and playing with a ball.

Manipulative play refers to activities by which a child learns to gain better control over her environment.

These activities include the use of puzzles and building blocks (which also require some physical play skills) as well as games that involve social manipulation ("What can I do to make Daddy come to me?").

Symbolic play involves manipulation, not of people, but of events and objects. These play activities would include the use of fantasy, pretend play, and nonsense rhymes.

In symbolic play, a child can change events, identities, emotions, and so on, for the sake of her play, thereby gaining more complete control over her newly created world.

In a child's life, play has important effects on development. We will discuss in particular the effects of play on the physical, cognitive, emotional, and social development of the child.

Physical development. Play activities that involve physical exercise help to promote a child's general health.

Specific activities that involve, for example, perceptual-motor skills also help to develop the child's eye-hand coordination.

Cognitive development. Through play a young child is able to try out her understanding of how the world works.

What we see in a child's play is not just trucks, dolls, teacups, and saucers. It is also the child's thoughts which are newly forming in her mind as she tries to conceptualize and understand the world as she experiences it.

At the same time, as children play together they need to use language to communicate with one another and these conversations aid language development

Emotional development. Perhaps the single most important contribution of play to emotional development is the role it has in the formation of a child's self-concept.

Play is also a means by which a child can deal with emotional conflicts (for example, by using puppets to talk about hurt feelings).

Social development. In play activities, a child has an opportunity to experiment with different roles, power relationships, and rules. For example, a young child may tell a doll or teddy bear to "sit in a corner" for some type of misbehavior.

As children play and interact with other children, these are also practicing social learning how to communicate and get along with others.

Because young children enjoy play, it becomes a very natural way for them to learn about themselves and about the world in which they live.

So, the next time you see your child engaged in play, you will know that she is not just "goofing off."

She is engaged in the "work of childhood," namely, promoting her physical, cognitive, emotional, and social development.■

He is capable of playing out, in his mind, an entire sequence of behaviors—before he tries out these same behaviors in the physical world.

His memory is also improving because of his improved rehearsal and representational abilities.

He is also better able to find lost or hidden objects because he can retrace his steps in his own mind before he retraces them in the physical world.

This is an enormous achievement which some child experts have described as "nothing short of miraculous."

But at this age a child is generally not yet capable of what Piaget called "concrete operations," which characterize the thinking of children between six and 12 years of age. This is when a child becomes capable of internal mental operations, such as addition and subtraction.

The thinking of a pre-operational child is clearly superior to the thinking of a sensorimotor child. As he enters the pre-operational period around age two, the child's way of thinking is very much like that of a sensorimotor child but, by age six, there is little resemblance.

To summarize, Piaget's theory emphasizes the qualitative changes which occur in a child's cognitive development.

To him cognitive development is the intellectual counterpart of biological adaptation to our environment.

Just as we eat food and change it into the living tissues of our bodies, so we receive information about our world through all of our senses and change these sensations into words, ideas, and actions.

And while the processes remain the same throughout life, our body structure changes from helpless infancy to capable adulthood.

Likewise our behavior, concepts, thoughts, and problem-solving abilities change as our cognitive structures mature.■

Family Size

Now that your child is four years old, you may have considered having another child in your family.

What effect might family size have on Youngster's development?

Do children from larger families have lower IQs? Is an only child always a spoiled child?

What are some characteristics of parents that need to be considered before deciding to have another child?

These are some of the questions which child development specialists have been studying in recent years.

The overwhelming evidence from these studies is that family size does have an impact on a child's personality and intellectual development.

Children from large families, for example, have been found, in general, to be more altruistic, cooperative, and responsible.

Later-born children, however, have been found to have lower IQs than the first-born in the family, and to have more learning problems in school.

However, if the children are spaced widely enough apart in age within the family—three or more years apart—these negative effects are less likely to occur.

In contrast, the single child has been found to benefit intellectually from increased interaction with adults. But single children also tend to be more self-centered, less outgoing, and sometimes have more problems with aggressive behavior.

It would be misleading to conclude from these research studies that the size of the family is either good or bad in itself.

In understanding an individual child, many other factors, such as family interactions and communication style, need to be taken into consideration.

Nevertheless these studies help to highlight various aspects of different family structures.

Since family size may affect how a family functions, parents who are aware of and sensitive to these differences can make appropriate adjustments—like those we are about to suggest—to benefit each child's personality and intellectual development.

For example, parents of a single child should try to make sure that she has adequate opportunities to interact with other children.

They should also make sure not to put an "old head" on young shoulders; that is, don't try to involve her in adult-type decision-making before she is ready.

On the other hand, parents of a large family have a very different set of concerns.

They need to make sure that too much responsibility is not thrust on the oldest child, that the middle child (or children) doesn't get squeezed out of their attention and affection.

Also the youngest child should be given opportunities for independent decision-making and for responsibility with family chores.

Parents also need to be aware of other important research findings related to having another baby. Studies have found that women over 35 years of age, as well as those 15 years of age or younger, have increased risk associated with childbirth.

They should therefore consult with a physician for an assessment of the various risks involved.

Good health, regular exercise, and good diet for the mother have been found to be important in having a healthy baby.

On the other hand, the use of tobacco, alcohol, and drugs (including medications) by the mother have been found to have harmful effects on the developing fetus. The greater the dosages used, the greater the potential harm appears to be.

In some ways, all these research findings seem to complicate our modern lives. But these research studies provide important information that every prospective parent needs to consider.■

Bad Dreams vs. Nightmares

Bad dreams are normal recurring events during the preschool years. Psychiatrists say that bad dreams appear to represent controlled anxiety.

Children between four and five years of age are known to have frequent bad dreams. For example, they may imagine during sleep that there are monsters coming in through the bedroom window.

At this point children usually awaken, sometimes with a pounding heart. They believe their dreams are external events.

By five years, however, they will come to know that their dreams are not real. Soon after they will realize that their dreams cannot be seen by others.

By about six years of age they are aware that their dreams are personal and take place inside themselves.

Nightmares are different from bad dreams. They are less common and are thought to represent uncontrolled anxiety. During the course of the day avoid anything which appears to induce fear or anxiety in your child.

While experiencing a nightmare, a child may panic or hallucinate until fully awake and in contact with the world.

In the case of nightmares, it is wise for at least one caregiver to stay with the child to provide comfort until the child is ready to go back to sleep.■

Classification: Things Alike, Things Different

We all use classification—things alike, things different—every day of our lives.

We know that aspirin and arsenic are alike in that they both begin with the letter "a." But we wouldn't survive if we couldn't tell the difference between them.

Children also learn to use classification. It helps them to create order out of what would otherwise be chaos in the world around them.

When a young child points to a stranger's dog and says "dog," adults are generally impressed that she has learned the *word* "dog."

What is even more impressive is that she has learned the *concept* "dog" and can apply it to a Chihuahua or a Great Dane.

She can also apply the concept "dog" not only to a real dog but also to a stuffed toy dog, a photograph of a dog, or a drawing of a dog.

What is the concept "dog" she has learned to recognize? How did she learn to apply it even to a kind of dog she had never previously seen?

Actually the child's concept of "dog" is only built gradually from experience using a classification system based on "same" and "different."

Try making a list of the special features that are the *same* for all dogs—but that make them *different* from all other animals.

It's not that easy to do. Yet that's how children learn to develop classification concepts in their minds. And that's why they need lots of practice with classification: getting a hold on what is the same and what is different.

You can help your child to develop classification skills in her everyday experiences by pointing out what things

are the same (and why), as well as what things are different (and why).

For example, in the supermarket you might point out that the soft drinks (Coke™, Pepsi™, 7UP™) are arranged next to one another on the shelves.

In what ways are they alike? You can drink them, they taste good, they're sweet, and they're fizzy.

Next you can ask your child in what ways these soft drinks are different. Would she prefer a 7UP or a Pepsi?

She will learn that these two soft drinks are not only different in color, but also in smell and taste.

A little girl, examining the floppy wings of a plastic grasshopper, proudly announced, "Butterfly."

"It's a grasshopper," her mother explained, "but it flies like a butterfly." "What else can fly?" asked the mother.

"Bats and airplanes—and capes fly too" answered the little girl. Her concept of flying was very basic, very practical.

A parent's comments and questions can greatly help a child to develop better clas-

sification skills.

Sometimes this involves a process known as "think aloud" in which you try to catch yourself in the act of thinking and then put words with your thoughts.

For example, if your child brings you a pair of red socks instead of the blue socks you wanted, your immediate—and unhelpful—comment might be, "No, not those ones, these ones."

The "think aloud" response (which is helpful) would be, "Please bring me the blue socks, not the red socks."

You could then put the blue socks next to her blue dress and point out to her that they would look good together because they are the *same* color.

You might also point out that the red socks and the blue dress would not look so good together because the colors are *different*.

Before you know it, your child may run to her wardrobe to see if there is a red dress that matches her red socks!

Children need to learn lots of ways in which things can be the same or different: wide, narrow; long, short; fat, thin; straight, curly; black, white. She will learn about which things flap or float, stink or sink.

In the course of a day, one can find innumerable opportunities to develop classification skills: drying the silverware, sorting clothes, and putting away toys.

The classification skills that you teach your child are ones which she will put into practice over and over again, even when you are not around.

After all, it is by means of these skills that she learns to create order out of her everyday experiences.

Being able to classify will make her life both easier and more enjoyable—and yours too!■

Improving Family Communication

Good communication within a family involves more than just exchanging words. It also involves free expression of ideas and feelings.

Improved communication results in a happier family environment.

Here are some ways in which parents can improve communication in the family.

Make communication a priority

1. The first step in improving communication in your home is to set aside a good time for the family to be together.

2. Avoid choosing times when family members have other things on their minds, such as a favorite TV show or game.

3. Remove distractions, such as a child's favorite toy, before getting together.

4. Provide a comfortable setting—preferably with soft seats rather than hard-back chairs.

5. Avoid interruptions by turning off the television set, and any other entertainment media. In that way, you make the point that family communication has a high priority in your life.

Develop good listening skills

1. Learn to be a good listener. Listen with an open mind even when you are shocked by what your child tells you.

Reserve judgment until later. Otherwise in the future, your child may withhold communication.

2. While listening, exhibit attentive nonverbal behaviors, such as showing interest and warmth toward your child.

3. Make use of silence. This gives your child time to re-think what he has said. He may sometimes even change his mind upon reflection during a long pause.

4. Observe your child's nonverbal behaviors, such as facial expressions or other outward signs of his inner feelings (such as trembling, for example).

5. Be attentive to the emotional tone of your child's speech, not just the words he uses. Sometimes his nonverbal emotional tone may contradict the verbal message (for example, if he shouts angrily, "I am NOT angry!").

Develop your child's expressive skills

1. Encourage elaboration of what your child wants to communicate. ("Tell me more about that.") Give him time to expand on his thoughts and ask him questions for clarification.

2. After giving him time to elaborate, give help if he needs it to express his thoughts, feelings, and actions more clearly.

3. Reflect back to him in your own words what you think he said for confirmation and clarification.

4. Suggest alternatives for him to evaluate if there are other thoughts you want him to consider.

5. Summarize what has been said so that there is general agreement about the outcomes of your discussion.

What to avoid

1. Avoid talking <u>at</u> your child. Instead talk <u>with</u> your child.

2. Avoid making any judgment until after all discussion is over. Harsh judgment by a parent may have a stifling effect on present or future communication by the child.

3. Avoid interrupting while your child is speaking.

4. Avoid asking "why" questions. Even mature adults don't always know why they behave in certain ways.

5. Avoid closed questions with a "yes" or "no" answer. Such questions usually provide a dead-end answer without facilitating further open communication.

6. Avoid being untruthful or insincere. Even though parents might want their child to think, for example, that they

Learn to be a good listener. Listen with an open mind, even when you are shocked by what your child tells you.

were "always good," the child is not likely to believe it.

Benefits of improved family communication

There are many benefits from improved communication within the family.

1. The child learns a sense of trust and love.

2. The child understands himself better and is more self-accepting.

3. The child learns to listen to good advice and use it.

4. Parents learn to understand their child better.

5. Parents experience fewer conflicts in the home.

6. Parents develop cooperative relationships within the family.

7. Parents establish a warm and friendly environment that will encourage future sharing of thoughts, feelings, and actions.

8. As a result of improved communication, the whole family will become more understanding, more loving, and more cohesive.

For more ideas on how to improve communication in your family, we suggest:

How to Talk So Kids Will Listen and Listen So Kids Will Talk. Faber, A. and Mazlish, E., (1980). New York: Avon Books.

Megaskills. Rich, D., (1988). Boston, MA: Houghton Mifflin.

Parenting Young Children. Dinkmeyer, D., McKay, G.D. and Dinkmeyer, J.S., (1989). Circle Pines, MN: American Guidance Service.■

Toy Safety

About fifty years ago it wasn't too difficult to select toys that were safe for a young child.

In those days, there just weren't so many toys to select from. And most of the toys available had been around for many years.

So the safety of most of them was already well-established and it would have been possible to give parents a list of toys that were considered unsafe.

Today there are about 150,000 toys available for young children. And it has been estimated that about 5,000 new toys appear on the market every year. So it is unrealistic to develop lists of safe and unsafe toys.

In place of such lists, it is better for parents to think about safety guidelines when selecting a toy for a preschool child. Here are some suggestions for choosing safe toys:

• Select toys that are developmentally appropriate for your child. In other words, match the toy with your child's age and level of development.

• Choose toys that are sturdy and not easily broken. Be aware that the toy will be dropped, thrown, or used in other ways not intended by the manufacturer.

• Look for a "nontoxic" label on the toy.

Here are some things to avoid:

• Avoid toys made of glass or thin plastic which could shatter and cause a cut.

• Likewise avoid toys with sharp points or sharp edges.

• Avoid toys that are flammable.

• Avoid toys with small parts which could be swallowed or become a choking hazard. This is especially important for children under three years of age.

Many times there are good toys and games that are not dangerous—but they do include small parts which are dangerous if a child puts one of them in his mouth.

An example would be the token or marker used to play board games. Some games do require adult supervision—even if it doesn't say so on the box.

• Avoid toys that need to be plugged into an electrical outlet.

Giving some thought to toy safety and being aware of possible dangers can greatly reduce the likelihood of injury to your child.

To report a dangerous product or a product-related injury, call the U.S. Consumer Product Safety Commission's (CPSC)hotline (1-800-638-2772) or visit CPSC's web site at:

www.saferproducts.gov

This web site also lists child safety publications that are available to consumers to print (free) from a computer as well as other publications available in hard copy.

Your report of a dangerous product may protect another child because the commission does monitor complaints and has the power to recall toys that are potentially dangerous for children.

The CPSC is charged with protecting the public from unreasonable risks of injury or death from thousands of consumer products under the agency's jurisdiction.

Their work to ensure the safety of consumer products such as toys, cribs, power tools, cigarette lights, and household chemicals has contributed significantly to the decline in the rate of deaths and injuries associated with consumer products over the past 30 years.

But, contrary to popular belief, the commission does not inspect ALL toys on the market, not even all toys imported from abroad.

It does, however, spot-check imported toys and follows up on leads or complaints it may receive about any toy.

Playing with toys is a wonderful way for a young child to learn. Toys can also provide many hours of enjoyment. Unfortunately, accidents sometimes occur, particularly with toys which are unsafe.

Ultimately it is your responsibility to determine the relative safety of the toys with which your child will play.

Take a good look at the toys you buy for your child — and other children — and the toys your child receives as gifts.

There are also others publications in local libraries and book stores that provide information about selecting good toys.■

Growing Child™

P. O. Box 2505 • W Lafayette, IN 47996
(800) 927-7289
www.GrowingChild.com

Contributing Authors
Phil Bach, O.D., Ph.D.
Miriam Bender, Ph.D.
Joseph Braga, Ed.D.
Laurie Braga, Ph.D.
George Early, Ph.D.
Carol R. Gestwicki, M.S.
Liam Grimley, Ph.D.
Robert Hannemann, M.D., F.A.A.P.
Sylvia Kottler, M.S.
Bill Peterson, Ph.D.

What It's Like To Be Four Years Old

A four-year-old child is eager to learn factual information about her world. But she still has difficulty distinguishing fact from fantasy.

Her well-developed power of imagination sometimes causes her to confuse reality with fantasy.

For example, she may report as "true" some elaborate stories she tells which are filled with themes of violence and death.

If she watches much television—and sees programs which use flashback techniques, depict an actor "dying," or encapsulate a person's whole life in 30 minutes—she is likely to be even more confused about distinguishing reality from unreality.

In trying to resolve conflicts in her mind between "fact" and "fantasy," between "good" and "bad," between "right" and "wrong," a four-year-old experiences inevitable frustrations.

Because of these frustrations it will not be too surprising to find that your child may sometimes exhibit problem behaviors at this age.

These behaviors may take different forms: open disobedience, bad language, resistance at bedtime, or even a bout of bedwetting.

In dealing with these problem behaviors, parents should keep in mind the inner conflicts their child is likely to be experiencing at this age.

Most of these conflicts are related to her newly-emerging feelings, thoughts, powers, and abilities.

In trying to sort out and cope with her experiences, she will inevitably make many mistakes. She will blunder repeatedly.

At times you may even wonder if she is deliberately testing your patience with

To help a child acquire more effective control over his actions, parents need to set firm, consistent, and reasonable limits for him. This should be combined with large doses of love and understanding.

her "impossible" behavior.

Through all of this turmoil she is learning to deal more effectively with her own behavior.

To help her acquire more effective control over her actions, parents need to set firm, consistent, and reasonable limits for her.

This should be combined with large doses of love and understanding.

In these ways your child will be helped to express openly and deal effectively with her conflicting emotions while at the same time unraveling the many mysteries in her mind.

Parents can also use problem behaviors as opportunities to teach positive, desirable behaviors, using praise and rewards for good behavior.

Instead of saying, "Don't jump around in your chair," you could make a positive statement, such as, "I'm impressed that you have worked so quietly until now."

In the words of the proverb, "You can do more with sugar than you can with vinegar."

Four years old can be a wonderful and expansive age for your child, physically, intellectually, emotionally, and socially.

By being able to participate actively as a parent in this exciting developmental process, you enrich not only your child's life but your own as well.■

The Influence of Television

Amost every American family owns or has access to a television set. In the average home, it has been estimated that the TV set is turned on for six or more hours every day.

Recent studies also indicate that, although the amount of viewing varies from one home to another, the average preschooler watches two to four hours of television each day.

Long-term TV viewing habits are usually established between 2-1/2 and six years of age.

It was also found that children from poorer families watched more television than those from more affluent families.

The amount of time spent in front of the TV set increases steadily during the preschool years.

The peak amount of TV viewing occurs during the early elementary school years.

By the time they graduate from high school, most students will have spent 12,000 hours in the classroom, and over 18,000 hours watching TV.

They will also have spent more time with the TV set than with their parents.

Positive effects

Given the great influence of television on children's lives, it is not surprising to find that in recent years many research studies have been conducted in this area.

In reporting the findings of these studies, we will begin with positive effects that were found.

Good educational TV programs can sometimes enhance young children's learning by providing information about the world outside their own immediate environment.

Research findings regarding the educational programs Sesame Street and Mister Rogers' Neighborhood were mainly positive.

These programs, of course, were spe-

cifically designed to stimulate a young child's social, cognitive, and language development.

In particular, three-year-old children who watched Sesame Street frequently, when compared with those who didn't watch the program frequently, were found to have larger vocabularies at age five.

By contrast, three-year-olds who frequently watched other noneducational programs did not have increased vocabularies at age five.

In other words, TV watching did not result in increased vocabulary unless the TV program was designed to improve language development skills.

The portrayal of children of various ethnic groups in a positive manner on Sesame Street was found to influence positively the behavior of young children who were later observed playing and interacting with children of these same various ethnic groups.

Research studies have also indicated that young children who frequently watched Mister Rogers' Neighborhood were considered by their parents to be more friendly and cooperative during play, to observe rules better, and to tolerate delays more patiently.

It was also found that the program stimulated reflective thinking in young children. The findings are not too surprising since this program was designed to help

children use imagination and creativity and develop positive self-esteem.

Some researchers point out, however, that even good TV programs deprive children of time that might be better spent in creative play and other more active developmental experiences.

TV and violence

Of all the influences of television on young children, the one that has caused the most concern is the impact of TV violence.

Research evidence accumulated over several decades and corroborated both by two Surgeon Generals' Reports and by the National Institutes of Mental Health, indicates a strong relationship between TV violence and children's aggressive behavior.

This research evidence indicates that:

(1) Up to 80 percent of primetime shows on television include violence.

(2) Although action-adventure programs intended for adults have a high frequency of violence (on average, eight violent acts per hour), the highest frequency of TV violence is found in children's cartoons (over 20 acts of violence in every hour).

(3) If verbal aggression was counted, the rate would be much higher.

(4) Children, both boys and girls, who watched violence on TV were found to be more likely to engage in aggressive behavior than those who did not watch violence on TV.

In particular, preschool children who watched TV cartoon shows with violence, later pushed, choked, and kicked their playmates a great deal more than a group of preschool children who watched non-violent TV cartoons.

(5) The amount of TV violence watched also makes a difference. The more TV violence a child watched, the more aggressive the child became.

continued on page 303

Developing a Love of Reading

One of the most precious gifts that any parent can give a four-year-old child is a love of reading.

It should be noted that at this young age we are not talking about teaching your child to become a precocious or "early" reader.

Research studies have indicated that, while some children can be taught to read at this early age, the practice should not be generally encouraged.

It was found, for example, that by age 10, "later" readers catch up with "early" readers and in some instances surpass them in reading skills and comprehension.

We are talking instead about ways in which to stimulate your child's love of reading.

If you help your child develop an interest in books at this age, you will open the gates to a world of wonder, knowledge, and entertainment—for the rest of her life.

One of the ways to instill in your child a love of reading is to help her choose books that will interest and excite her.

A good place to start, in selecting an appropriate book, is your public library. Librarians are usually trained to identify books that are suitable for your child's age level.

After the librarian has directed you to several books that are appropriate for your preschool child, let her browse through them to select the ones she wants you to read to her at home.

Be aware that her choices will most likely not be the ones you would have picked!

By now your child should have her own library card. From one library visit to another you can take care of it so that it won't be lost.

Let her use it when it is time to check out the books. In this way she will feel more involved—and more self-assured.

Some libraries have children's books on tape. These tapes are particularly useful on days when you have many chores to do around the house.

Youngster can be taught to push the "start" button to listen to her favorite stories or nursery rhymes. You can listen also in the distance while getting your own work done.

It is very important to occasionally set aside some special time during the day for reading: after dinner, before bedtime ... anywhere, anytime can be good reading time.

Just make sure to give priority to this special time with your child.

In this way she will learn that: (1) She is an important person in your life, and (2) You place a high value on reading.

If you find that there is one library book in particular that has captured her interest—for example, one that she has asked you to read and re-read to her five or six times—consider buying a copy of her very own to keep in her room.

Giving books as gifts is a wonderful way to let your child know that you think books are special. Be sure to put her books on a low shelf where she will have easy access to them.

Have plenty of reading material—books, magazines, brochures—around the house.

When you read to her, try lots of different reading materials. There is a book or magazine for every taste.

The more you read to your child, the more you will become aware of her particular interests and tastes.

Be prepared to be amazed by some of the things which spark her interest!

Lastly, let your child become aware of your own love of reading. Talk to her about the things you like to read.

Your own good example—more effectively than any words—will instill in your child a lifelong love of reading.■

continued from page 302

(6) The effects of TV violence also appear to be long-term. It was found that the amount of TV violence a child watched at age eight was related to the seriousness of criminal acts performed as an adult.

In another study, the amount of aggressive behavior exhibited by over 1500 12- to 17-year-olds. was related to the amount of TV violence they had watched.

(7) It has also been found that one of the effects of watching TV violence is that children eventually become insensitive to the pain and suffering that results from violent behavior.

(8) It was also found that "good guys" are just as likely as "bad guys" to commit violent acts.

Subtle techniques are used in TV programs and films to encourage the viewer to want a violent act to be committed.

(9) On TV programs, in general, violence is rewarded and is portrayed as a satisfying and successful way for people to get whatever they want.

Next month we will discuss ethnic and sex-role stereotypes as well as children's food commercials on TV.

The following month we will discuss the influence of television on a child's cognitive development.

We will conclude with fourteen very practical steps parents can take regarding their child's TV viewing habits.■

Parent Involvement in a Young Child's Play

It has been remarked that a parent is a young child's first and most important teacher. How then can parents take a more active part in their child's learning through play?

We will discuss four different types of parent-child play activity: (1) instructional, (2) observational, (3) interactive, and (4) self-directed play.

Instructional play

In this type of play activity, the role of the parent is to instruct, and the role of the child is to learn.

This form of interaction is most appropriate when a child needs guidance and direction in tackling a new and challenging task.

When working on a new puzzle, for example, the parent might say: "I am going to try putting this piece here because this shape matches that space, and this color matches that color."

By thinking aloud the parent is actively instructing the child in a method of problem solving which will enhance the skills of the child.

It is important to give the child an opportunity to practice the newly-learned skill immediately after the parent has taught it.

Observational play

In this form of play, the parent demonstrates a skill without formal instructions while the child observes.

A parent might initiate observational play by saying, for example: "Let's see what I can build with these blocks."

The parent then starts to build with the blocks, modeling the particular play skill which the child will learn.

Although this form of play does not involve direct verbal instruction, the parent may make some comments or ask questions ("Do you think this piece will fit?")

to help focus the child's observation and attention on the skill being modeled by the parent.

Parents can also model how to adopt a role in pretend play, or to expand concepts in play. A parent might pick up his (play) cup and say, "Hm, this is delicious. What are you cooking us for dinner?"

Interactive play

In this type of play activity, both parent and child take a co-equal active part. The parent might say, for example, "Let's work on this together."

Parent and child then become engaged in the same activity either working cooperatively or taking turns.

This assumes that the child has already acquired the basic skills to participate even though the parent may be more skillful.

Children particularly like to be praised ("You're doing a good job.") whenever they engage in interactive play with an adult.

Self-directed play

In this type of play, the child assumes a more independent role and, in general, directs his own activity. For example, the child may decide what game to play and may even decide what the rules will be.

The role of the parent in this type of play activity is to give the child as much freedom as possible while at the same time being ready to step in if the child becomes destructive, or if he may cause injury to self or others.

How to decide which type of play activity to use

It is important for parents to be aware when to become more involved in their child's play and when to assume a less active role.

In general, a child needs instruction when faced with a new and difficult task. But for instruction to be successful the child must

be in a frame of mind to learn.

If the child shows signs of fatigue, it is best to try another approach. Likewise the parent must be in a good mood—not rushed or irritable—in order for this activity to be a fun time together.

The more familiar a child is with some play activity, the greater the likelihood that self-directed play will be appropriate.

A great deal of learning can take place during self-directed play as the child uses different methods—such as trial-and-error—to face a challenging task.

With this type of play activity, inappropriate intervention by an adult may actually disrupt the child's learning.

It should be noted that the same playthings may be used with any one of these four types of play activity.

For example, with a new puzzle, a parent may begin with some direct instruction ("I'm going to put this piece here because ..."), then move later to observational play where the parent models the play skills needed and the child observes before practicing the skill.

Once the child has acquired the basic skill, parent and child can engage in interactive play during which they work side by side to solve the puzzle together.

Eventually the child can engage in self-directed play in putting together the puzzle unaided by any adult.

In summary, having some awareness of the different types of play activity can help parents assume a more effective role in their child's learning experiences.

In advancing from instructional play, (in which the child is greatly dependent on the parent), to self-directed play, (in which he assumes a more independent role), the child progresses from being a passive learner to being an active doer.∎

Psychosocial Development

In recent years educators and psychologists have been studying an important area of child development called psychosocial development.

This term refers to the psychology of social development which, as we shall see, covers a wide range of social behaviors.

An important contribution to our understanding of the psychosocial development of young children has been made by the eminent psychoanalyst, Erik Erikson.

Although Erikson's theory includes eight stages of development which cover the entire life span, we will discuss only the first three stages which relate to the preschool years.

Each psychosocial stage involves a "crisis" which shapes later development. For Erikson, a "crisis" is a developmental challenge which one faces, rather than a catastrophe in one's life.

According to Erikson's theory, the crisis during the first year of life is one of **trust versus mistrust.**

How an infant's needs are met on a regular basis during this period determines whether he develops a basic sense of trust or mistrust.

If his physical and emotional needs are consistently met in a caring manner, he will develop trust.

In turn, this trust will enable him to be open to new experiences in his environment. By contrast, a child who is deprived of a caring and loving environment may develop a sense of mistrust toward the world.

A child who has learned to trust others progresses to the next positive stage— **development of a sense of autonomy.**

By becoming more aware during toddlerhood of the meaning of the words "I," "my," and "mine," he develops a better sense of his own independence.

On the contrary, when a young child is frequently punished harshly or when his behavior is too strictly controlled, he may develop what Erikson has called "a sense of shame or doubt" which can lead to later psychological problems.

The next crisis, **initiative versus guilt,** normally occurs during the preschool years.

A four-year-old who has developed a sense of autonomy during toddlerhood is now ready to show more initiative in exploring his world.

He is learning to determine what kind of person he can become.

A preschool child is ready to take more initiative in his environment because of:

(1) His newly acquired language abilities which enable him to ask innumerable questions about anything and everything that interests him;

(2) His improved mobility skills which enable him to explore the physical world more freely; and

(3) His newly developed cognitive abilities which enable him to expand his imagination.

In his mind he can now become whatever and whomever he imagines he wants to be.

At this stage you will notice his descriptions of himself will frequently be related to his physical capabilities (for example, "I can jump this high!"), or to his possessions ("I have a pedal-car.").

By initiating his own activities, he now shows more purpose in everything he does. He also shows greater satisfaction in his activities. And he takes greater pride in whatever he accomplishes.

If you watch a four-year-old and a two-year-old child playing, for example, you are more likely to see the older child show initiative by building a tall tower with wooden blocks, whereas the younger child will want to assert autonomy by knocking down the tower.

A four-year-old who has developed a sense of autonomy during toddlerhood is now ready to show more initiative in exploring his world.

With an energy that at times seems inexhaustible, a four-year-old child is eager to learn whatever he sees someone else doing.

His enthusiasm helps him overlook any temporary failure on his part. He is ready to start over or undertake some new challenge.

On the contrary, when a child fails to develop a sense of initiative, the result, according to Erikson, is the development of a sense of guilt.

This feeling can arise when a child experiences repeated failure, sometimes related to unrealistic parental expectations.

This feeling can also be brought about when the child's primary caregivers are overcritical or too harsh in their discipline.

The child feels guilty for attempting to become independent.

Parents can help a preschool child develop a basic sense of initiative by:

(a) Providing appropriate toys, such as wooden blocks, for creative learning experiences;

(b) Encouraging exploration and initiative in play;

(c) Giving recognition to new accomplishments, and

(d) Being supportive in times of failure.

Parents also need to be patient whenever they see their preschool child make mistakes or occasionally be overly aggressive in his actions or words.

The child who develops a strong sense of initiative during the preschool years has formed the basis for later psychosocial growth and development.

Such a child develops self-confidence and a positive self-image, enabling him to face life's challenges with even greater vigor and enthusiasm.■

Bedwetting Again

Although your child may have already been successfully toilet trained, don't be too surprised if some additional bedwetting occurs during the preschool years.

Although most bedwetters are dry by age six, approximately 10 percent of all school-age children experience bedwetting problems.

In this group, for reasons not well understood, boys outnumber girls by three to one. Bedwetting can cause considerable upset and embarrassment for both the child and the parent.

Some parents mistakenly punish their child—such as by putting him in diapers—for this behavior. Such punishment will most likely only make the problem worse.

There are several possible causes for a child to wet the bed. Physical causes would include such factors as: (a) The child's bladder may not yet be sufficiently developed to hold a full night's urine; (b) His muscular responses may not yet be adequately developed to inhibit urinating; (c) He may have a hormonal imbalance, or (d) He may not awaken with a full bladder due to a pattern of unusually sound sleep.

Bedwetting may also occur if a child experiences emotional stress, such as when sleeping away from home or if a death or divorce occurs in the family.

Daytime wetting may occur even past age five whenever a child is frightened or laughs too heartily, or just forgets to go to the bathroom because he is having a really good time.

Approximately 75 percent of four-year-olds outgrow bedwetting problems without need for any form of intervention.

Although most other bedwetters would probably eventually outgrow the problem on their own, it would generally take many years for them to do so.

Among adults only one in 100 experience bedwetting problems.

Here are some suggestions for parents

on how to handle a child's bedwetting problems:

1. In most cases the best way to deal with occasional bedwetting is to treat it as normal behavior. In other words, avoid punishing the child.

Discuss the behavior with the child in a matter-of-fact manner.

2. If the bedwetting continues to occur at least two or three times a week, some common sense remedies for your child should be used, such as:

(a) Avoiding drinking large amounts of liquid before bedtime, and (b) Using the toilet immediately before getting into bed.

Growing Child

P. O. Box 2505 • W Lafayette, IN 47996
(800) 927-7289
www.GrowingChild.com

Contributing Authors

Phil Bach, O.D., Ph.D.
Miriam Bender, Ph.D.
Joseph Braga, Ed.D.
Laurie Braga, Ph.D.
George Early, Ph.D.
Carol R. Gestwicki, M.S.
Liam Grimley, Ph.D.
Robert Hannemann, M.D., F.A.A.P.
Sylvia Kottler, M.S.
Bill Peterson, Ph.D.

3. If both of these remedies are insufficient, parents can try dry-bed training which consists of waking the child to use the bathroom immediately before the parents go to bed.

With this method, the child may also be awakened at regular intervals during the night to use the bathroom.

4. If none of these remedies work, parents should consider purchasing a urine alarm device.

This consists of a moisture-sensitive pad which is connected to a battery-operated alarm. At the first sign of dampness, the alarm sounds to remind the child that it is time to use the toilet.

5. A physician may prescribe medication, such as imipramine hydrochloride (trade name, Tofranil).

Only 50 percent of children taking this drug become dry and almost all resume bedwetting when the drug treatment is discontinued.

Hence it is usually regarded only as a temporary solution. Possible side effects include increased heart rate, increased blood pressure, and loss of appetite.

A more recently developed medication called desmopressin acetate (trade name DDAVP) has been successful in some cases. It comes in the form of a nasal spray and must be prescribed by a physician.

Whatever method parents decide to use, it is best to remain calm and deal with the problem in a matter-of-fact manner. A child's feelings can easily be hurt due to the embarrassment of a wet bed.

Scolding will most likely only increase the child's anxiety which, in turn, could result in even more bedwetting.

A helpful resource for parents is a book by R. Mercer titled, "Seven Steps to Nighttime Dryness: A practical guide for parents of children with bedwetting," (Brookeville Media LLC, 2004).■

Growing Child

Discipline: Ten Rules That Can Work For You

Discipline is something that concerns all of us who care for children. We need to know how to deal with the hundreds of small and large problems that arise.

Discipline is more than punishment for misbehavior. It is the means by which we teach our children good conduct now and for the future. Every mistake a child makes can become an opportunity for new learning.

• We all want our children to grow up to be responsible adults.

• We want them to know right from wrong.

• We want them to know how to stand up for their own needs, rights, and convictions without interfering with the rights of others.

• We want them to learn inner controls rather than rely on someone else to tell them how to behave. These are the long-term goals of discipline.

It can be hard to achieve these goals. Some of the methods of discipline we use to bring a problem under control may make our children too dependent on outer control.

The time to help Youngster learn the good habits of self-discipline is now. Here are ten rules that can guide you.

1) Teach by your example. Try to act in ways you'd be proud to see Youngster copy, now and when she's grown up.

Especially at this age, Youngster learns from your example. For instance, if she

hears you lie to others, she will learn to tell lies. If you punish her for hitting another child by spanking her, she'll learn that hitting (spanking) is an acceptable action, at least for big people.

But if you show concern for Youngster's feelings, needs, and rights, she'll learn to show the same concern for others.

2) Be fair. Try to be fair in your discipline. Give Youngster a fair hearing when she does something wrong. Let her tell her point of view.

Make your punishment "fit the crime." For example, if she breaks one of her own toys, the loss of the toy is punishment enough. She doesn't need a spanking or to be told she's careless or clumsy.

If you point out to her—with kindness and sympathy—that this is why you sometimes remind her to be careful, she'll learn the lesson much more readily than if you make her feel bad.

Perhaps she'll listen better when you caution her in the future.

3) Remember the Golden Rule. Next time you reprimand or punish Youngster when she misbehaves, think about how you would feel if you were in her shoes.

Would you feel hurt, misunderstood, or angry if people treated you the way you are treating her? Or would you feel they understood your point of view even though they weren't pleased with what you had done?

If someone yelled at you or made you feel bad because you'd misbehaved, what would you learn? Would you learn to commit acts for which you were punished when you thought you could get away with it?

Would you learn to hide the truth from your parents in order to avoid punishment?

Wouldn't you prefer that Youngster trust you rather than be afraid of you?

Wouldn't you prefer that she learn not to do something because she understands why it's wrong rather than from fear of punishment?

If so, try to remember to treat her as you yourself would like to be treated.

4) Discipline with kindness and respect. When Youngster makes a mistake, let her know you don't like what she did without making her feel she's a bad person for doing it.

For example, if she hits her baby brother, take her aside and explain that you won't

continued on page 308

continued from page 307

allow her to hit him even though you understand how mad she gets when he takes her toys or interrupts her games.

Listen to her side of the story, and try to work out a solution to the problem together. Try not to make her feel guilty and ashamed.

We all make mistakes. Mistakes are an excellent opportunity to learn better ways of behaving.

5) Accentuate the positive. Let Youngster know you appreciate her doing things that are important to you. For example, thank her for helping you keep the house neat by picking up her toys and clothes.

If she forgets, gently remind her that it makes your work harder when you have to do all the work yourself. And ask for her help.

Compliment her when she takes responsibility for herself in any way, even if her efforts are awkward.

Point out the times she does things the way you've told her. For example, thank her when she asks for something instead of whining.

6) Minimize the negative. Pay more attention to the things Youngster does well than to her mistakes.

Without thinking, we often take for granted those behaviors of others that please us. Then we exaggerate out of proportion the things they do wrong.

This approach can backfire with Youngster because children tend to repeat those behaviors that get the most attention. For example, the more you ask her to stop an annoying habit such as playing with her food, the more she may do it.

Try ignoring it instead. Then, when you notice her eating neatly, compliment her. It won't take long before you begin to see a change.

7) Explain your expectations. Let Youngster know what you expect of her.

Try to keep your expectations fair, reasonable, and sensible. Spell them out to her.

If she knows what you expect of her, it will be easier for her to please you and avoid your disapproval. You will prevent unnecessary misunderstandings and hurt feelings.

For example, explain that you expect her to be in bed by a time that is acceptable to you. Let her know that she can lie in bed quietly for a short time before going to sleep. Offer to read or tell her a story. Or just talk with her during that time if she wishes.

But explain that you will not want to spend the time with her if you have to remind her several times every night that it is time to go to bed.

Let her know what you expect as well as what she can expect when she doesn't fulfill her part of the bargain.

8) Be consistent. Decide what's important to you. Then, try to be consistent in your expectations and responses.

For example, suppose you set up a rule that you don't want Youngster playing on the living room sofa with her shoes on.

Don't let her do it one day when you are feeling good and yell at her the next because she's getting on your nerves.

Try to remind her, gently but firmly, that you do not want her to do it. Ask her to leave the living room until she can do as you ask. Thank her when she remembers

to take off her shoes.

9) Cultivate patience. No matter how much you love her, there will be times when Youngster's behavior will exasperate you.

Try to remember that she will never be this age again and that this, too, will pass.

Let her know how you feel when what she does upsets you. But try to keep your sense of humor and perspective.

Be patient with her attempts to do things for herself. She may not do them well at first. But she will learn with practice. Like every other skill, responsibility for oneself takes practice and lots of room for mistakes before it's mastered.

10) Think, don't react. When we were children, we all swore we'd never treat our children in some of the ways our parents treated us when they got angry.

Now that we are parents, we may find ourselves reacting in many of those same ways we swore we would not repeat.

Try to think before you react to Youngster. Try to remember how you felt when you were small—how easily you could be hurt and frightened by those on whom you depended for guidance and comfort.

When you do react in a way you think was unfair or overly harsh, let Youngster know.

It's helpful for her to see that you too can make mistakes—and acknowledge them. It will build her trust in you. And it may make her more considerate of your feelings in the future, as well.

It's not always easy to behave toward our children as we would want. Try to accept yourself as you are, and do the best you can.

No one can be kind, considerate, fair, patient, and respectful all the time. Be as understanding of yourself as you are of your child.

Just by trying you will succeed. And Youngster will learn from your example.■

Perspective-taking Skills

In previous issues of *Growing Child* we have discussed some of the persistent efforts of a young child to make sense of the world around him.

At two or three years of age, for example, a child is preoccupied with questions about interpreting and understanding the many stimuli which his senses (seeing, hearing, smelling, tasting, touching) receive from his environment.

What is this thing? What does it do? How does it work? What will it do next?

Jean Piaget, the well-known child development theorist, noted some years ago that in interpreting and understanding the world around, him, a young child starts with an *egocentric* viewpoint.

That is, he tends to see things only from his own point of view.

This does not mean that the young child is being arrogant or selfish. It simply means that at first, he can only perceive the world from his own unique vantage point.

He also presumes that everybody else perceives the world exactly the same way he does.

There is a very simple way to test a child's egocentric thinking. On a large sheet of paper draw a simple stick figure of a person (see the first diagram in the next colum).

Then on each of three small cards, draw similar but smaller stick figures that look like the large one.

Next place the large figure on a table in front of the child.

Then arrange the three small cards on the table in front of the child so that one is right side up, one is upside down, and the other is on its side, as shown in the diagram.

Point to the large picture and ask your child: "From where you are sitting at the table, which of these three smaller pictures looks like the way you see the big picture?"

Your child should not have any difficulty selecting the correct card on the left hand side.

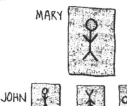

Next, point to the large picture again and ask: "From where Mary is sitting at the table," (use a doll, if you wish, to represent Mary) "which of these three cards looks like the way Mary sees the big picture?"

If he answers incorrectly, you may let him go to the other side of the table where Mary sits. Then have him return to his own side of the table to select the correct card.

Next, point to the large picture again and ask: "From where John is sitting, show me the card that looks like the way John sees the big picture from his side of the table."

After he has mastered this test, a more difficult task is to turn the card on the right in the opposite direction. Then ask whether the card on the right is how John or Joe sees the big picture.

By engaging in this type of activity, a child is helped to progress from purely egocentric thinking to perspective-taking; namely, being able to perceive the world from another person's viewpoint and not just his own.

The egocentric nature of young children's thinking is also revealed in their speech. Researchers have found a simple way to test this ability by having two preschool children sit opposite one another at a table.

Place a small upright screen between the children so that they cannot see one another. Put identical sets of objects in front of each child. Designate one child to be the speaker, the other to be the listener.

The task of the speaker is to describe one item on his side of the table without actually naming it.

The task of the listener is to identify correctly on his side of the screen the object which has been described.

The two children can engage in dialogue, with the listener asking more questions (but not asking for the object's name) and the speaker providing more descriptive information.

It has been found that, without practice, children younger than four years in the role of the speaker usually do not give enough information for the listener to be able to identify the object.

Likewise, a young listener doesn't have enough skill to ask helpful questions when given the opportunity to seek more information.

With practice, however, both the speaker and the listener can improve their skills considerably.

By about four to five years of age, many children are capable of developing better perspective-taking skills.

Perspective-taking skills—namely, the ability to think about someone else's perspective being different from one's own—is a most important developmental achievement.

It enables a child to consider not only another person's perspective of the physical world, but also to think about how another person's intentions and emotions might be different from one's own.

It is such perspective-taking skills that enable a person to interact successfully with others, by predicting or anticipating how another person might think, feel, or behave.■

Television Viewing

Last month we discussed some of the positive effects of children's television shows as well as some of the implications of watching television violence.

This month we will discuss research findings about the effects of television viewing on children's cognitive development, eating habits, and their ethnic and sex-role stereotyping.

Effects on cognitive development

A special concern about the influence of television viewing on preschoolers arises from the fact that, at this age, children have neither the cognitive maturity nor life experience needed to distinguish between fantasy and reality.

One of the most important developmental tasks for a preschool child is learning to know the difference between what is make-believe and what is real.

For the preschool child, even those things she already knows are not possible may sometimes become "real."

One child, for example, jumped from a window because he presumed he could "fly" like Superman.

Another child, aged four, was hospitalized after swallowing 40 vitamin pills which a television commercial told him would make him "big and strong real fast."

In a study of young children's reactions to television commercials, it was found that two-thirds of three- to four-year-olds believed that the characters in the commercials could actually see into their homes.

Almost half of them thought they could communicate with a television cartoon character.

Another important cognitive developmental task for preschool children is learning to understand the concept of "time" in the real world.

Time perspectives on television unfortunately tend to confuse a young child because time is presented in television

shows in a distorted manner, such as with the use of flashback techniques, or presenting a person's entire life in a one-hour "special."

Researchers have indicated that even watching good television programs may sometimes do more harm than good.

Watching television programs can train a child, for example, to become a passive, nonverbal observer rather than an involved, active learner simply because the programs generally require little mental effort.

Television can also deprive a child of valuable active playtime which would stimulate physical, intellectual, and social development.

Research evidence also indicates that children who have spent too much time watching television perform relatively more poorly than their peers in later school years.

It was found that children who watched fast-paced television programs were more restless and performed more poorly on tasks requiring sustained attention, such as solving a puzzle.

Among school-aged children, it was found that those who had watched television the least were the ones who had read books the most.

When television time was restricted for a group of first grade children in another study, it was found that their test scores and overall school performance improved.

Unhealthy habits

Television commercials were also found to have undesirable effects on children's eating habits.

Research evidence indicated that nine out of 10 preschoolers demand food items they have seen advertised on television.

Because preschool children accept information uncritically, they generally believe that all food products advertised on television are good for them.

By contrast, the American Academy of Pediatrics has indicated that less than five percent of daytime food commercials recommend good, nutritious foods, such as vegetables and fruits.

Another health-related side effect of television watching is obesity. Recent research evidence indicates that every hour spent watching television increases a child's likelihood of being overweight.

Researchers have suggested three possible explanations: (1) Children consume many snacks while watching television; (2) They burn fewer calories; and (3) They are encouraged by television commercials to eat less healthy food which is fattening.

Ethnic and sex-role stereotyping

Another area which has received much attention in recent research studies is the portrayal of ethnic and sex-role stereotypes in television programs.

This area of study is important because, for many children, television has a greater cultural influence than family, school, or church.

A review of these research studies indicates that:

(1) Some educational programs such as Sesame Street and Mister Rogers' Neighborhood present cultural diversity in a positive manner.

(2) But, in general, ethnic minorities—particularly African Americans, Hispanics and Native Americans—have been underrepresented in television programs.

(3) When members of these minority groups appear in television shows, they are generally among the supporting cast rather than in lead roles.

(4) They are also generally portrayed as having lower status jobs.

(5) They are more likely than Caucasians to be cast either as servants or criminals.

continued on page 312

Some Sorting Games

In order to think about and understand our world, we have to develop the ability to organize our experiences—our sensory information, in particular.

By grouping our experiences into categories, we acquire knowledge and understanding.

As adults we generally use this organizational ability automatically—without even thinking about it.

If we see a new style of chair, for example, we can classify it immediately as "chair" without much, if any, mental effort—even if we had never seen another chair exactly like it.

For a young child, however, who is trying to understand and make sense of his world, the ability to organize sensory experiences is not quite as automatic. It requires a lot of practice in order to develop.

At four years of age, organizing life's experiences into categories is a major intellectual challenge.

One of the best ways for your child to develop this organizational ability is by learning to sort objects into categories.

Here are some simple sorting games which will provide your child with valuable practice in organizing and classifying objects according to their appearance, function, and location.

In addition, these games will provide both you and your child with endless hours of fun and entertainment.

Sorting by appearance

There are two considerations which are important when sorting by appearance:

(1) Start with only *two* objects to identify at a time. When your child has mastered grouping two objects by appearance, you can then move on to sorting three or more similar objects at a time.

(2) Begin by identifying only *one quality* at a time, namely, either color, shape, or size. After your child has mastered the ability to

categorize by one quality, you can increase the challenge by specifying two or more qualities ("Show me the *big red* blocks).

Even though your four-year-old child may not be able to name an object's size or shape, he should now be ready to sort items by these categories. You will need:

• Items that are similar to one another in either size, shape, or color (example: combs, shoes, balls).

• Items that are different from one another.

• Receptacles (such as boxes or trays) into which the sorted items can be placed.

With the containers in place, you're ready to start. Begin by:

(a) Sorting by *color:* Have Youngster identify two objects that have the same color.

You can start the game by saying: "Here is a *red* block. Can you find the other thing that is *red?*"

(b) Sorting by *shape:* Have Youngster identify two objects that have the same shape (triangles, circles, squares).

If he doesn't recognize the word "triangle," you may show him one saying: "Here is one *triangle.* Can you find the other *triangle?*"

If he is incorrect the first time, you may say, "Here is one *triangle.* And here is the other *triangle.* Now, *you* show me the two *triangles.*"

If he is correct, you can say, "Yes, those are the two *triangles.* Now find another *triangle.*"

As he develops more skill, you can introduce new categories, such as pictures of dogs, cats, flowers, or trees, so that he can categorize them by their shape.

(c) Sorting by *size:* Have Youngster identify two objects that are similar in size. For example: "Pick out the two *big* ones."

"Show me the two *long* ones."
"Show me the two *short* ones."

If Youngster chooses correctly, you may say, "Yes, those two things are the *big* ones."

If he chooses incorrectly, you may say: "This one and this one are the two *big* ones. Here is one of the *big* ones. Now you show me the other *big* one."

Sorting by function

This sorting game requires skills beyond those needed for sorting by appearance. It requires your child to *think* about an object's *use.* Some examples:

"Pick out two things you can *eat*" (a carrot and an apple, for example).

"Show me two things you can *wear*" (a sock, a shirt).

Again, it is best to start with only *two* items which you think your child can categorize easily.

When that ability has been mastered, you can move on to three or more items.

Likewise, you can gradually increase the complexity as your child demonstrates newly acquired skills: "Show me the *three blue* things which Daddy *wears*" (shirt, tie, sock).

continued on page 312

continued from page 308   continued from page 311

(6) Italians are frequently stereotyped on television as gangsters and Latin Americans as drug smugglers.

(7) Likewise, although most women in American society have a job outside the home, few women in television shows are seen in such work roles.

(8) Although some television programs show women in working roles, these roles are frequently in strongly sex-stereotyped jobs such as nurse, teacher or secretary.

(9) On television shows, females talk less than males, more often need help, and seldom are shown as problem-solvers.

(10) Females also tend to be depicted on television shows as weak, emotional and passive, whereas males are more often portrayed as active, strong, and rational.

(11) It was also found that children who watched more than 25 hours of television weekly had acquired more traditionally sex-role stereotyped opinions than children who watched less than 10 hours per week.

(12) Television commercials aimed at females were found to use different techniques, such as fading and soft background music, whereas those aimed at males used more action, rapid cuts, and louder music.

(13) In general, television commercials were found to depict women as inferior beings who spend most of their time putting on cosmetics, shopping, or seeking men.

(14) It was found that older people were generally depicted as useless, cranky, and forgetful.

Next month we will discuss some other effects of television viewing on young children.

We will include 14 very practical steps parents can take regarding their child's television viewing habits.■

Sorting by location

Another form of sorting game is to group items by their proper location.

For example: (1) Putting away the silverware after a meal: "All the *forks* go *here*. Show me *where* the *spoons* go."

(2) Sorting the laundry: "The *socks* go in *this drawer*. Show me *where* the *shirts* go."

(3) Putting away the groceries: "The *vegetables* go *here*. *Where* do the *paper towels* go?"

Be sensitive to your child

In playing these sorting games, it is important to remember that no two children are exactly alike.

One child may show great interest in sorting, while another child may not yet be ready, or may just prefer watching you do all the work.

It is also important to be sensitive to your child's mood on any particular day. One day he may want to spend many hours playing these sorting games.

On another day, he may show no interest. It is best to adapt your rhythm to that of your child.

Growing Child

P. O. Box 2505 • W Lafayette, IN 47996
(800) 927-7289
www.GrowingChild.com

Contributing Authors

Phil Bach, O.D., Ph.D.
Miriam Bender, Ph.D.
Joseph Braga, Ed.D.
Laurie Braga, Ph.D.
George Early, Ph.D.
Carol R. Gestwicki, M.S.
Liam Grimley, Ph.D.
Robert Hannemann, M.D., F.A.A.P.
Sylvia Kottler, M.S.
Bill Peterson, Ph.D.

Repetition is essential for learning. Each time your child repeats a sorting game, he learns something new.

During the preschool years, especially from three to five, your child's intellect is developing rapidly.

Even if a learning activity doesn't go well one day, it may go better the next day.

The more fun an activity is, the more likely Youngster will want to return to it.

Repetition is, of course, essential for learning. Each time your child repeats a sorting game, he learns something new.

This new knowledge was already there for him to learn earlier. But he may not have been developmentally ready.

Today he is no longer the child he was yesterday. Now he brings to the activity all that he has experienced and learned.

So enjoy playing these sorting games. Your home will become an ideal classroom for your child's intellectual development.

And while he is learning, he will most likely also enjoy every moment of your attention and your love.■

Understanding Youngster

At four years of age, Youngster is generally curious about the world around her, especially the people in it.

She has fun trying to imitate people she knows, has heard about, or has seen on television. She likes to help out. She's usually easy to get along with.

Sometimes, though, Youngster can be unpredictable and hard to understand. She may get very excited about an activity, only to leave it suddenly without explanation.

Sometimes you may have to tell her the same thing a hundred times. Still she forgets to do what you've asked.

She can be adorable one minute and whiny or pouting the next. And, she may—for no apparent reason—begin to be afraid of all sorts of things which never bothered her before.

In other words, Youngster is experiencing some rough spots which are normal on her journey from four to five years of age.

Why is this happening? How can you help Youngster—and yourself—get through these rough spots? A good first step is to try to see the world through her eyes.

1. Youngster is no longer a baby. You have expectations of her taking some responsibilities for herself. This is good. Most of the time Youngster probably is proud to be able to do things for herself.

But there are times when she wishes someone else would take care of her responsibilities.

This shows up, particularly, if there's a

younger child in the family from whom less is expected.

Try to understand how Youngster feels. And let her know you understand her feelings: "You don't want to put away your toys now. You're tired and you wish I'd do it for you. Let's pick them up together."

2. Youngster will sometimes get frustrated because she is not yet old enough to do many of the things she'd like to do. This is made harder if she has older siblings who are allowed privileges she is denied.

For example, she may want to go out without supervision. So she may slip out on her own while you're not looking. Naturally, if this happens, you're going to be upset and worried.

Be honest with Youngster about your feelings. But try, also, to let her know you understand her feelings. "You wanted to go out by yourself like the big kids. You got mad when I wouldn't let you. So you went anyway. I understand how you feel. But I can't let you go out alone. I get very worried and upset that

something might happen to you."

3. Youngster is also having a hard time finding her place in the world. It isn't easy to be "in-between"—too young for some things and too old for others. It's not just that she isn't allowed to go places and do things. There are many things she simply can't do yet.

Youngster needs your patient support when she gets overwhelmed by tasks that are too big for her. Explain that everyone has trouble doing some things. Offer to help out if she wants. But don't take over. That would only increase her feelings of incompetence.

She needs reassurance and encouragement to help her see the things about herself that are special. Compliment her, for example, on how good she is at making other people feel happy or on what a wonderful smile she has.

Youngster needs your help to see and develop her own special talents. For example, tell her how much you love to hear her sing her "made-up songs." Ask her if she'd sing a little each day with you. Let her teach you.

4. Youngster sometimes has a hard time keeping her mind focused on one idea for a long time. For example, she may start out drawing a picture she says is supposed to be a car. By the time she finishes her drawing, it may have changed identities several times.

Or she might tell you a story in which each thing she says makes her think of something else. So she never completes any of her thoughts.

continued on page 314

continued from page 313

Don't worry about this. The average attention span for this age spans 10-12 minutes. As she grows older, Youngster's thinking will become more organized and conventional. She'll be able to pay attention to an activity for a longer time.

For now, encourage her to stick with things she has begun. But be flexible. Don't force a child this age to follow too rigid a schedule.

This is a time when young children use their minds in creative ways. They need to practice these thinking skills.

5. Youngster's memory, at this stage, may not be as good as you think it should be. This can cause problems when you give her too many directions at one time.

For example, you might say to her, "Go upstairs and get your hat, your coat, and your gloves. While you're up there, don't forget to put away the toys you left in the hallway. Then put on your new shoes, and we'll go to the store."

With so many things to remember, she's likely to forget at least some part of what you told her. The most she can remember is two to four things.

She'll remember more if the instructions are short, simple, and related to one another.

Also, she'll remember better when it's something important to her. That's when she really will pay attention.

Otherwise, you'll need to take the time to tell her slowly what you want. Ask her to repeat it.

Try to be understanding if she still forgets. Her memory will gradually improve with practice and as she gets older.

6. Youngster can sometimes be moody when things don't go her way. Her mood can change quickly from joy to anger, for example, if someone doesn't pay attention to her or if she can't make a toy work the way she wants.

Often you may not even know why she's upset. She may have some idea inside her head of what she expects.

When her expectations aren't met, she might pout or stomp about without ever letting you know why.

Try to put yourself in her shoes. See if you can figure out the problem: "I'll bet you're mad because you got tired of waiting for me to get off the phone."

Be sympathetic, even if you think her reason is not important. It's important to her. If she feels you understand, she'll get over her moodiness more quickly.

7. Youngster is becoming more aware of how little control she really has over her life. As a result she may try to boss other people around, both adults and children. She may behave in some pretty "bratty" ways at times.

Let her know you don't like being bossed around any more than she does. Tell her you'll try to be fair with her. But you expect her to be fair, too, with you and others.

Give her as much control as you can in as many areas of her life as possible.

For example, let her have input about the clothes you buy for her. Let her sometimes pick out what she wants to wear even if you don't always approve of her selection.

Try not to pressure her—even by the tone of your voice—into always doing things your way.

If you've decided she has to do something a particular way, tell her directly what you expect. Don't make Youngster guess what you expect and then get upset if she doesn't meet your expectations.

If a choice is possible, really give her the choice. Don't try to influence her.

8. Youngster may also be developing fears of things that never used to bother her.

This is because of her present feelings of powerlessness.

She doesn't have the complete protection she had as a baby (nor should she). But she's not yet capable of caring for herself in many ways.

She knows just enough about the world around her to know there are many things she doesn't understand and can't control.

Thus, she fears lots of things but especially the unknown—dark places, loud noises, strange-looking people, unfamiliar places and things.

Some of Youngster's fears may seem silly to you. Don't try to talk her out of her fears by telling her, "There's nothing to be afraid of. It can't hurt you."

Try to understand that her fears are very real to her. And don't accuse her of being a baby for being afraid. We all get afraid sometimes.

You will help Youngster more effectively overcome her fears if you tell her that it's all right to be afraid.

Let her explain to you what frightens her. Tell her you understand how she feels. Ask how you can help.

As a general rule the best way to understand and help out Youngster is by trying to put yourself in her shoes.

Remember your own thoughts and feelings when you were a child. Treat her the way you liked to be treated as a child.

Be honest and straightforward with her about how her behavior affects you. And try to understand how your behavior affects her.

Assert your own rights and needs, but not at Youngster's expense.

She is too young to stand up for her own rights, needs, and feelings, so you have to protect them for her.

As you treat her, so will she learn to treat other people later in her own life.■

A Child's 'Theory of Mind'

Last month we discussed how a young child develops "perspective- taking skills," the ability to perceive the world from another person's viewpoint.

This month we will discuss a related but more complex topic, namely, what researchers call a child's "theory of mind."

"Theory of mind" is a term used to describe a developmental change in the thinking of children when they show some understanding of:

(1) characteristics of their own thinking, and

(2) how their thinking may differ from that of another person. This usually seems to occur around four years of age.

In recent years researchers have begun to seek answers to important and intriguing questions about the development of thinking skills in children: When do children begin to develop some basic understanding about how their own thinking occurs?

When do they become consciously aware of their own mental representations, which are their own thoughts in the mind (such as, for example, thinking about a drink of water), as distinct from things in the real world (actually drinking the water)?

When do they begin to realize that what a person thinks can affect what that person does?

Even though these are complex questions to consider, we would like readers of *Growing Child* to be aware of some of the findings in this important area of research in developmental psychology.

While the term "theory of mind" sounds complex and abstract, it has very practical implications.

For example, as adults we use a theory of mind whenever we interact with other people.

For such social interactions to occur, each one of us needs to develop some understanding of the complex interactions—both within ourselves and in others—of thoughts, feelings, and behaviors.

The better we develop such a theory of mind, the better we can interpret and understand human behavior.

It has been found, for example, that the development of a theory of mind during the preschool years is a key factor in enabling a five-year-old child to be a more alert and active participant in social interactions with other children.

By developing the ability to infer other people's thoughts, feelings, wants, and intentions—that is by using a theory of mind to think about what others say and do—the young child is able to acquire essential skills needed to get along well with other people.

There is some evidence to suggest that children may begin to develop a theory of mind as early as two years of age.

A two-year-old may say, for example, "Mommy, don't get mad," indicating some understanding that another person's feelings may differ from one's own.

It was also found that two-year-olds play differently and even talk differently when they are in the company of older playmates.

But this understanding is quite primitive in two-year-olds whose thinking is still egocentric.

Even for three-year-olds there is an assumption that the "real" world is identical with their own perceptions of that world.

In other words, they assume that everyone experiences reality in exactly the same way (remember last month's article on the development of perspective-taking skills).

What appears to change at about age four is the young child's ability to develop mental representations.

This means that at this age a child is learning to distinguish between his own thoughts (thinking about an ice cream cone) and the real world (the ice cream cone itself).

There is much research evidence to indicate that before age four children confuse appearance and reality.

In one experiment, for example, young children were shown a sponge which had been painted to look like a rock.

Children younger than four years of age either said it looked like a rock and was a rock, or that it looked like a sponge but really was a rock.

On the contrary, the four- and five-year-olds indicated correctly that even though it looked like a rock, it really was a sponge.

It appears that at four years of age a child is also beginning to understand that:

(1) different people experience the "real" world in different ways;

(2) a person's beliefs about the world may sometimes change; and

(3) a person will act according to his own belief, even if that belief is, in reality, false.

continued on page 316

A Healthy Family Life

continued from page 315

All of us probably know some families that are happy and close-knit. All of us probably also know other families that are dysfunctional.

A healthy family life—in which the members truly care for and about one another—is a great joy and blessing. It's worth taking time to consider how interpersonal relationships in a family might be improved.

Here are some characteristics of a healthy family life.

1. In healthy families, the members make time to be with one another. For the sake of good family relationships, Mom may have to reschedule a hair appointment or Dad may have to cancel his golf outing.

These actions say louder than any words: "My family is important to me."

2. Family members try to share as an entire family in the activities of each member of the family. Four-year-old Joey needs to know that others consider him to be an important member of the family by attending his preschool play.

Likewise, it is important for Joey to learn at this age that he is not the center of the universe, that he also needs to make time for other family members.

For example, he might be able to help a younger family member or join in celebrating a sibling's birthday or success in school.

3. Healthy families try to involve all members, as far as possible, in decision-making. When buying a new car, for example, even though four-year-olds won't know much about the car's engine, Joey's color preference could be taken into consideration.

4. Healthy families go places together. This may involve something as simple as a trip together to the park or as complex as extended vacation travel.

5. Healthy families show appreciation for one another. They say "thank you" even for everyday actions such as cleaning one's room or cooking a meal.

Sometimes a little note is a good way to let other family members know they are valued and appreciated.

6. Healthy families learn how to deal with problems. All families have problems at one time or another.

It's not the problems that make or break family life. Rather it's how the family learns to deal with those problems. In a healthy family, each new problem can be viewed as a new opportunity for growth.

7. Healthy families have fun together. This can bring family members closer to one another. Shared fun breaks down barriers, such as age group differences.

It can also help to bring out a family member's hidden talent for comedy. Family fun may be as simple as sharing a few jokes or watching a comedy movie together.

8. Children learn how to talk, behave, and take turns around the family table at mealtime. They learn how to be polite, not interrupt when someone else is talking, how to share, and when you have guests, how to entertain. These are all good lessons for success in life.

There is a body of research to support the conclusion that families who have a family table and eat there together on a regular basis have children who do better in school and are less likely to smoke, drink or take drugs.

Every child and parents needs a sense of community. Your family IS a community where you can share your days with one another. Laughter is the best dinnertime music, and the atmosphere at the family table should be that laughter is welcome.

This is also a good time to pass on those family traditions and stories from your own childhood.

Building a healthy family life is a truly great challenge. But it's a challenge which will provide inestimable rewards.■

An example may help to clarify these distinctions. A child is told that a dog is really hiding under a couch but a person looking for the dog thinks the dog is outside in the garden.

Will the person first look under the couch or in the garden?

A three-year-old will most likely answer that the person will first look under the couch—because that is where the dog really is.

By contrast, many four-year-olds will usually answer correctly ("in the garden") because they are able to distinguish between where the dog really is and where the person thinks the dog is.

To an adult it will be obvious that people will act according to their own thoughts and beliefs rather than according to "what really is."

For a four-year-old such an understanding, however, represents quite an accomplishment since it indicates the child has developed what has been called a "theory of mind."

Whenever parents respond to a child's request by saying, "I want to think about that," they are helping the child to realize that a person can have more than one thought or perspective about a request.

Likewise when parents ask a child, "What would you like for lunch?" they are getting the child to think about various options.

Some four-year-olds have more difficulty than others in processing multiple thoughts and comparing one thought with another in their minds.

By using a theory of mind, a four-year-old not only learns to distinguish between thoughts and reality, but he also learns that the thoughts and feelings of others may differ from his own.

The development of these thinking skills will be an important factor in helping his social interactions with other people in the years ahead.■

Children's Television Viewing: Some Practical Steps

Last month we discussed the effects of TV viewing on children's cognitive development, eating habits, and their ethnic and sex-role stereotyping.

This month we will discuss some other effects of television viewing on young children.

We will conclude with 14 very practical steps parents can take regarding their child's television viewing habits.

Psychologists have expressed concern that as long as the TV is "turned on," other more valuable experiences are "turned off."

For example, it has been found that television viewing often prevents the members of a family from interacting with one another.

Extensive television watching also prevents a young child from engaging in more creative self-generated activities.

From watching TV commercials, children not only want to eat less healthy foods, they also feel deprived if they can't have the exciting and sometimes expensive toys they saw advertised, which, in turn, can lead to family discord.

Children learn values from television which are often at variance with their parents' values.

They can learn, for example, that success is measured by the type of car you drive or by the clothes you wear.

Success is attained by manipulating people rather than by hard work. There is a pill or a drink to bring instant relief from life's problems.

Such messages not only impart values, they also give an unrealistic view of the world we live in.

For many years citizens' groups and public policymakers have lobbied to have some limits applied to advertising aimed at young children, to reduce the amount of violence on television, and to get more educational television programs for children.

Unfortunately these efforts have been strongly resisted both by advertisers and by the television industry.

What Parents Can Do

1. *Consider turning off the television set completely except for educational programs which are beneficial to your child.* Remember that as long as the TV is turned on, other activities which could benefit your child—such as creative play and family communication—are turned off.

2. *Set some limits, at least, to the amount of TV time your child is allowed.* In research studies preschool children whose television watching was the most severely restricted were found to be better developed physically, intellectually, and socially. They also did better in school in later years.

Some researchers have suggested a maximum of one hour of television per day for a preschool child. But even that one hour may be harmful if the material is inappropriate.

3. *Identify the specific programs which your child may watch.* Be sure to turn off the TV as soon as that program ends. Otherwise your child may become fascinated with the next program which may be undesirable.

Programs, including some cartoons, that include inappropriate behavior related to violence, sex, drugs, or alcohol, should be avoided.

As your child grows older you can review together what television programs are acceptable.

4. *Avoid using TV as a babysitter.* Since television will have such an important and powerful influence on your child, avoid allowing yourself or your child to drift into a pattern of random television watching.

If your child develops a habit of watching too much TV, it is a habit that will be difficult to break later. Make a conscious decision, therefore, about the role of television in your family life.

5. *Encourage your child to watch good educational programs,* like Sesame Street and Mister Rogers' Neighborhood; Reading Rainbow, It's a Big, Big World and Arthur have good ideas to offer.

Programs like this can help a child's intellectual and social development provided they don't interfere with other more beneficial developmental experiences.

6. *Watch television with your child and later discuss the program.* Through such discussion, for example, a child can be helped to understand the difference between acting and real life, between fantasy and fact.

Even a "bad" program can be used by a parent to discuss more appropriate behavior.

Research studies indicate that when young children watch a television program in the company of an adult with whom they can discuss it, they learn more from the program.

7. *Teach him critical skills for watching television commercials.* Explain, for example, the difference between some unhealthy foods that may be advertised on TV and the nutritious food found in your home.

He also needs to learn that he is not a deprived child if he doesn't get every toy

continued on page 318

Vygotsky's Theory

continued from page 317

Though similar to Piaget's ideas in suggesting that children construct knowledge through action and move through stages of intellectual development, the Russian psychologist Lev Vygotsky proposed that thinking and learning are highly influenced by language, social interaction, and culture.

For Vygotsky, language and thinking are distinct and separate processes, in the early years.

What he called *self-directed speech* is a behavior that shows young children are learning language to guide their learning. Here we see children talking to themselves, naming their actions, particularly as they solve problems.

So language is not just a method of expression, but a basic tool for constructing knowledge, a method for thinking at higher levels.

Thus a quiet classroom or home where children just sit and listen is not optimal for learning from this viewpoint; rather, encouraging children to use language enhances thought as well as speech. Later, self-directed speech is internalized as thinking.

Vygotsky also argued that children's thinking is influenced by interaction with other people. When getting support from more competent peers or adults, children are *scaffolded* to use their best thinking or problem solving.

When presented with tasks that are slightly beyond their present mental capability—what Vygotsky called the *zone of proximal development*—the more knowledgeable parent or sibling asks questions or gives hints to guide the child to move ahead in their thinking.

For example, a child who can solve a 10-piece puzzle is given one with 20 pieces.

Rather than show the child how to do the puzzle, the parent may suggest that the child look for all the pieces with straight sides, or ask the child what color piece would show the bird.

Thus as parents scaffold a child's problem solving and thinking, they do not perform the tasks for them but provide a supportive structure for problem solving, with the actual solution left to the children.

Vygotsky was a major proponent of pretend play, saying that play is a major source of mental development.

He identified two critical features of play for development. One is the opportunity to practice using *symbolic thought.*

This is the ability to use an abstract symbol to stand for an idea or an object that is not present, as in when a child holds a block to his ear and speaks into it as a telephone.

This ability will later be used in understanding that the letters and words on a page are symbolic, and the ability is best honed in the dramatic play of early childhood.

The second feature of pretend play is that it contains understood rules for behavior that children must follow to successfully play the pretend scene, such as, "Pretend you be the father and first you have to go to work and then you come home for dinner." Thus pretend play promotes children thinking and acting in deliberately self-controlled ways.

It can be seen that Vygotsky's theory has major implications to guide adults' interactions with children, and the environments they provide.■

Growing Child

P. O. Box 2505 • W Lafayette, IN 47996
(800) 927-7289
www.GrowingChild.com

Contributing Authors

Phil Bach, O.D., Ph.D.
Miriam Bender, Ph.D.
Joseph Braga, Ed.D.
Laurie Braga, Ph.D.
George Early, Ph.D.
Carol R. Gestwicki, M.S.
Liam Grimley, Ph.D.
Robert Hannemann, M.D., F.A.A.P.
Sylvia Kottler, M.S.
Bill Peterson, Ph.D.

which an exploitive television commercial tells him he should have.

8. *Use information gained from television to stimulate your child's interest in reading.* When your child shows an interest in something seen on TV, go together to the library to find some appropriate books on this topic.

9. *You can also use information from television programs to stimulate your child's interest in indoor and outdoor activities.* This could include, for example, nature study or a child's favorite hobby.

10. *Take your child to a museum,* a cultural event, or to the zoo. This will build on whatever television program or topic stimulated his interest in the world around him.

11. *Consider using high quality educational videotapes or CDs.* They have several advantages over TV programs.

• As a parent, you can monitor ahead of time what your child will see.

• You can stop the tape at any point for discussion.

• You can set your own limits on the amount of viewing time, depending on such factors as your child's alertness, attention, and interest.

• You can also replay segments which were clarified through discussion.

12. *To improve children's television programming, call or write to your local television station* to let them know your opinions, both pro and con.

13. *Contact the manufacturers of products advertised during a TV program* which you consider offensive or inappropriate.

14. *Consider joining and supporting a citizens' group or parents' organization* which lobbies for better educational television programming for young children.

Parents who are concerned about good schools, good education, and good social experiences for their children need also to be actively involved in promoting better television programming for young children.■

Childhood Memories

Remember the baby book you kept when your child was an infant? Maybe it's tucked away on the shelf in a closet or in a drawer.

Wherever it is, take it out. It will provide many hours of sharing and learning and fun for you and your child.

A memory book is a particularly great resource for any special time you set aside to spend with your child such as a rainy day or a story at bedtime.

She will delight in hearing stories about herself at a time she can't remember— when she was a baby and a toddler.

It can also help you to see better her point of view of her life as she shares her memories. You may be amazed to hear her tell of things you'd forgotten, or to listen to her versions of shared events.

Obviously it's great for her language development. It can also help with those thinking skills we've talked so much about— understanding time, space, and order, as you talk about things that happened "last year," "when you were a baby," "in the old house," "before your baby brother was born," and so on.

The memory book is also a good way to help your child see how skilled and competent she is now compared with the ways she used to do things.

"Oh, look at this picture of you before you could walk."

"When you were a baby, it was so hard for you to hold onto anything." "Now, you're so good with your hands, the way you use scissors and crayons and put on your own clothes."

"I really appreciate how you help me with setting the table. That takes a lot of skill with your hands."

The memory book will probably give you many ideas of ways you can share with her how she's grown and learned since she was a baby.

It will help her to understand herself and grow in positive self-concept as she realizes her accomplishments.

If you never kept a baby book for your child, or if it's been a long time since you added any material, now is a good time to start a current memory book.

Keeping a memory book of her life can be a useful and enjoyable project that she'll love having for years to come. Here are some of the things you could include:

1. Photographs. Take pictures of her—eating; sleeping; having fun with friends and family; enjoying favorite activities such as playing with special toys.

Be sure to keep a record of each photo—with a short description and a date.

Have a special "Photograph Day" and have your child help in planning the project.

Her creativity, visual awareness, thinking and social abilities will gain much stimulation through such involvement with you and others who are a part of her memory book projects.

2. Artistic creations. Keep samples of your child's art work in her memory book. Save early scribbles as well as her work with fingerpaints, crayons, watercolors, collages, self-portraits and treasured colorings.

Keeping a memory book of your child's life can be a useful and enjoyable project that a child will love having for years to come.

You don't need to save everything she does. Have her help you choose a few favorites. Remember to date them.

3. Physical measurements. Make a growth chart marked off in inches.

Every few months, measure your child and make a notation on the chart of the date on which she reached that height. Alongside make a note of her weight on that date, if you have access to a scale.

Help her make handprints and footprints every few months using finger-paints. Again, be sure to date them.

4. Transcriptions of verbal creations. Write down stories that your child makes up, songs she composes, interesting or funny things she says, insights she has about life and people.

Include any particular things she'd like kept in her memory book, such as favorite stories or songs.

5. Voice recordings. If you have a tape recorder, or can borrow one, make a sound recording of her voice. Record her singing, telling a favorite story, or talking on the telephone.

Include her conversations with friends and family. Do this every few months, if possible.

continued on page 320

continued from page 319

6. Video recordings. If you own a video camera, or have access to one, use it to record special events such as holidays, birthdays, and other significant happenings.

7. Anecdotal record. Keep a written record to go with the pictures, tape recordings, creative products, and other records of your child's development.

Make a few notes about what she likes to do at different age levels. Describe the skills she's learning. Note the things she likes and doesn't like (foods, toys, colors).

Write down interesting comments others have made about her. Be sure to record experiences she has particularly enjoyed.

Keep your notes anecdotal, as if you were telling someone a story about your child.

With the collection of these kinds of materials and notes, you're creating a gift for your child more valuable than any toy that money could ever buy.

You're keeping a record for her of a time when she would otherwise have only glimpses and sketchy memories.

You're also helping her develop self-confidence by providing her with a record of her growth—a word-and-picture story of who she was and who she has become.

As she grows older it will become a special treasure not only for her but for others too who will come to know and love her.

Ashley Montagu once wrote that "... the most important job in the world is the making of another human being, one to whom we have given roots and wings."

In providing your child with a memory book, you are not only helping her to establish her own "roots" by informing her about her past, but you are also helping her to grow her "wings" with which she will soar into the future.■

Self-Concept: How Does Your Child See Himself?

Self-concept or self-image is how a child thinks of himself in relation to the people and things in the rest of the world.

What is your child's concept of himself? Is he a very important person in his own eyes? Or does he think he's not too good a person?

It is very important that a child have a very genuine feeling that he matters in the world, that he is important.

Psychologists have developed several measures of self-concept. An extensive body of research on school-aged children shows that a child's self-concept is directly related to achievement in school.

Children who have a poor self-concept tend to do poorly in school learning tasks. Those who feel good about themselves generally do well in school.

In one of the research studies, researchers gave two tests to a group of kindergarten children.

One was an IQ test which measures intellectual functioning, and the other was a test of self-concept.

Two years later these same children were given a test of achievement in school to measure how well they performed in reading, writing, and spelling.

It turned out that the measure of self-concept was a better predictor of their school achievement than was the measure of intelligence.

Parents can influence their child's self-concept development. Here are three general principles which will help your child develop a good self-concept.

Principle No. 1: Let your child know that you love him.

A child needs to know that he is important to you, that he has your love—even when he has engaged in some unlovable activities. ("I love you, but I don't like what you have just done.")

Principle No. 2: Help your child handle his failures. What messages are you giving

him when he fails? He needs to know that you're on his side, that you accept him—win or lose—for who he is. Your corrections should reflect what he's done, not what he "is."

Principle No. 3: Don't be dishonest. Your child knows when he hasn't done well, when he has failed.

If you acknowledge that you know this, but that it isn't the end of the world, your child gains confidence in you to reflect an honest value to him.

At this age your child is trying to find his place in the world. He's experimenting with different ideas and concepts, looking to you for guidance and support.

Make sure you give him the room he needs to learn and make mistakes. But also make sure he knows you're on his side—win or lose.

Helping to develop a positive self-concept is one of the most important things any parent can do for a child.■

The Chalkboard Experience

Children love to draw on a chalkboard. The chalkboard need not be an expensive slate.

A discarded piece of wallboard or Masonite™ painted with several coats of chalkboard paint—green or black—will serve the purpose.

For young children scribbling is the fore-runner of form perception—the recognition and reproduction of geometric forms and letters.

They first scribble lines, angles, and curves. They will later go on to produce the complicated combinations of lines, angles, and curves that form letters and numbers.

It has been found that young children don't scribble in a random manner. They follow a certain sequence in their scribbles.

There are 20 basic scribbles. From a combination of these scribbles there are structures which are identifiable by age.

According to Rhoda Kellogg the evolution of scribbling into pictorial drawing goes something like this:

20 Basic Scribbles

For the three-year-old:

The four-year-old takes the basic scribbles and turns them into new forms or aggregates.

For the five-year-old:

Here are some variations of the chalkboard experience:

1) Chalk on dry paper. Paper may be highly textured, sand-paper, butcher paper, or newsprint. Varieties of colored chalk on dark paper or dark chalk on light paper will enhance your child's enjoyment.

In addition to learning about different shapes and forms, your child is also learning about the effects of his strength on what he is drawing. The more pressure he exerts on the chalk, the more intense the color becomes on paper.

2) Chalk on wet paper. Moisten heavy-duty paper with water.

Your child will observe the differences in the use of chalk on dry and wet papers. On the latter the colors become more brilliant on contact with moisture.

He must also use greater control—a lighter touch is needed to prevent tearing the wet paper.

3) Chalk on wet paper, moistened with buttermilk or liquid starch.

In addition to learning about shapes and forms and how the intensity of a color can change depending on the amount of pressure used, your child will also learn about different cause-effect relationships.

For instance, he will discover that when the paper is moistened with buttermilk or liquid starch, the effect will be that the colors won't rub off when the paper dries.■

Listening Skills

Our senses let us see and hear and taste and smell and touch the world. Children need experiences with their senses, to develop them, to sharpen their awareness of the qualities of things. Here are some listening games to help your child learn to tell the differences between sounds.

Say, "Close your eyes." (Be sure there's no peeking.) Now, make a noise. "What noise was that?"

Now, make a different noise and ask each time, "What noise was that?" Knock on the floor, on the wall, on a table. Knock on the refrigerator door. Knock on a box of cereal. Tap on the counter with your fingernail, with a fork, a pencil, a pie tin. It's more fun for your child when you take turns. Close your eyes and let her make a noise which you are to identify. It's not as easy as you might think!

Another game to develop listening skills is to play "What Sounds Do You Hear?" Again, take turns. For example, your child might identify the sound of birds singing, while you say you hear the church bells ringing. She hears the sounds of a truck going by, you hear the sound of a passing train.

These games help to develop awareness of sounds in our environment. They also help to sharpen your child's attention skills.■

Catch Them Being Good

A few years ago some teachers decided they wanted to give more attention to good behavior in the classroom than to bad behavior.

So, instead of correcting the student with bad behavior ("Bill, you're not paying attention again"), they decided to give a 'Gotcha' award for good behavior ("Joe, you just won a 'Gotcha' award because I 'Gotcha' being good: listening to what I was telling you.")

Parents can use a 'Gotcha' award just as effectively as teachers.

Create a certificate which says in large letters: 'GOTCHA' AWARD (see box).

Each time, you can fill in your child's name, the good behavior that you noticed, and the reward that you wish to give (the 'value' of the award).

You can award the certificate for any good behavior you wish (a cheerful smile, a courteous 'thank you,' or a neatly kept bedroom, for example).

Your child will particularly enjoy receiv-

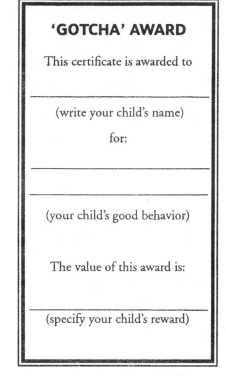

'GOTCHA' AWARD

This certificate is awarded to

_____

(write your child's name)

for:

_____

_____

(your child's good behavior)

The value of this award is:

_____

(specify your child's reward)

ing the 'Gotcha' award when it comes as a surprise.

So, try to be creative and innovative in selecting the good behavior for which you give the award.

Continue recognizing positive behavior as you normally would with a smile, comment or pat on the arm.

Likewise, be creative in deciding the 'value' of each individual 'Gotcha' award (50 cents, a big hug, a piece of fruit, or a candy bar, for example).

It's a good idea to ask your child what are some rewards he might like to receive.

They may be as simple as accompanying you to the grocery store, a visit to you or your spouse's place of work, an outing to the park or a play date with a good friend.

If you compile a list of possible rewards, you can then choose the one most appropriate for each occasion.

By getting a 'Gotcha' award, your child will learn that good behavior (not just bad behavior) is noticed, that good behavior is important, and, because it is important, good behavior is often rewarded by parents.■

Pool Safety

For some families, swimming is a summer activity. For others, who have access to an indoor pool or who live in a warm climate, it can be a year-round source of fun.

Unfortunately, the fun can turn to tragedy if basic safety rules are not observed.

Here are some pool safety guidelines:

• Never leave young children unattended—even those who know how to swim—near a swimming pool area.

If the supervising adult has to leave for any reason—such as to answer the telephone—make sure first that all children are out of the pool area. It only takes 30 seconds for a toddler to drown.

• No diving should be allowed in an above-ground pool.

• In an in-ground pool, no diving should be permitted unless the pool has at least 8 feet of water at the diving end.

A safety nylon rope with a colored buoy attached should be installed to distinguish between the shallow and deep ends of the pool.

• Don't allow your child to use flotation devices, such as inflatable animals or mattresses.

Your child might slip off them or they may deflate unexpectedly in water that is too deep for him.

• No glass containers should be allowed in the pool area.

• No running near the edge of the pool.

• Horseplay, such as pushing others underwater, should not be permitted.

• If you have an outdoor pool at home, it should be surrounded with a high fence and a gate that is kept locked. Consult your insurance company to determine how high the fence should be.

• Keep a safety ring and a rope near the pool at all times. Don't let children use the

continued on page 323

A Word of Caution

Although much is known from recent research studies about young children's amazing cognitive abilities, does this imply that it's time to start them on school-like activities in reading, writing, and mathematics?

Some children, in trying to be "parent-pleasers," will "polly-parrot" rote answers. And parents need a word of caution to distinguish rote answering from true learning.

Children who "polly-parrot" rote answers, without any real grasp of the relevant underlying concepts, are actually developing an unsound foundation for later learning.

They merely learn to mimic behaviors and sounds in a mechanical parrot-like fashion.

Unfortunately these inappropriate behaviors are reinforced if they hear their parents boasting to other adults about how "bright" they are ("Nancy is already doing algebra!").

For good learning experiences to occur it is important to provide Youngster with a high level of choice in play. Allow lots of opportunities for her own initiative and creativity.

The secret is to surround the child with appropriate materials—books, puzzles, blocks, and other educational toys—which provide opportunities for academic-type learning in a playful environment.

A young child's room can be given a highly attractive appearance by decorating it with colorful alphabet letters or numbers and with pictures and labels of familiar objects (such as bears and dolls).

Youngster first gets to like her room because of the colors, shapes, and objects.

Later she will gradually become familiar with the various written symbols in the room and with their meaning.

In this way academic learning is integrated into Youngster's life experiences in a manner that is pleasant, enjoyable, and age-appropriate.

Young children's best learning occurs when their interest is aroused. ("What's that?" "What's she doing?" "Why?") That's the time for responsive and supportive teaching on the part of the parent.

Our advice is to avoid turning this valuable teaching into formal school-like academic training.

Although some preschool children can be taught to read, most experts in early childhood education consider it unwise to engage at this age in formal academic training.

Such training usually requires a child to sit quietly and to be attentive for long periods of time.

These demands on a young child are not appropriate for her developmental level and often have an adverse effect later on school learning.

They also take time away from more appropriate developmental activities such as interacting with peers and adults and learning through play.

So how can we use important findings on early childhood cognitive development to give Youngster the type of learning experiences she needs?

Youngster will learn best when important learning experiences—such as language and simple number concepts—are embedded in everyday fun activities.

To the child the focus is on *play*, even though to the adult who engages in a play activity with the child, the primary focus may be on *learning* some new concept. ■

---

continued from page 322

Healthy Handwashing

safety ring as a toy because otherwise it may not be available when needed.

• If your child doesn't know how to swim, now is a good time for him to learn.

• If you don't know how to perform CPR, now is a good time for you to learn. It could mean the difference between breath and death.

Swimming is meant to be a safe and fun activity for children and adults. By observing basic safety rules, you and your child can enjoy many hours of fun. ■

If you have not done so already, four years of age is a good time to help your child develop healthy handwashing habits.

In that way she will be prepared to practice cleanliness when she goes to kindergarten.

Proper handwashing can prevent the spread of many communicable diseases.

Water alone, however, won't kill germs. Soap, preferably liquid soap, is needed too.

Drying the hands with a disposable paper towel will help stop the spread of germs.

Here are some appropriate occasions for your child to practice handwashing:

• When she comes into the house after playing outdoors.

• After using the toilet.

• After sneezing or using a tissue.

• After petting an animal.

• Before eating food.

Good habits, learned during the preschool years, can last a lifetime.

So help your child develop the good habit of washing her hands. ■

When Someone Teases

Sooner or later your child will experience teasing. Teasing occurs when someone says or does something to bother another.

It may take the form of one child calling another a name ("You're a nerd!") or doing something to annoy (for example, poking someone repeatedly in the back).

Child psychologists have noted that, between the ages of two and six years, physical forms of aggression, such as shoving or hitting, decrease.

At the same time, however, non-physical forms of aggression, such as teasing, tend to increase.

Whereas two-year-olds are likely to struggle physically to establish ownership of some toy (which probably neither two-year-old really wants!), a five-year-old is more likely to tease than to hurt another child in a physical manner.

As preschool children develop perspective-taking skills, that is, the ability to see things from someone else's point of view, (which we discussed in the 4 years 3 months issue of *Growing Child*), they are better able to understand specific characteristics of another child.

They may use these newly developed skills—being able to surmise what another child may be thinking or feeling—to engage in teasing behavior.

How can you help your child deal with teasing?

Usually the most effective way to deal with people who tease is to ignore them.

So teach your child to look away or even walk away without answering or reacting in any other way.

Sometimes a group of children may pick on one child to tease. If she responds in an angry manner, the other children will most likely laugh because she behaved in a predictable manner.

They teased her in order to make her angry. The angrier she becomes, the more likely the other children will tease her again and again.

If, on the other hand, she just looks away or walks away, the other children have nothing to laugh about. So they will most likely just leave her alone.

This probably won't happen immediately, so help her by explaining patience, and that her behavior and patience will more

Growing Child

P. O. Box 2505 • W Lafayette, IN 47996
(800) 927-7289
www.GrowingChild.com

Contributing Authors

Phil Bach, O.D., Ph.D.
Miriam Bender, Ph.D.
Joseph Braga, Ed.D.
Laurie Braga, Ph.D.
George Early, Ph.D.
Carol R. Gestwicki, M.S.
Liam Grimley, Ph.D.
Robert Hannemann, M.D., F.A.A.P.
Sylvia Kottler, M.S.
Bill Peterson, Ph.D.

than likely be rewarded with an end to the teasing.

Teasing can be a difficult problem for some children to deal with. If parents are aware that their child is being teased by others, they may help in the following ways:

1) Talk to your child about why other children tease and what outcomes they expect. This will help your child avoid provoking more teasing from others.

2) Let your child know that the most effective way to deal with teasing and to prevent future teasing is to look away or walk away without saying or doing anything else.

3) Role-play for your child what you would do if someone teased you. ("Here's what I would do if someone called me 'stinky pants').

4) Have your child practice role-playing a similar situation ("Show me what you would do if someone pushed you to annoy you.").

5) Once your child knows how to deal with one form of teasing (for example, being called names), have her role-play a different form (such as when someone pulls her hair or pushes her aside).

By anticipating such situations and by role-playing what to do, your child gains the self-confidence she will need to ignore the teasing behavior.

Teach her also to not retaliate by teasing others herself. If your child doesn't want to role-play the situation, you can use two puppets.

One puppet engages in teasing behavior while the other puppet demonstrates how to deal with it by looking away.

Even though the teasing by other children may not immediately stop—it may in fact even increase initially—ignoring the teasing has been found to be, in the long term, the most effective way to deal with this problem.■

Growing Child

'I'm Now Four and a Half'

If you refer to your 54-month-old child as "four years old," he will probably correct you by saying, "I'm now four-and-a-half" or "I'm almost five."

To parents it's only six months difference. But in a young child's time frame, that seems like an eternity. Furthermore, his self-identity at four-and-a-half is different from what it was at three years old, or even at four.

If you ask a three-year-old what he is doing with his blocks, he would probably reply: "playing."

But when you ask your four and-a-half-year-old the same question, he will most likely tell you what he is making: "I'm building a bridge."

In other words, his play activities have become more purposeful. He is beginning to experience a need to achieve.

It's a desire to express oneself by what one can do. Four-and-a- half shows he wants to do things and do them well.

He is also showing more curiosity about the world around him. As a result he is forever asking questions.

He is also showing more interest in numbers and the letters of the alphabet. In particular, he is interested in the letters of his own first name and sometimes his last name.

In seeking to understand his environment, he is now better able to classify objects by color, size, shape, and texture.

He is also better able to compare objects by size (big/small, long/short) and to order events in simple sequences. When you read a story to him, he is able to repeat the main idea, and he likes to predict what will happen next.

His attention span has also improved so that he can now attend to a story for about 10 minutes. When reading to him, it is best to let him take a break rather than forcing him to listen for longer periods of time.

At four-and-a-half, he also likes to use his acquired gross motor and fine motor skills. He loves to run and jump, walk forward and backward, and balance on one foot for about five seconds.

His ability to draw and color has also improved, and he can fold a sheet of paper in halves, quarters, or diagonals.

He enjoys listening to music, especially when he marches, claps, or uses other body movements to the rhythm of the music.

His vocabulary is also expanding very rapidly. And he can sometimes use as many as 10 words in a sentence. As his vocabulary improves, he also develops better sensory and perceptual abilities.

For example, with his improved vocabulary, he is better able to identify different objects by smell (roses, oranges, onions) and he can better describe different tastes (sweet, sour, bitter, salty.)

He has also developed a better sense of touch, being able to distinguish rough from smooth, thick from thin, just by feel.

As he learns to identify more and more objects by name, his vision and observation skills also show improvement. He is also better able to differentiate sounds: soft, softer, softest; loud, louder, loudest.

In other words, his improved ability to use language has an important influence on the development of his sensory and perceptual skills.

His improved vocabulary also helps him develop a better sense of his own self. By now he can probably name most of his important body parts: head, eyes, ears, nose, mouth, arms, hands, feet.

He can also give his own full name, address, telephone number, birthday and age—all of which helps his development of self-identity.

His improved language skills also enable him to interact socially with both adults and peers. This opens up for him a whole new world of social development.

In short, he has become a more adventurous and active learner. He knows that there is still a great deal more he wants and needs to learn. But he also wants some recognition from adults for all that he has already learned, especially in the past six months.

That's why he asserts so strongly: "I'm now four and *a half!*"

Making Books With Your Child

Several months ago we talked about choosing books to read to your child. Some of the very best books for her are those she can make herself with your help.

You can begin now to help her build a library of her own homemade books.

These books will give her a special sense of pride. At the same time, they will help her learn the simple but often overlooked idea that books are words written down so that you can read them later and share them with others.

Here's how you and your child can make a simple book.

Start by using the cardboard backs from notebook pads for the front and back covers.

You can make the pages from plain white paper, or paper with lines like that used in the primary grades at school.

Help her design and plan what will be on the covers. This alone can be a special project.

Help her cut the paper to the size of the cardboard. You can fold or draw lines where she should cut. Then let her practice her fine motor skills by cutting the pages.

Use a hole-puncher to make three holes on the side of each piece of paper and the two cardboard covers. Your child can probably do this if you mark for her where to make the holes so they'll line up evenly.

Then you can use brass paper fasteners, yarn, or pieces of string to hold the pages and cover together.

Now the real fun begins. The ideas for what to put in the books are unlimited. Here are just a few suggestions:

1. A Day in the Life of a Preschooler. You can take photographs of your child going through her usual daily routine.

Paste one on each page and write a caption together underneath, describing the picture.

It's best to let your child tell you what's happening. Write it in her own words: "There's me sleeping. Time to get up." "I'm brushing my teeth." "Mommy's fixing my hair."

Make your lettering large, even, and easy to read.

2. Family and Friends. For this kind of book, take pictures (or drawings by your child) of people, pets, and favorite toys or places in her life. Again, ask her to describe each picture and write down what she says.

3. Theme Books. For these, you and your child can go through magazines looking for pictures and ideas which fit a theme the two of you have chosen.

Some possible ideas for theme books are:

A Book about Animals;

A Book about Trees;

A Book about Feelings;

A Book about People's Jobs;

A Book about Color;

A Book about Gardens;

A Book of Smells;

A Book of Big Things;

A Book of Hands;

A Book of Flowers;

A Book About Good Things to Eat

A Books About Nature

A Book of Little Things;

A Book of Funny Pictures;

A Book of Things that Use Electricity;

A Book About Dogs, Cats or Pets

A Book of Things that Smile;

A Book of Things I Like.

Label and describe each picture in each book you do together.

Working together on such projects will help develop your child's ability to work cooperatively—an important social skill she will need in school and later in her life.

4. Multisensory Books. These books can include things with different textures to

feel, things that make noise, and things with different smells.

For example, your child might want to make a recipe book, describing in pictures and words how to make a food dish she likes. She could put a little vanilla or cinnamon or even peanut butter on the pictures to make them smell.

Or, the two of you could go to a store that sells materials and patterns and ask for obsolete sample swatches. Then you can make a book of things that are soft, rough, smooth, scratchy.

A nature book could be made with leaves, acorns and seeds, a piece of pine cone, or shells pasted onto cardboard pages.

5. My Own Fairy Tales. Ask your child to make up a "Once upon a time ..." story. Write it down as she tells it.

If you have a video camera or tape recorder, record it. Then write her story, a few sentences to a page, in large, neat letters.

Let her illustrate it with her own drawings or with pictures she finds in magazines.

If you have recorded it, she can "read" along in her book as she listens to herself on tape. This is a good activity for reading readiness.

continued on page 327

continued from page 326

6. **"How I Feel About ..."** books. Have your child choose a topic she'd like to write about: my baby brother; love; bugs; going to kindergarten; snow; rain; television.

If she needs help, suggest topics you know are things which she likes.

This is a good opportunity for you to help her develop skill in expressing her feelings, an ability that will help her to understand herself and get along better with others.

The book can be just a few pages long, depending on how much she has to say on the subject.

She might want to have a longer, open-ended book in which she comments on how she feels about a series of topics, adding new ones as she thinks of them.

Write whatever she says about her chosen topic, leaving space for pictures or drawings which will illustrate each topic. Once you and your child have begun making

books on a regular basis, you probably will come up with endless ideas for topics.

Be sure to put a date on each book so you'll know later when it was made.

You might give some thought to buying some bookplates she can put on the inside cover of her books: "This book belongs to_____." Or you can make your own bookplate: "This book was written and illustrated by_____."

On the cover of each of her books, print in large letters the title of the book and her name. Have her color and decorate front and back covers according to her own design.

The books you and she make will be fun to do. They will also add a very special quality to her personal library.

Having "written" them herself, she will be better able to "read" her own books. It will help her make the connections between an

object, its picture, its written word, and its spoken name.

Normally when a child repeatedly hears a favorite story read to her, she comes to memorize the words of that story.

This is one of the first steps in eventually learning to recognize familiar words by connecting the words on the page with the ones she knows.

This process is strengthened with her own stories since she knows right away what the words in the book are, because they're her own.

Making her own books, along with being read favorite stories, are the kinds of activities which will make your child see reading as something that's fun and easy.

Encouraging such a positive attitude toward reading is one of the best things you can do to help her get ready to read when the time is right.■

Sibling Relationships

More than 80 percent of all children growing up in the U.S. have at least one sister or brother.

In a survey of parents which asked why they decided to have more than one child, the most frequent response was "to provide social companionship for our first child."

It has been found that four- to six-year-olds spend more than twice as much time with siblings than with parents.

Not surprisingly, therefore, siblings exert an important influence on one another's development.

Sibling interactions—which can be either positive or negative—help to foster social awareness of another person's needs, feelings, intentions, and ways of thinking.

They also provide opportunities to learn about loyalty, cooperation, and affection,

as well as how to deal with conflict and competition.

In the past, when researchers studied sibling relationships, they focused almost exclusively on a negative aspect, namely, sibling rivalry.

Child psychologists today indicate that more attention needs to be paid to the positive influences which siblings can have on one another.

In this article, therefore, we will focus on some of those positive influences. Next month we will address the issue of sibling rivalry.

What are some of the positive influences which siblings can have on one another?

It has been found that, with the help and encouragement of parents, a rich emotional relationship can begin with

the birth of a baby brother or sister.

By helping to care for a newborn infant, the older child can develop greater social competence.

By the end of the infant's first year, many siblings have become social partners and friends.

Research shows that preschool siblings interact differently with one another than with their parents. They are more likely to confide in one another—sharing thoughts, feelings, interests—than with their parents.

They will also talk with one another more than with parents about their friends, and even sometimes about sexual questions.

With parents, they are more likely to listen without interrupting and show greater

continued on page 328

continued from page 327

concern and affection for one another than for a child who is not a family member.

It has been found that siblings can provide great emotional support for one another in times of adversity.

For example, if there was chronic disharmony in the family—with parents not getting along—it seemed to bring siblings closer together.

Likewise, in times of personal stress—such as not getting along with other children—siblings were found to draw closer together and to depend on one another for emotional support.

An older sibling can also be an excellent teacher and role model for a younger brother or sister. Research shows that older boys tend to exert dominance and to rely more on physical power.

Older sisters, on the other hand, are usually more skillful as teachers, being more patient and more willing to explain. Not only do these interactions benefit the younger child, but they enhance the self-esteem and sense of responsibility of the older child.

The influence which siblings have on one another is often *direct,* such as the effects of mutual interactions on language development, personality, and intelligence.

But research studies indicate that they also influence one another's development *indirectly,* such as when younger children take to heart the advice they hear a parent giving to an older child.

It should be noted, of course, that sibling relationships vary considerably from one family to another, depending, for example, on the age, sex, and number of siblings.

In order to understand sibling relationships, it is not sufficient to look simply at how the children get along with one another.

Research studies indicate that it is even more important to look at each child's

relationships with the rest of the family members, especially the parents.

How parents react and respond to the unique characteristics of each of their children greatly influences sibling relationships.

It has been found, for example, that when parents are warm and affectionate toward all their children—fostering secure parent-child attachments—the siblings are more likely to develop warm relationships with one another.

On the other hand, when parents are cold and hostile, the children are more likely to develop antagonism toward one another.

It is sometimes difficult for parents to strike a balance between treating all their children with equal affection, yet at the same time recognizing the unique strengths and weaknesses of each child.

Family meetings can often provide opportunities for individual characteristics of each child to be identified and recognized in an atmosphere in which all family members feel prized and loved.

Contrary to popular opinion, the absence of siblings is not necessarily harmful to the development of an only child.

An only child has sometimes been characterized as a self-centered, overly dependent, "spoiled brat."

But researchers have recently presented quite a different picture of the only child as being achievement oriented and usually well-adjusted when interacting with both peers and adults.

This is most likely to occur when parents of an only child provide appropriate opportunities for their child to interact with other children, such as in play groups and childcare settings.

Next month we will discuss the negative side of sibling relationships, namely, sibling rivalry. We will then make several recommendations on how parents can deal with and prevent this particular problem.■

Talking Games

Here are two "talking games" which parents can use to stretch their child's imagination and build vocabulary.

Hand Game: "My Hands"
My hands upon my head I place,

On my shoulders, on my face,

On my lips, by my side;

Then behind me they will hide.

Now I'll hold them way up high,

and let my fingers gaily fly.

Now I'll hold them down in front of me,

And clap them—one, two, three.

My eyes can see. (Make eyeglasses with hands.)

My mouth can talk. (Move thumb and index finger as if talking.)

My ears can hear. (Cup hand and place it behind ear.)

My feet can walk. (Make second and third fingers of hand "walk.")

My nose can smell. (Touch nose with index finger.)

My teeth can bite. (Move fingers together and apart as if chewing.)

My lids can flutter. (Hold hands up to eyes and flutter fingers.)

My hand can write. (Pretend to hold a pencil and write.)

Finger Game: "My Hands Are Grand"
I squeeze a lemon just like this, to get the juices out.

I hold a pitcher just like this, to pour milk from the spout.

I crack a nutshell just like this, to get a peanut.

I peel an orange just like this, when I want the inside out.

Oh, me! Oh, my!

My hands are grand, they do so many things.■

Shyness

Most people have experienced shyness at some time in their lives.

Shyness may be exhibited in a number of ways: blushing, trembling hands or knees, a queasy stomach, dryness of the mouth, a quickened heartbeat, or simply being overly quiet in the company of others.

Among adults, as many as 40 percent consider themselves to be too shy in public and wish they could change this behavior.

A shy preschooler will cling to her parents, fearful of encountering any new person or social situation.

A shy child will also generally be reluctant, for example, to participate in a summer camp or join in any normal group activity, preferring instead to watch others from a safe distance.

Excessive shyness frequently causes emotional discomfort and embarrassment.

Overly shy children usually develop negative feelings—including inferiority—toward themselves. As a result, they fear they will be perceived by others as unattractive, unpopular, and inferior.

The problems of the shy child can become a vicious cycle. In other words, because they lack basic social skills, they withdraw from social experiences and interactions which, in turn, deprives them of the opportunity to develop the very social skills they need.

In a preschool child, excessive shyness can also have other detrimental effects.

Social interaction is needed not only for a young child's social development, but it is also essential for good physical, emotional, and cognitive development.

That is why shyness is such an important topic to consider during the preschool years.

Parents of a shy child often feel frustrated because they are at a loss to know what to do.

Unfortunately, they frequently may have

difficulty hiding their frustration from their child.

What to avoid

Here are some behaviors parents should try to avoid when dealing with an overly shy child:

1. Don't express your frustration in front of your child. Being angry with her will only cause the child to lose her self-esteem and thereby become more socially withdrawn.

2. Don't ignore the child who is shy. Because shy children rarely speak up or act out, they are often ignored or overlooked by both parents and teachers, which, of course, also results in lowering their self-esteem.

3. At the same time, it is not wise to be overly protective of the shy child. Over-protectiveness often leads to greater social withdrawal and more clinging to parents. Be supportive, but not overprotective.

4. Above all, don't ridicule a child because of her shyness. Shy children are particularly sensitive about their inability to interact socially with others.

5. Don't force a shy child to engage in social interactions for which she is not yet ready.

When forcefully thrust into a new social situation for which she has not been prepared, a shy child will usually want to

retreat immediately—and, as a result, may become even more socially withdrawn.

6. Don't allow siblings to make the problems of the shy child worse. It has been found that two-thirds of all excessively shy children had older brothers or sisters who bullied them or made fun of them.

Basic understanding

What then can parents do to help a child who is excessively shy? A good starting point is to have some basic understanding of what causes a child to be shy.

From recent research studies, it would appear that several factors are involved including *genetics, temperament, environmental influences, and lack of basic social skills*. We will consider each of these factors in turn.

Researchers have found that between 10 and 15 percent of all babies are born with a *genetic predisposition* to be shy and socially withdrawn.

From the moment they are born, these children exhibit higher levels of motor arousal and a higher heart rate than other infants.

About three-fourths of the children identified as shy at birth continue, during the early childhood years, to be overly self-conscious and overly anxious in social situations.

These research findings lend support to the viewpoint that shyness may be part of a child's basic *temperament*.

But there is also evidence which indicates that the child's *environment* can greatly influence the degree of shyness.

It has been found, for example, that shy children usually have at least one parent who is shy.

Thus the child's shyness may not only be genetic, but also the shy parent may become an environmental role model of shy behavior;

continued on page 330

continued from page 329

It has also been found that shy children generally lack some basic social skills. Hence they need to be taught directly how to interact socially with other children since they have not been able to acquire these skills on their own.

What to do:

Here are some considerations for helping an overly shy child:

1. Shy children are generally helped the most by persons who show understanding and sensitivity toward their problem.

2. A shy child will learn how best to interact socially by being placed in a small group, preferably of friends and acquaintances, with clearly defined, structured activities.

3. Placing a shy child in a small group with children who are younger can sometimes help boost self-confidence.

4. An older child who is found to be sensitive and caring can be trained to help a shy child become more involved in small group activities.

It should be noted that the friendship and encouragement of peers is often more effective in overcoming shyness than any interventions by an adult.

When an adult intrudes into children's interactions—even if it is to praise or encourage the shy child—attention immediately focuses on the adult and the child-to-child communication ceases. When this happens, the shy child may feel isolated, embarrassed, or more dependent on the adult.

5. When facing a new social situation, parents should generally allow a shy child to set her own pace in adjusting to a new experience. Just make sure not to let her completely avoid all new social situations.

6. It will also help to discuss beforehand with the child what a new social situation will entail and even to role-play

what she will say or do.

7. Treat your child's shyness as a fairly normal developmental challenge. In seeing your relaxed approach, others will be less likely to ridicule or make fun of a shy child.

8. One of the most effective ways for parents to help a preschool child overcome excessive shyness is by building the child's own self-esteem (See "Ten Ways to Help Build Your Child's Self-esteem" in month 47).

Growing Child

P. O. Box 2505 • W Lafayette, IN 47996
(800) 927-7289
www.GrowingChild.com

Contributing Authors
Phil Bach, O.D., Ph.D.
Miriam Bender, Ph.D.
Joseph Braga, Ed.D.
Laurie Braga, Ph.D.
George Early, Ph.D.
Carol R. Gestwicki, M.S.
Liam Grimley, Ph.D.
Robert Hannemann, M.D., F.A.A.P.
Sylvia Kottler, M.S.
Bill Peterson, Ph.D.

9. If a child continues to be excessively shy in most group situations over a long period of time, it would be wise to seek the help of a mental health professional who specializes in dealing with children's problems.

Lastly, three considerations should be noted:

• It is important to remember that some degree of shyness is perfectly normal, and is to be expected in young children.

• Being shy will not necessarily be a barrier to success.

Many shy people (the composer Beethoven, poets T.S. Eliot and Robert Frost, Presidents Abraham Lincoln, Theodore Roosevelt and Jimmy Carter, historical figures such as Tomas Edison and Albert Einstein, as well as entertainers such as Brad Pitt, Lucille Ball, Tom Hanks and Julia Roberts)have not let their shyness impede their ability to perform in a public arena.

• One of the greatest gifts that a parent can give to a shy child is the love, understanding, and encouragement she will need to deal with or overcome her shyness and thus truly enjoy new social interactions.■

Getting Ready to Read

Some children learn to read with ease during the preschool years. Others still may not be ready to read in the first grade.

It's important to respect each child's particular skills and interests. As we've said before, it's important not to push Youngster to read before he's ready and eager for the task.

However, there are some games you can play with your child now which will help him get ready to read.

Does your child recognize his favorite foods in the grocery store by their wrappers or boxes?

This is a good sign that he's ready for some prereading games. The grocery store is a rich storehouse of prereading materials.

One of the skills Youngster needs in order to read is the ability to recognize the general appearance of a particular word and distinguish it from others.

For example, the word cookies looks different from the word vegetables even if you don't know how to read either one.

Grocery store items make good material for learning this skill because each product has a clue such as a colored picture of the product which helps distinguish one item from another.

Many products are easily recognized because of their well-known trademark symbols. These clues can help Youngster recognize a familiar product before he can actually read its name.

There are many fun games you and Youngster can play using products com-

monly found in the supermarket or grocery store. We will describe a few. Then you and your child can probably invent and create more of your own.

For these games you will need to begin saving empty boxes and cans. Save duplicate examples of products.

Open a can from the bottom rather than the top. This will allow you to have ones that look just like those in the store.

You and your child can save labels from cans, bottles, boxes, or advertisements. Mount each one on a large index card.

Make the "cut-outs" large enough that Youngster can easily recognize the product.

Try to make at least five cards for each product-name so you can use them in different games. Following are some games you can play with these materials.

1. Card Games. Give Youngster several product-name cards. Keep in your own hand at least twice as many cards, including duplicates of the ones you gave Youngster.

Hold up one of your cards and ask, "Do you have Campbell's Tomato Soup?" (or whatever name card you have).

If Youngster correctly states that he has a duplicate of that card, he can take your product-name card and put that pair aside.

When he has no more cards in his hand, he wins. Then he can be the "caller."

You can make up many variations of this game as Youngster's skill increases.

When you first play the card game, put a picture of the product along with the word on each card. This will give Youngster an extra clue to use in matching his cards to yours.

Later you can play the same game using cards which have letters and words like those he will have to learn and use in school.

2. Lotto. Cut several pieces of lightweight cardboard four times as big as the product-name cards you've got.

Divide each one into four squares, and paste a product name label on each square.

Give Youngster a lotto card and four matching product-name cards.

Show him how to match each product-name card to the space on the lotto card containing its match.

When he can do this easily, give him several lotto cards plus all the matching product-name cards and let him play the game on his own.

Let him show you his finished lotto cards

continued on page 332

continued from page 331

to check that he's matching them correctly.

As his skill increases, you can increase the challenge by making some new lotto cards with eight or more squares.

You can also increase the difficulty by finding product-names which are somewhat similar yet different such as four different kinds of Campbell's soup labels.

3. Bingo. Make bingo cards from lightweight cardboard. Divide each card into nine squares. Leave the center square "free," and paste eight product-name labels on the other squares.

Cut a piece of lightweight cardboard into squares to make markers which can cover the product-names on the cards.

Call out a product-name and show Youngster how to cover with a marker the square of the name you called.

When Youngster has covered a row of squares up and down, across or diagonally, he wins and can say "Bingo!"

At first, call out only product-names which are on Youngster's bingo card. Later you can make the game harder and call out names which are not on his card.

This game can be made more challenging by writing only the written word on the bingo card so that he has to find the written word on hearing its name. He doesn't have the visual clue as he did earlier.

If he has a lot of difficulty, give him some more practice with card games first.

Bingo will be even more fun for your child if a friend or an older brother or sister joins the fun. Let everybody have a turn being "caller."

If Youngster enjoys bingo, you can make up other cards with his help, using pictures, letters, or words.

4. Grocery Store. Set up an area of your home like a small "grocery store," putting the empty cans and boxes you have saved on shelves low enough for Youngster to reach.

Make labels of lightweight cardboard which identify a general category of food (soups, vegetables, fruit, cereal, and cookies).

Put the labels on the shelves, and remove all the cans and boxes.

Have Youngster restock the shelves according to category. Help if necessary, but let him do the work.

This activity will give Youngster practice in classification as well as prereading skills as he figures out where to put the canned peaches, the cereal, and the other products.

Direct him to "shop" for different items: "Get me one can of tuna fish and a box of cereal."

As you increase the number of instructions, you'll be giving Youngster practice and experience in paying attention and remembering. But don't expect him to remember more than three to five things at a time.

Make shopping lists for the "grocery store." At first, use cut-out labels to make the shopping list.

Later try just printing the product names. This will be more difficult for Youngster because the card will have the printed words but will not contain the picture of the product.

Using just the printed words will help stimulate simple word-recognition skills.

Give Youngster a shopping list and a box or basket as a grocery cart. Then let him "go shopping."

When he is done, "check him out" at a pretend "cash register." Check to see if his groceries match the names on his shopping list.

Youngster can help in making future "shopping lists." This will help him learn about the things used about the house.

At the same time it will provide a good opportunity for you and your child to work cooperatively at something which is an important part of family life.

As you play these games you will get a better idea of which kinds of food he most enjoys.

You will also discover which things he finds easy and which ones give him difficulty. Keep the games fun and challenging but not too difficult.

Praise him when he does well and give him a chance to "pat himself on the back" for a job well done.

If you discover that a game you've planned is too hard for him, put it aside and go back to something more familiar that he's already done successfully. In this way he won't become discouraged or frustrated with the tasks.

As always, keep in mind the importance of exposing your child to good children's literature as he's getting ready to read.

Enlist the help of your librarian as you continue to provide inviting and interesting books.

The goal is to increase Youngster's interest and reading readiness as you show him that reading is important, useful and fun!

He should feel good about his skill, understanding that it will increase with practice and use.■

Exaggerations—Lies or Fantasy?

Four-year-olds are fascinated by words—and love to use them for their sounds as well as for their effect on the listener.

The results sometimes range from amusing to astonishing, if, in fact, the listener is not actually stunned.

At the same time, four-year-olds are often great tellers of tales. Four often seems to feel that what he has to say must be bigger and better than life if anyone is to pay attention to him.

This is quite understandable when you consider that his experiences, although exciting to him, may be pretty humdrum to adults.

Also, what seems very large to him may, through the experienced eyes of his parents, look pretty small.

So, he may announce importantly one day, "The blackbirds came today! Jillions and jillions of them, all over our backyard!"

Or, "Mama, come look! There's a great big spider on the screen. He's big and black. He's really BIG—big as a house!"

Don't put him down, even indulgently, by saying, "Now, the word is not a 'jillion,' it's a million! And you know that a million blackbirds couldn't fit in our backyard!"

What does Four know about a "million"?

He only knows that it means "a lot." To him the 50 or so starlings strutting around his backyard is an uncountable number!

How much better to acknowledge his important news by saying, "Wow! There must really be a lot of those birds. I'll have to look! I wonder where they came from?"

When you share his important news, he feels important. He learns again that language is an important tool of communication.

Further, you might add to his knowledge by commenting, "Those are big birds, aren't they? They are called starlings. I wonder what so many of them are doing in our yard."

On the subject of the spider, it's best not to say: "How could a spider as big as a house sit on the screen? You shouldn't tell such lies!"

How much better to accept the fact that you agree that it is a bigger-than-usual spider.

Talk about the fact that most large spiders are garden spiders, that they eat insects, and that the spider is probably more afraid of us than we are of the spider!

We can give children a chance to enjoy the exaggerations of childhood. Never again will things look so big, so bright, so exciting to them. Why not enjoy it with them?■

The Wonders of Water

Children are curious about the world around them. You can use this natural curiosity to help your child learn about the wonders of water.

Begin with three different bowls of water—one cold, one lukewarm, and one hot (but not too hot for your hand).

Have your child put his hand in each bowl so that he can feel the different sensations.

Then let him watch you boil some water in a saucepan with a lid. He will discover that water has changed into steam.

Next let him fill an ice cube tray with water which can then be put in the freezer.

Ask him if he already knows what will happen. Later let him see and feel the solid ice cubes.

You can also discuss with him some of the uses of water:

(1) To drink when I'm thirsty.

(2) To wash myself when I'm dirty.

(3) To swim in when I'm hot.

(4) To cook vegetables.

(5) To water flowers and house plants.

Later you can come back to the same topic to see how many of the uses he remembers.

Then teach him some other uses, such as to wash clothes or to provide heat by hot water pipes, or a hot water bottle.

Your child can also learn that some objects float on water while others do not. Let him engage in this scientific experiment:

Have him collect a variety of objects which he can put, one by one, in a large tub of water: a stick, a stone, a feather, a flavored ice stick, a nail.

Before he drops each object in the water, ask him to predict whether the object will float or sink.

At first his predications will not be very accurate. But with practice, his ability to predict will greatly improve.

By teaching your child about the wonders of water, you are also helping him to be more observant and more aware of other wonders of nature in his immediate environment.■

Perception of Time

Our modern technological society is extremely "time" conscious. It is even said today that "time is money." We have become a nation of clock-watchers.

In earlier times, people had a simpler lifestyle. Without clocks and watches to regulate their day, they used a more relaxed, less demanding time frame (for example, sunrise, midday, sunset).

It is important to realize that a young child's perception of time is more akin to the old world lifestyle than the modern one.

That is because a young child's perception of time is different from that of an adult. A young child's understanding of time develops slowly over a number of years.

Concepts such as specific times and dates are not mastered until about age eight.

Likewise, preschool children have great difficulty understanding the inverse relationship between time and speed. (The faster one travels, the less time a journey will take.)

They can more easily learn the positive relationships between speed and distance (the faster one goes, the farther one will travel) and time and distance (the longer one travels, the farther one will go).

Only after these two relationships are understood will the young child understand the relationship between time and speed.

Young children also tend to order events in the time sequence in which they are presented—which parents may often interpret as defiance of their authority!

For example, when a parent tells a preschool child, "You can go outside to play after you clean up your room," the parent may be dismayed to find that the preschooler interpreted this message in the following time sequence:

(1) Play first and (2) clean up later.

In other words, a preschool child is less

When using time-out as a discipline technique, use a kitchen timer which your child can see rather than a clock. In this way she can see the time limit actually change.

likely to focus attention on a little preposition (like the word "after") than on the time sequence in which he heard the message: (1) "go outside to play," followed by (2) "clean up your room."

It has also been noted that preschool children have difficulty interpreting correctly a sentence in which the passive voice is used: "Johnny was pushed by Jim."

A preschooler is likely to think that since Johnny's name was mentioned first, he is the one who did the pushing.

Preschoolers are accustomed to thinking that when Johnny's name is first in time sequence ("Johnny hit Jim"), then Johnny is the one who performed the action (hitting or pushing).

As children develop better perspective-taking skills (which we discussed some months ago), they eventually learn to interpret correctly who was the pusher and who was the one pushed.

Now is a good time for parents to help

improve their preschool child's perception of time. Here are some suggestions:

• Establish a routine for everyday events (rising, getting dressed, eating meals).

• Talk to your child about the order in which events will occur during the day.

• Instead of using an adult time frame ("at 9 o'clock"), use your child's frame of reference (for example, "after breakfast").

• At the end of the day, discuss the events of the day in a certain order. Youngster may need some prompting since preschool children tend to focus on the here and now rather than on the past or future.

• When giving your child a command, express the events in the order in which you want them to be carried out. ("First pick up your toys; then you can go outside to play," rather than "You can go outside after you pick up your toys").

• When using time-out as a discipline technique, use a kitchen timer which your child can see rather than a clock. In this way he can see the time limit actually change.

• A three-minute time-out is usually as effective with a preschool child as any longer one. Three minutes is about as long as you can expect a healthy preschooler to sit still.

• When traveling in the car, talk with your child about the places you will visit in sequence, the distance you will travel, and the amount of time it will take.

Even though a preschool child cannot organize information to draw a map of his own, research studies indicate that children as young as three years of age can use a simple map to find their way through places they have never seen before.

Even though your preschool child may not yet fully grasp the concepts you discuss and their relationships, he is learning new vocabulary and becoming aware of important new concepts which will help him better understand his world.■

Sibling Rivalry

Last month we discussed some of the positive aspects of sibling relationships.

This month we will address an issue which every family with more than one child will most likely experience—sibling rivalry.

Sibling rivalry refers to feelings of jealousy, resentment, or hostility which develop between children of the same family.

Parents usually become concerned about any animosity shown by one family member toward another. Actually sibling rivalry is an inevitable and normal part of family living.

Sibling rivalry may begin while the mother is still pregnant. The first-born child witnesses the air of excitement and the preparations being made for the new arrival.

It eventually dawns on the young child that she will no longer be "cock-of-the-walk" in the family. Another child will be demanding and receiving Mom's and Dad's attention and affection.

Research studies indicate that, with the arrival of a newborn baby, parents become less involved with any older child in the family. It appears that this pattern may last for some years.

In other studies it was also found that when mothers are with two or more of their children, they are more attentive and more responsive to the younger one.

As a result, an older child can develop feelings of jealousy and resentment toward the younger one.

These feelings may express themselves in outward actions, such as shaking the baby's crib.

Or they may take the form of deliberate disobedience or regression to infant-like behaviors in feeding or toilet training.

Protest-type behaviors will most likely be exhibited whenever the parent is actively engaged in taking care of the younger child. It is during the preschool years that sibling rivalry is most in evidence.

A preschool child is still highly dependent on her parents because she has usually not yet established secure relationships with anyone else.

Not surprisingly, therefore, sibling rivalry is most likely to occur when the children are less than three years apart in age and when they are of the same gender.

Other factors which cause added stress in the preschooler's life, such as divorce or family mobility, can provoke or intensify sibling rivalry.

Rivalry between siblings will often be at its worst whenever a parent is present.

Once the parent leaves the room, the siblings may resume playing cooperatively

together. This is merely a sign that the children are competing with one another for the parent's attention or affection.

One of the most important steps in understanding and dealing with sibling rivalry is to realize that it is an inevitable and normal part of family life.

This is because parents, by necessity, must deal differently with each of their children.

For example, it would not be appropriate for parents to use the same discipline technique with a -one-year-old that they

would use with a seven-year-old.

They should also expect better table manners from the older child, which, of course, causes resentment leading to more sibling rivalry.

But the older child should also have more privileges appropriate for his age, such as more freedom in play activities and style of dress.

It is these inevitable differences in treatment that usually lead to feelings of jealousy and resentment.

Parents should make it clear to their children that treating all family members fairly does not mean treating them identically. ("When you are as old as Johnny, you will be allowed to go to bed later.")

It is also wise to point out that with new privileges go new responsibilities. ("Yes, Johnny can stay up later, but he also has to help with the dishes.")

It is inevitable that parents will compare one child with another in their own minds.

But if they make those comparisons in the presence of their children, they fan the fires of jealousy and resentment.

Next month we will present some recommendations for parents to reduce sibling rivalry.

It must be stressed, however, that there is no single "blueprint" or "magic wand" for dealing with these problems.

Parents must always take into consideration not only each individual situation but also the unique characteristics of each one of their children.■

Fire Safety

Every year thousands of children die needlessly in fires due to inadequate fire safety education.

Parents teach young children how to tie their shoelaces, how to dress themselves, and how to get along with others. But all too frequently they fail to teach their child about fire safety.

Young children are curious about fire in all its forms, whether it be the burning of a log, the flames of a newspaper, or the flick of a cigarette lighter.

Yet this same curiosity, if unchecked or unsupervised, can become the cause of tragedy.

Children playing with matches are still the leading cause of fire-related deaths and injuries for children under five years old in the U.S.

It is important therefore to consider what parents need to do and what young children need to know in order to prevent tragedy.

What parents need to do:

• Teach your child about the dangers of fire. Your fire safety lesson (see below) may save your child's life and yours too.

• Teach your child what to do if his clothes catch fire: First STOP, then DROP to the floor, and ROLL to put out the flames. It is important to teach this maneuver which can prevent severe burns.

• Keep matches and other flammable materials away from children.

• Store all flammable liquids (such as gasoline, kerosene, flammable cleaning supplies, and charcoal lighter fluid) outside of the home.

• Replace frayed electrical cords immediately. Don't overload circuits or extension cords. Do not put cords and wires under rugs. Turn off and unplug any appliance that overheats, sputters, sparks or emits an unusual smell.

• Keep any heat source (such as an electric heater) at least three feet away from drapes, furniture, or anything that could ignite.

• If there are toddlers or young children in the house. cover any outlets that are not in use

• Keep a screen in front of the fireplace whenever a fire is burning.

• Check to make sure all appliances—stove, hair dryer, iron.—have been turned off whenever you leave the house.

• At Christmas time, make sure to unplug all Christmas tree lights if no adult is in the house and when you leave the house.

• Make sure all your child's clothes are flame-retardant.

• Keep a fire extinguisher in any room with a potential fire hazard, such as kitchen or garage.

• Make sure to have a separate smoke detector on each level of your home.

• Have your child help you check the smoke detector's batteries periodically to make sure they are in good working order.

• Have an escape plan for every room with at least two possible ways to get out in an emergency. Talk about what to do if there's a fire in the house.

• Practice a fire drill. Remember, before opening any door, touch it to see if it's hot—if it is, don't open it.

• Designate a meeting place a safe distance outside the house where everyone can be accounted for.

• Store a flashlight in each bedroom for use in an emergency.

• Keep an inventory of each room's valuable items in a separate location.

• Keep all important documents and papers in a fireproof box.

• If candles are lit, keep them out of reach of children and pets and away from fabrics and furniture.

• If your house does catch on fire, shout a warning to everyone in the house and leave as quickly as possible—on all fours if necessary to stay below the smoke level.

• Cover mouth and nose with a moist towel or clothing to protect from dangerous fumes.

• Check to make sure all occupants are safely out of the house. Call for help as soon as possible.

What your child needs to know:

• Never play with fire. Even though a fire is fascinating to watch, it can be highly dangerous.

• Never play with matches or any other flammable substance.

• Never turn on any electric appliance—such as an electric heater or stove—unless an adult is present.

• If you see a fire starting—even if you were the cause of it—get help immediately. Otherwise the fire may quickly get out of control.

• Learn how to dial an emergency number for help. Never dial this number for fun because by doing so, you may put someone else's life at risk.■

P. O. Box 2505 • W Lafayette, IN 47996
(800) 927-7289
www.GrowingChild.com
© 2011 Growing Child, Inc.

Contributing Authors

Phil Bach, O.D., Ph.D.
Miriam Bender, Ph.D.
Joseph Braga, Ed.D.
Laurie Braga, Ph.D.
George Early, Ph.D.
Carol R. Gestwicki, M.S.
Liam Grimley, Ph.D.
Robert Hannemann, M.D., F.A.A.P.
Sylvia Kottler, M.S.
Bill Peterson, Ph.D.

Growing Child

Encouraging Special Gifts and Talents

In *Growing Child* we tend to focus on "typical" growth and development. We tell you what you can expect from your child at different ages and how you can help her grow.

We also talk regularly about how you can recognize any special learning problems she might have so you can help her cope with them successfully.

We think it's equally important that you learn to recognize those special gifts and talents your child might have so you can help her develop these skills to their fullest capacity.

What do we mean by special gifts and talents? A gift or talent is something that a child is blessed with as a birthright. It is a seed which—with proper nourishment—will grow and flower.

How do you know what special gifts or talents your child may have? How can you best help her develop her special gifts?

Here are some guidelines that may help you answer these questions:

1. Giftedness may be expressed in many different ways. If you were told your child was highly gifted, what would you expect?

That she would be able to read, write, or do mathematics far ahead of most children her age? That she would have a special gift for drawing, acting, or playing a musical instrument?

Most people have ideas of giftedness that are limited to these kinds of talents. In

actual fact, areas of giftedness have very broad limits.

Your children might be especially gifted in their ability to understand other people's feelings. Or some might have an outstanding ability to remember past events.

The skills a human being possesses are indicators of potential giftedness.

Howard Gardner has developed a theory that incorporates eight ways of being smart (see "Frames of Mind: The theory of multiple intelligences," Basic Books).

2. Some children may be highly gifted in one area but average or even below average in others. There is a well-known artist in Japan who is mentally retarded. Though unable to speak well, he is able to communicate beautifully through his drawing.

He was fortunate enough to have a caring and talented teacher who, in searching for a way to reach this man when he was a child, discovered and encouraged his natural talent for drawing.

Some children are smarter, more talented, better coordinated, and generally more outstanding than others in almost everything they try. These are the ones who are most likely to be noticed and labeled as "gifted."

But even these children have areas in which they are not outstanding.

And there are many more children whose special gifts may go unnoticed because their talent lies in an unexpected area or because they seem ordinary in other ways.

It is your challenge— and your responsibility—to discover your child's special gifts and talents and to give her the chance to develop them.

3. Every child has the potential to be creative. Creativity is the way in which a child uses her special gifts to express her own unique qualities.

Creativity is self-expression. It is a basic human need. It is not something reserved only for certain people, though many adults have never learned a means through which to share with others their own unique outlook on life.

People who have never developed their ability to express who they are can feel a sense of frustration and lack of fulfillment.

continued on page 338

continued from page 337

You can help your child develop her unique talents so that she can express them creatively.

There is no other human being just like her. She comes into the world with the seed of potential gifts which will make her different from anyone else.

She will respond in her own special way to each experience she has. She will be drawn to some things and to some people over others.

Given appropriate opportunity, and with your encouragement, she will learn to express what she thinks and feels about life in her own special way.

4. A child's giftedness requires nurturance.
It is in the nature of an apple seed to become an apple tree. No matter what, it will never be an orange tree.

But in order to grow into an apple tree, the apple seed must be planted and given the right soil, lighting, moisture, and other conditions.

Your child will naturally be drawn to activities which give her a chance to grow the "seeds" of the special gifts that are a part of her nature.

But she needs opportunity and encouragement in order to develop her natural talents.

For example, you might notice your child singing along whenever she hears music on the radio, on television, or on CDs you play.

Some CDs of her own—not just "children's music" but a variety of selections of good music—as well as your encouragement will give her a chance to expand her auditory perception and interest.

5. A child needs to develop basic skills in an area before she can use those skills creatively.

For example, she needs to know how to cook before she can combine ingredients in new and interesting ways to invent her own special recipes.

To be creative, she must first have "know-how." Then she will be able to use the basic tools and information in an exploratory way, playing around with what she knows in order to come up with a variety of unusual, interesting, and unique combinations ... and that's what creativity is all about.

People often mistakenly think it involves no skill to be creative—that creativity simply is an unconventional approach to something.

This kind of misunderstanding can lead to hesitation in teaching children basic skills for fear of interfering with their "spontaneous creativeness."

In fact, we handicap children by not teaching them the basic skills as much as by discouraging their spontaneous efforts.

There is no reason why a command of basic skills should interfere with your child's spontaneity in creating.

The key lies in how the foundations, the basic skills, are taught.

6. A child needs to use her gifts in order to develop them.
There is an ancient Chinese proverb that can help you guide your child in learning the basic skills necessary for her to express her gifts and talents creatively:

I hear, and I forget.

I see, and I remember.

I do, and I understand.

This sounds so obvious, but it requires some thoughtfulness to put into practice.

For example, how many times have you told your child how to do something and become impatient when she doesn't do it "correctly" right away?

How often have you shown her how to use something and ended up doing it completely yourself while she simply watches? It's easier to take over than to let her do things herself.

But it's important to take the time to let

her try things until she can do them and eventually do them well.

Perseverance is an important part of learning to use one's special gifts. It takes a while to learn a new skill, and a child needs the chance to practice it until she masters it.

She needs your support, encouragement, and interest in her attempts to learn and your loving patience when she is not yet successful. She needs to do in order to learn to do with greater skill and creativity.

7. A child signals her areas of potential giftedness by how often and how long she shows interest in an activity.

She will naturally be attracted to certain activities and will want to engage in them whenever she gets the chance.

For example, your child might particularly enjoy pretending to be someone she's seen on television or in books you've read to her.

Or she might be very observant when you're taking care of your garden or house plants. Whatever her interest is, you can best encourage it by:

• Noticing and commenting on her interest. "I see you like to be with me when I'm fixing something that's broken."

• Giving her the opportunity for involvement. "Would you like to try to fix this yourself?"

continued on page 339

continued from page 338

• Offering guidance without taking over or pushing too hard. "Here's how I do it. Now you try. I'll help, if you want, but see what you can do by yourself."

• Giving her encouragement and being patient with her efforts. "That's a good try. It takes a while sometimes to get things just the way you want. Want to try again?"

• Being accepting, but allowing her to judge her own achievements. "You worked so hard at that. How do you feel about what you did?"

• Providing her with materials and the time and space in which to work on her own. "I'll be here if you want me. Why don't you try it on your own now?"

8. One of the best ways to encourage and support a child's development of her gifts is to be careful not to discourage them.

There are so many offhand comments, made without thinking, which can turn off a child's interest and excitement in an activity. And once turned off, it's hard to

rekindle again.

Here are some of the kinds of "roadblocks to creativity" to watch out for:

• "Don't bother me now. I'm too busy to look at your picture."

• "What's this mess? Didn't I tell you to stay out of the kitchen?"

• "That's for girls (boys). I don't want to see you do it again."

• "That will never work."

• "That's a what?" "What is this stupid (ugly, weird) thing?"

• "What would people think if they saw you do that?"

• "Come on now, is that the best you can do?"

• "That's nice." (said without interest or even noticing what your child is showing you).

• "That's not the way to do it. It doesn't look right."

• "Why can't you do it like your sister?" (brother, cousin).

We all have busy times and we have our moments of impatience and annoyance with our children, no matter how much we love them.

It's hard to be alert to the effects of your reactions (or non-reactions) to your child's every word and deed. But it's worth the effort because your opinion is so very important to her.

With your help and encouragement, she can develop her special gifts and talents to their fullest capacity so that she can grow to be all that she is capable of becoming.■

Fairy Tales

In a research report from the National Council of Teachers of English, the author urges parents and teachers to use fairy tales more frequently, particularly when reading aloud to children.

According to this report, children from kindergarten age onward who are sheltered from terrors such as those which appear in fairy tales are prevented from learning the strength necessary to cope with them.

Needless to say, some children witness more horrors on television.

The author suggests that fairy tales also provide a necessary respite from the struggles of dealing with the real world.

He cites evidence that children who read fairy tales may be engaged in a "sober striv-

ing to deal with the crisis of experience (children) are undergoing." At around eight years interest in fairy tales peaks. Fairy tales confirm the child's beliefs about the world. The protagonist, whom the child identifies with, is the center of the universe. The world has magic. Finding the right magic will transform important events.

A good child conforms to a parent-figure's rules, an example of which is Snow White not

being allowed to let anyone into the house while the dwarfs are at work.

Adversity must be confronted, but hopefully everything will turn out all right in the end. No extenuating circumstances will save the violator from being punished.

Finally, reading fairy tales to children exposes them to a variety of rich language and grammatical patterns which they are not likely to get from television.■

Reducing Sibling Rivalry

Sibling rivalry is an inevitable and normal part of life in any family in which there is more than one child. Nevertheless, there are some actions parents can take to help reduce sibling rivalry.

The recommendations which are presented below deal mainly with the first occasion for sibling rivalry, namely, the arrival of another offspring.

These same general principles will also apply—while taking into consideration each child's unique characteristics—when dealing with rivalry among older siblings.

• **Involve the older child in the preparations for a new baby.** Research studies indicate that sibling rivalry begins even while the mother is still pregnant.

The first-born can help, for example, in getting the baby's room ready and in selecting which toys to pass on to "my baby brother" or "my baby sister."

The amount and type of involvement will, of course, depend on the first-born's age and level of maturity.

• **Dispel unrealistic expectations by describing to the older child what the newborn baby will be like.**

Preschool children sometimes have unrealistic expectations about having an immediate playmate or having a little "doll" who can be picked up and laid down at will.

• **After the birth, try not to be overprotective of the baby at the expense of older children.** It has been found that, even as children get older, parents give more attention and affection to a younger child, which can cause feelings of jealousy in an older child.

• **Try not to make the older child's life more restrictive than before the birth,** such as by demanding quiet in the house whenever the baby is sleeping. It's better to let the baby adapt to the normal noise level in the household.

• **Avoid disrupting the older child's routines and lifestyle as much as possible.** Some changes will be inevitable, such as, perhaps, having to share a bedroom. It will help to keep other changes to a minimum.

• **When the older child is between three and five years of age, it is wise to provide him with his own private space,** in which he can feel secure with his own possessions. Toys which are used in common can be kept in a different shared area.

Even with older children, most quarreling can be avoided by providing each child with his or her own special area and possessions, as well as having a common area for items which are shared.

• **Give the older child the opportunity for input into family decision-making.** Use of a democratic approach—even while maintaining clear rules and structure—can help reduce sibling conflict.

• **When taking care of a newborn baby, invite an older sibling to help,** such as by assisting at bath time, or changing a diaper. This is a good time for parents to treat the older child as a partner, rather than by assigning him a chore which would only cause resentment of the baby.

• **Be sensitive to how the older child may be feeling.** So much attention is given to the baby not only by parents but also by friends and neighbors.

For example, if friends bring lots of gifts for the baby but nothing for the older child, it would be a good idea to provide the older child with some special treat.

Parents can also talk openly about feelings, initiating the topic and including things like, "I imagine you might sometimes feel ... " or "Lots of kids with a new brother sometimes feel ... "

• **Plan ahead for the older child to have something enjoyable to do** whenever you are going to be actively involved in caring for the younger one.

This might mean the older could spend time with the other parent or watch a favorite educational program on television.

• **Talk with the older child about the younger one's needs and feelings.** It has been found, for example, that when mothers talked about the newborn as a person with specific desires and needs, preschool-age siblings displayed greater interest and nurturance toward the baby.

• **Sometimes it is necessary to teach the older child appropriate social skills,** such as by role-playing a particular experience. This will likely also help the child later with peer relations. Research studies indicate that children who develop poor sibling relationships have difficulty later in getting along with peers.

• **When older siblings get into a minor conflict, it is generally best to let them settle their own quarrels.** Otherwise they may use the parent to escalate the conflict. Obviously parents should intervene if the situation is likely to become violent.

• **It is a good idea for parents to try to spend some uninterrupted quality time with each one of their children individually.** A child who is assured of a parent's love and attention is less likely to provoke sibling rivalry.

• Even though these recommendations should help to decrease rivalry, it must be remembered that some degree of sibling rivalry is to be expected in every family.

Feelings of jealousy and resentment are a child's normal reaction to the attention given to another family member. Parents may be relieved to know that research studies indicate that sibling rivalry rarely persists into the adult years.■

What Makes a Good Kindergarten?

The word "kindergarten" means "garden for children." It implies a place for children to grow.

It should not be a place where a child is forced into patterns of behavior and learning—a sort of prep school for first grade—for which he is not yet developmentally ready.

A good kindergarten provides a wide variety of experiences through which the child can increase his knowledge, understanding and appreciation of the world around him.

It affords opportunities to explore the use of eyes and hands together through a variety of materials: sand, water, fingerpaint, paint, crayons, clay, wood, a hammer, and nails.

It also affords opportunities to run, climb, push, pull, build—and take apart again. The imaginative child is free to develop his creativity in his own way as he learns to distinguish between fantasy and reality—and to enjoy them both.

Group experience with age mates teaches cooperative play, role-playing, sharing, taking turns, and consideration for others.

The shy child is drawn into group participation. The aggressive child learns to moderate and control his self-indulgent demands and to appreciate the feelings of other children.

The gentle routine of a good kindergarten leads the child into social awareness. It helps him develop self-control and consideration for others. It feeds his excitement about learning. It does not make the rigid behavioral demands of first grade.

Beware the kindergarten which boasts of teaching children to read and write all the letters of the alphabet, to count to 100, before they "graduate" to first grade. Experience has shown that even at age six, a number of children, many of them of average or above average intelligence, are not developmentally ready to read.

A good kindergarten will provide a child with a wide variety of planned sensory and motor experiences. These experiences will help him develop form perception, visual and auditory discrimination of similarities and differences, good listening habits, expressive language, and the logical concepts which underlie an understanding of numbers as an expression of quantity.

A child with this kind of active learning experience will move easily and confidently into his first year of formal schooling with the necessary tools to make academic learning meaningful.

The period between ages four and six is a period of rapid perceptual-motor development during which the child integrates, organizes, and associates information received through sensory channels, including feedback from body movement.

"Hot-house" forcing of academic learning during this critical developmental period can only be done at the expense of broadening the base of sensory and motor experience upon which higher abstract learning must later depend.

The change to academic instruction in nearly every kindergarten in the country shoiuld be noted as something parents will have to deal with. Parents should be enlisted as advocates along with teachers for keeping appropriate practices.

Avoiding the too-academically- oriented kindergarten does not mean that you should also avoid the kind of situation-related teaching which may arise from your child's questions.

A four-year-old may ask such questions as, "What does that say?" "Show me my name!" "What is that letter?"

Answer his questions. Print his name for him to look at or to try to copy if he shows interest.

Show your pleasure when he recognizes and points out a letter on a billboard or newspaper headline.

Capitalize on his interest without going beyond it. Don't assume that if he asks about one letter, he is really interested in learning the whole alphabet!

Use similar tactics with numbers and quantities. "Yes, you may have two cookies—one, two!" We commonly teach a young child to tell his age by showing the appropriate number of fingers. By also counting "one, two, three, four"—as we touch each finger—we associate verbal symbols with quantity.

A four- or five-year-old is curious about the world around him. He is busy exploring his own capabilities and the possibilities of the objects and places he experiences.

He is ready, willing, and eager to expand his knowledge of the "whos, whats and whys" of his world in the company of his same-age peers.

Five-year-olds learn best by moving, doing, experiencing, observing, listening, talking, exploring.

A good kindergarten will capitalize on this learning style. It will avoid tying the child down to rote memorization or pencil and paper copying tasks for which he is not developmentally ready.

Some of the characteristics of a good kindergarten program would include:

• A clearly stated child-centered philosophy of early childhood education based on sound principles of child development.

• A curriculum which is designed to stimulate the child's interest in learning rather than one based on rote memorization.

• School leaders and administrators who are knowledgeable about early childhood education and who encourage and support continuing professional development for all staff members.

• Caring teachers with training and experience in working with young children both individually and in small groups.

• An ongoing, active parent-teacher partnership.

• A warm, friendly learning environment which stimulates and builds upon young children's natural curiosity about the wonderful world around them.■

Artful Answers

One of the joys of being a parent is being able to answer your child's questions. You are constantly filling a small mind with new ideas.

This joy is sometimes, however, replaced with annoyance. As your child's understanding grows, so do the number and difficulty of his questions.

And they tend to pop up at times when you are busy or your mind is occupied with something else.

Sometimes he will ask a question just to gain your attention, but more often than not he has been doing some hard thinking about something and has run up against a mystery.

Whatever the circumstances, the way you answer his questions can have an important effect on the direction of his thoughts, both now and later. Your response can influence his appetite for learning.

There are two easy but not-too-useful ways to answer a young child's questions. One is simply to say, "I don't know." The other is to tell him everything that comes to mind about an answer.

Unfortunately, neither type of response gives the child the kind of information which is most useful to him.

The first obviously provides no information. The second floods him with too much.

Some of your child's questions will put a strain on your own knowledge. Unless you are an electronics expert, you may be in trouble if your child asks, "How do the people get inside the television set?"

Rather than say, "I don't know," do the best you can with what you do know.

The best short answer might be that the picture floats through the air. It goes into the set, even though you can't see it.

This will fire his imagination. Later he will be back with questions, like "How does the picture get into the television set?" (through the antenna, dish or cable)

or "Where does the picture come from?" (from a television station).

Again, the answers are simple and center around the one most important fact that has to do with the question.

It is easy to be overzealous in giving an explanation, forgetting that each word or phrase may be a new idea to him. A few too many words and all is lost. A young child simply can't hold on to it all.

There is an artful middle ground between these two extremes. It takes more care, but the results will be well worth the effort.

The artful answer gives the child an explanation he can remember for the present. It also plants the seed for further questions and a fuller understanding sometime in the future.

Growing Child™

P. O. Box 2505 • W Lafayette, IN 47996
(800) 927-7289
www.GrowingChild.com
© 2011 Growing Child, Inc.

Contributing Authors

Phil Bach, O.D., Ph.D.
Miriam Bender, Ph.D.
Joseph Braga, Ed.D.
Laurie Braga, Ph.D.
George Early, Ph.D.
Carol R. Gestwicki, M.S.
Liam Grimley, Ph.D.
Robert Hannemann, M.D., F.A.A.P.
Sylvia Kottler, M.S.
Bill Peterson, Ph.D.

This can be illustrated by comparing two ways of answering a question that your child might ask: "What makes a car go?"

A conscientious but overloaded answer would go something like this: "A car has an engine that makes its wheels turn. When you push on the accelerator with your foot, the engine turns around and that makes the wheels turn so the car can move."

Engine, wheels, accelerator, foot, provides too many ideas. It is more than he can digest. He may not understand any of it.

A more effective explanation would be to say, "A car has an engine. The engine makes the wheels turn."

"Engine" is a new word that will require all of his attention. You can illustrate engine by lifting the car hood and giving him a look, again without too much explanation.

A good rule of thumb is to look for the shortest explanation that will answer the question. This will give your child a single, important fact which he can chew on. After he has digested the main idea he will be ready, in his own time, for more details.

A few minutes or a few weeks later he will come to you with another question: "What makes the engine go?" or "How does the engine make the wheels go?"

Then you can pause for a moment and select the best single fact to answer the question.

It takes a little time and thought to give an artful answer. A short answer will get your child started on the right track and provide the fuel for further thinking.

You will save yourself some time in the actual explanation and possibly the trouble of reanswering the same question later.

A helpful hint: Before answering a questions, you can ask a question to see what the child already knows or thinks.

Your artful answers will lead to more and better questions, building his understanding in the most effective way. ■

Growing Child

"Will My Child Be Ready for Kindergarten?"

Now that your child is almost five years old, the question of readiness for kindergarten begins to loom on the horizon. "Will my child be ready for kindergarten?"

Most school systems automatically accept children for enrollment based on a chronological age of five years.

This approach is not necessarily the best for each individual child. Each child grows and develops in a pattern which is unique to himself.

The concept of readiness for academic learning rests on three basic principles:

• Learning is most likely to occur when a child is *ready* to learn.

• A child's readiness is *not* predictable by chronological age alone.

• Most of the efforts directed toward "forced" learning—before a child is ready—are lost.

Failure to learn because of lack of readiness often produces a distaste for school which interferes with later learning.

Whatever you decide about your child's most appropriate entry date for kindergarten, we are confident that over the past several years you have provided him with a wide range of learning experiences—such as those we have suggested month by month in *Growing Child*—all of which were intended not only to be enjoyable activities in themselves, but also to provide the type of preparation needed for later learning in school.

This month is an appropriate time to review some of the learning that should normally have taken place by now to prepare your child for kindergarten.

We will focus on three important areas, namely, social-emotional development, motor skills, and intellectual readiness.

Social-emotional development. When a child enters kindergarten, he will have to deal with group situations—group expectations, group activities, group interactions—rather than the one-to-one relationships he has previously enjoyed at home.

For some children this experience can be difficult.

Research studies indicate that those children who have had the opportunity to interact regularly with other same-aged children—such as at a community playground, childcare, or Sunday school class—are more likely to have a smooth transition to kindergarten.

The latest large research study on school success pinpoints an absolute need for social emotional factors as most important for kindergarten success.

The development of good social skills is very important for a child's successful adjustment to the school setting. He needs to be able to interact with other children in a cooperative manner, such as being willing to share and take turns.

Research studies also indicate that a child's ability to make friends is a good predictor of later achievement in school.

In kindergarten a child must be able to control his own feelings and behaviors, not pushing, shoving, or fighting with others in order to have his own way.

He must also be able to relate to non-family authority figures, namely the kindergarten teacher and classroom aides.

Children who have had opportunities to interact with adults and other children outside the home generally have less difficulty adjusting to the social and emotional demands of kindergarten.

Motor skills. By now your child has probably developed appropriate motor skills which he can put to good use in kindergarten.

These motor skills would include large muscle activities such as walking a straight line, running forwards and backwards, hopping on each foot, and throwing a ball.

continued on page 344

continued from page 343

They would also include small muscle activities such as drawing, coloring, using scissors and paste, as well as being able to zip or button a jacket.

Intellectual readiness. There are some general intellectual skills which will make for a smoother adjustment to kindergarten, including the following:

• Colors: identify three or more basic colors (red, green, blue, yellow, white, black).

• Numbers: count to 10.

• Sequencing: repeat four numbers in sequence (for example, 6-3-1-8).

• Letters: identify at least some letters of the alphabet.

• Puzzles: assemble a simple puzzle with four to six pieces.

• Shapes: identify simple shapes (triangle, circle, square).

• General knowledge: demonstrate awareness of his environment (for example, "How many wheels does a bicycle have?")

• Vocabulary: know the meaning of simple, everyday words (such as hat, shoe, cat, house).

• Similarities: identify likeness (for example, "In what way are a coat and a pair of pants alike?").

• Differences: identify differences (for example, "In what way are a coat and a pair of pants different?").

• Opposites: identify opposites (for example, long-short, hot-cold, big-little).

By considering these intellectual readiness skills we are not advocating that parents engage in formal instruction of these skills.

Such formal academic training will generally be counterproductive when used with young children.

It has been found, for example, that in France where state-mandated reading instruction begins at age five, as many as 30 percent of the children experience reading disabilities.

By contrast, in Denmark where reading instruction does not begin until age seven, considerably fewer children experience any reading problems.

A young child learns best in a playful, enjoyable environment. And learning occurs most effectively when the child is ready to learn.

Helping your child get ready. Parents can stimulate their child's learning by being aware of appropriate skills and activities—such as the ones we have identified in this issue and in previous issues of *Growing Child*—which help to prepare the child for later learning.

It has also been found that a young child adjusts more easily to kindergarten if he already knows some of his classmates.

Before school begins, therefore, it is wise for you to invite some of your child's future classmates to your home so that they can play together and become friends.

Your child will then be looking forward to the first day of kindergarten as a fun time to be spent with friends, rather than dreading the traumatic experience of being alone among strangers.

Here are three practical recommendations which could greatly help your child's adjustment to kindergarten:

• Arrange for you and your child to visit the kindergarten he will attend.

• Talk with the kindergarten teacher ahead of time about the program and about any readiness skills your child will need.

• Arrange for some of your child's future classmates to play at your house where they can become friends.

Entry into kindergarten marks an important milestone in your child's life. Your support will help him begin this new experience and your positive attitude will encourage him along the way.

Help him make it a good experience!■

Songs and Rhythm

Singing songs can help a young child:

• Acquire better rhythm.

• Develop better listening skills.

• Improve attention.

• Have some fun.

1. "On This Summer Day"

Music: "Mary Had a Little Lamb."

(Actions should follow the words.)

Everybody clap your hands,

Clap your hands,

Clap your hands;

Everybody clap your hands,

On this summer day.

Variations may include "swing your arms," "stomp your feet," "shrug your shoulders," "wash your face."

2. "Around We Go"

Music: "Lazy Mary, Will You Get Up?"

Around we go, around we go,

One big circle marching so.

(Walk in a circle.)

Down we go, down we go,

One big circle sinking so.

(Walk with bent knees.)

Up we go...rising so.

(Walk on tiptoes.)

In we go...shrinking so.

(Walk on inside of feet.)

Out we go...stretching so.

(Walk on heels.)■

Creative Movement

Creative movement involves activities which can be practiced outdoors on a sunny day or indoors on a rainy day.

Purposes: These activities serve many purposes including:

• Improving one's body image.

• Acquiring better rhythm and balance.

• Developing better organization in space.

• Improving listening skills.

• Enlarging vocabulary.

• Stimulating creative thinking.

Types of movements: There is a wide variety of basic movements including (1) locomotor, (2) non-locomotor, and (3) manipulative movements.

Locomotor movements involve activities such as walking, running, rolling, hopping, skipping, sliding, galloping, jumping, creeping, and crawling.

Non-locomotor movements include swinging, stretching, bending, turning, twisting, and climbing.

Manipulative movements which involve use of the hands include pushing, pulling, lifting, catching, throwing, striking, and hammering.

"Let's pretend." Through pretend play the child uses his imagination. This requires listening, thinking, and exploring in space and time.

(1) Locomotor activities

Here are some suggested creative movement locomotor activities:

• Walking: "Show me how (a) a giant, (b) an elf, (c) a robot, walks."

• Running: "How would you run if (a) a monster were chasing you, (b) you were a very old person, or (c) you were a baby?"

• Rolling: "Can you roll (a) over and over like a log, (b) back and forth like a rocking chair?"

What's nice about pretend play activities is that every child is "a winner" because there is no single right way to perform them.

• Hopping: "Show me how you would hop if you were (a) a rabbit, (b) a kangaroo?"

• Skipping: "Show me how you would skip if you were (a) a grasshopper, (b) a big gorilla."

• Sliding: "Show me how you would go down a slide with (a) a ball, (b) a broom, in your hands."

• Galloping: "Show me how you would gallop if you were (a) a donkey, (b) a horse."

• Jumping: "Show me how you would jump if you were (a) the cow jumping over the moon, (b) a basketball player shooting a basket."

• Creeping or crawling: "Show me how you would get from this side of the room to that side if you had to go under a barrier."

(2) Non-locomotor activities

Here are some suggested non-locomotor activities:

• Swinging: "Show me how a branch on a tree swings in the wind."

• Stretching: "Show me what it would be like to be 10 feet tall."

• Bending: "Show me how you would bend to pick up (a) a small flower, (b) a heavy box."

• Turning: "Show me how (a) a small car, (b) a big truck, turns around a corner."

• Twisting: "Show me how you would unwind if you were a piece of string that had been twisted many times."

• Climbing: "Imagine you are climbing stairs all the way to the moon."

(3) Manipulative activities

Here are some suggested manipulative activities that involve the use of the hands:

• Pushing: "Show me how you would go through a door with the sign 'Push' on it."

• Pulling: "Show me how you would pull in a big 20-pound fish."

• Lifting: "Show me how you would lift (a) a feather, (b) a piece of paper, (c) a paperweight, off the table."

• Catching: "Let's pretend you are going to catch (a) a baseball, (b) a large beach ball. Ready? Catch!"

• Throwing: "Pretend you are throwing me (a) a glove, (b) a frisbee, (c) a ball."

• Striking: "Show how you would strike the table if you were angry."

• Hammering: "Let's pretend you have a hammer in one hand and a nail in the other. Start hammering."

What's nice about pretend play activities is that every child is "a winner" because there is no single right way to perform them.

Research studies indicate that, in general, children who engage in these kinds of activities develop longer attention span, nicer imagination, and a larger vocabulary. ■

Family Relationships

How the members of a family get along with one another can make the difference between a happy family life and one that is chaotic.

It can influence whether you are able to enjoy your children or instead find them too draining.

Family relationships are important both now and in the future. They will set many of a child's life patterns for how she will deal with others who are close to her. And they will strongly affect her feelings about herself.

Interactions within a family can be stormy or calm, loving or angry, cooperative or competitive—and often all occur within any given day.

Following are some guidelines to help you improve the quality of family life.

1. Try not to compare one child with another. Each child has her own ways of reacting to the things that happen to her. Each has special strengths and weaknesses.

Each one has her own rate of growth and development. Each child is drawn to different activities, things, and people.

It is natural for parents to compare the times at which a first and second child walked or talked or were toilet trained.

It's understandable to wonder why a third child is afraid of the water when the first two children learned to swim when they were preschoolers. But it's important to let each child be herself.

Notice the things that make each child unique, and encourage each of them to develop their own special talents.

Accept children's differences and you will help them to accept themselves and each other.

2. Try to spend some time each day alone with each child. It would be desirable to set aside some time each day—at least 10 or 15 minutes—to spend alone with each child. The child can count on this time as her own special time with you.

For example, you might plan to spend 15 minutes each afternoon with one child while her little brother takes his nap.

Or you might give an older sister 15 minutes in the evening after a younger child's bedtime.

If you can't do this every day, try to find a regular schedule you can stick to at least once a week.

We've talked before about a "special time." Let this be a time for each child to use as she wishes. You can offer a story, a game, or simply an understanding ear, but let her choose.

These special times with you will help you to get to know and enjoy each of your children more while you help each one of them to feel special to you.

You may also find this gives you more time for yourself as your children stop competing for your attention at other times.

3. Try to provide your children with opportunities for cooperating with each other in planned activities or daily routines.

For example, when you go to the supermarket, you can have one youngster sitting in a grocery cart looking for items you need in each aisle. Then have an older child get it and put it in the cart.

Or you can ask an older child to help teach a toddler how to use the toilet when he's ready.

An older child can make simple toys for the baby such as a "touch and feel" book or a "reach and grab" stuffed mitten toy to hang from his crib. She can show him how to use them.

In addition, be sure to notice and compliment your children any time you see them working and playing together cooperatively: "Tommy, thank you for helping Michelle get dressed. You're really a help to me." "Angela and Ann, I'm so glad to see you're enjoying playing together."

4. Set limits that you think are fair for each of your children. Let your children know what the rules are and what the consequences of breaking them will be.

Then try to stick to these rules as well as you can, changing them (with your children's knowledge) when they no longer seem appropriate.

This kind of "planning ahead" can avoid many fights and jealousies over such things as who goes to bed at what time and who gets to do what.

You will probably still get some protests. ("It's not fair that I can't stay up as long as she does.") But it is fair for children of different ages to have different limits, privileges, and responsibilities.

When they know what to expect, each child can look forward to growing up.

5. Try to plan time for the family to meet together. You probably already do this informally, at mealtimes, or at special family times you share on weekends.

Sometimes it's hard to get everyone together at the same time, especially if either parent works odd hours or if your children are involved in many different activities.

It is important to try to have some time to enjoy each other's company.

Also, each family member has responsibilities to the family as well as expectations and needs.

These might be worked out to everyone's satisfaction when the family gathers together and tries to understand and support each other.

For example, if squabbles occur frequently between siblings over household duties, this problem might be discussed at a family meeting.

Sometimes it helps to make a chart listing each family member's duties for the week or month. Then household tasks nobody likes can be assigned on a revolving basis.

continued on page 347

Separation Anxiety

Four- and five-year-olds may suddenly turn from being happy, independent, out-going children who enjoyed their nursery school or kindergarten to clinging, terrified children who refuse to leave their parents even to go outdoors to play!

This change from happy independence to fearful, tearful clinging can come as quite a shock to parents.

Mommy wonders if something has happened to frighten her child. She wonders if her child feels rejected and unloved because of something she did.

Daddy says, "She must be sick! Take her to the doctor!" Both parents wonder what could have happened to change their child so drastically.

The name given this phenomenon is "separation anxiety." It is quite common among children in the preschool years.

Separation anxiety occurs among preschool children or those whose entrance into kindergarten marks their first separation from home or parents.

Separation anxiety is a very natural response but one which is sometimes difficult to cope with.

The child is experiencing her own shortcomings and for the first time recognizing her own dependency on her parents. She is testing herself in terms of dependency and independency, and she is testing her parents as well.

Sometimes the episode can be related to a father's illness which requires hospitalization or even a period of bed rest at home.

Sometimes a mother's absence for the birth of another child will precipitate the anxiety. Sometimes no one can put a finger on the cause.

In searching for a reason, parents sometimes begin to feel more and more guilty.

They make excuses for the child. They wonder if they have been "bad" parents.

In their guilt and fear, they may allow the child to manipulate them and disrupt family life.

Meanwhile, the child feels less and less secure as she "gets away with" more and more. She recognizes her lack of experience. She fears a new experience.

Through tears, clinging and temper tantrums, she is saying again and again,

"Reassure me. Tell me what I should do. Help me grow in confidence and independence."

She needs to feel that her parents love her enough to guide her properly, to set boundaries on her behavior, and to make decisions which are best for her.

Separation anxiety becomes worse if parents allow themselves to be manipulated into staying home from a party because their child cries and clings to them, or by permitting her to stay at home and cling to them instead of going to school or outdoors to play.

It is not easy to carry a kicking, screaming child to the car and take her to school.

It is not easy to pry open her desperately clinging hands and turn away from her tear-stained face. But it can be done.

It is wise to anticipate separation anxiety problems. So the day before, she should be told in a calm but firm voice that Mommy and Daddy decide when she goes to bed, what she eats, and where she plays; that they have decided that she will go to school.

Tell her that you are sorry if she's not happy about it, but you have decided that she will go. Then take her—and leave her.

Each succeeding day this process will become easier for both you and your child.

You will have regained control of your family life. She will know what is expected of her.

Although she may fight against these expectations for a short time, she will eventually feel secure in the knowledge that Mommy and Daddy care enough to make grown-up decisions for her.

Her world will no longer be a scary place with no protective boundaries to keep her safe.

Instead it will become an orderly world in which she will feel more secure knowing that her parents love her and that they do whatever is best for her.■

continued from page 346

The attempts and perseverance in trying to resolve matters constructively and supportively in a family provide a good example for your child of how to resolve conflicts peacefully.

In addition to working out family problems, you can use this family meeting time to help your children understand and like each other better.

• Give each child, even the youngest, a time to express herself.

• Try to pay attention equally to each child, even the quietest.

• Show interest in what each child shares.

• Try to keep any one child from monopolizing the conversation.

• Be kind and supportive but firm about giving each person an opportunity.

The children will learn from your example (in time, if not right away) to respect each other as you respect each of them.■

Gun Safety

Gun safety begins with you.

Even if you don't own a gun, for your child's safety you need to instruct him about the dangers of guns.

If he encounters a gun in a friend's home, he won't know how to behave appropriately unless you teach him.

He needs to learn from his parent that guns are not toys and should not be played with—not even touched.

Why is it necessary for parents to discuss gun safety with their child?

Recent statistics indicate that dangerous weapons are part of an epidemic of violence among young people.

The National School Safety Center estimates that about 100,000 students carry a handgun to school every day.

According to the Bureau of Alcohol, Tobacco and Firearms, there are over 200 million privately owned guns in the United States.

It is estimated that half of all families in this country own at least one gun. Most times the gun was purchased for protection and is kept loaded, ready for use.

What to tell your child about guns:

1. Guns are not toys. They should never be touched—no matter how safe a friend says it is.

2. If he sees one of his friends with a real gun, assume it is loaded. Leave the place immediately and tell an adult what he saw.

3. Explain the difference between actors who use guns in movies or on television and the tragedies of real-life gun violence. Use newspaper stories to back up what you say.

4. Children have a natural curiosity about guns. Frequently repeat the message: "DON'T PLAY WITH GUNS."

Should you keep all guns out of your home?

Some persons (such as some farmers, police officers, or security guards) are required by their jobs to have a gun in their home.

Most other people have a choice.

In deciding whether to keep all guns out of your home, the Children's Defense Fund recommends that you consider the following:

• Every year hundreds of children accidentally shoot themselves or someone else.

• Over 5,000 American children are killed

Growing Child™

P. O. Box 2505 • W Lafayette, IN 47996
(800) 927-7289
www.GrowingChild.com

Contributing Authors
Phil Bach, O.D., Ph.D.
Miriam Bender, Ph.D.
Joseph Braga, Ed.D.
Laurie Braga, Ph.D.
George Early, Ph.D.
Carol R. Gestwicki, M.S.
Liam Grimley, Ph.D.
Robert Hannemann, M.D., F.A.A.P.
Sylvia Kottler, M.S.
Bill Peterson, Ph.D.

every year with guns.

• By the time a child is one year old, he can squeeze your finger with seven pounds of pressure, which is approximately the same amount needed to squeeze the trigger of a gun.

• If you keep a gun in your home, it's 18 times more likely to kill someone living in your home than to kill an intruder.

If you keep a gun in your home:

1. When you use the gun (for hunting, for example), don't ever leave it where a young child can have access to it.

2. At home, always unload a gun before putting it away.

3. Store the gun in a locked cabinet which no child can open.

4. Keep all bullets locked in a safe place separate from the gun.

5. Locate gun storage keys separately from "regular keys" in an area where children are unable to find them.

The best solution: If there are children in your house, do not have guns in your house.

It is a small price to pay to protect your child—or any child—from an accident. ∎

Your Child's Unique Characteristics

In some months time, your child will be going to kindergarten.

That's when teachers and other professionals are likely to ask parents:

• "What can you tell me about your child?

• What are some of her unique characteristics?

• What are some of her specific strengths?

• What are some of her weakest areas?"

Some parents are ready and able to answer these questions. Others are somewhat dumbfounded if they find that, after watching their child grow and develop for all these years, they really don't know much about her *unique* strengths and weaknesses.

Fortunately, there are a number of things parents can do in order to get to know their child better.

First, parents can use developmental milestones, such as those we provide in *Growing Child,* to determine in which areas their child is ahead or above average, in which ones she is behind or below average, and in which ones she is typical or just about average.

Second, parents can develop better observational skills by which to determine their child's unique characteristics and identify how she is like or unlike other children of her own age.

We can discuss these observational skills in more detail.

Observing a child means more than just *looking* or *watching.* We can sometimes *watch* children play, for example, without really *observing* the quality of the interactions between them.

Observation implies knowing something about the type of information that is needed.

The following consideration will help parents improve their observational skills while their child engages in play or other social activities:

• What are some of her favorite activities?

• What are some of her toy preferences?

• What games does she like to play the most?

• Are her actions self-directed or does she prefer to get directions from others?

• Does she initiate contact with other children or does she wait to be invited by them?

• Does she prefer to play with children of her own gender or does she prefer to interact with children of the opposite-gender?

• Does she have many friends or just a few?

• Does she usually prefer to stay with one activity or does she shift frequently from one activity to another?

• How long does she usually stay with an activity that interests her?

• Does she prefer indoor activities or would she rather play outdoors if given the choice?

• Does she display great curiosity about the world around her or is she rather cautious about exploring new territory?

• When she is required to change from one activity to another, can she make a smooth transition or does she get upset?

• Are there some age-appropriate tasks which she finds difficult to perform?

• How well does she handle frustration?

• Does she engage in imaginative play?

• Does she prefer to play alone or with other children?

• With whom does she appear to enjoy playing the most: (a) children who are older, (b) younger, or (c) those who are her own age?

• While she is engaged in one activity, is she alert to other sights and sounds in her environment, such as someone else's presence in the room or the ringing of the doorbell?

• In what ways does she appear to be like other children her own age?

• In what ways does she appear to be different from other children her own age?

By seeking answers to these questions, parents can improve their own observational skills.

By doing so, they will be able to provide valuable information to teachers and other professionals who ask: "What can you tell me about your child's unique characteristics?"

That information can greatly help a teacher and others who will work with the child.■

"My Child Lied To Me"

Many parents view truthfulness as the most important characteristic of a good child, more important than cleanliness, obedience, or friendliness, for example.

Not surprisingly, therefore, these parents get very upset whenever a child utters an untruthful remark.

To understand why most all young children at some time tell lies, it is important to be aware that children and adults have very different perceptions of what it means to tell a lie.

To an adult, lying usually means the deliberate telling of a falsehood. In a young child, however, saying something untruthful is a much more complex phenomenon.

There are many different kinds of untruths told by children who are under six years of age. And there are many different reasons why young children make untruthful statements.

That's why it is important for parents to understand how a young child's mind works.

As a result, parents will be better able to deal with the issue of lying and to prevent it from later developing into a harmful habit.

Why do young children lie?

• **Lying is the use of creative imagination.** Children begin saying things that are untrue at about age three or four.

At this stage of development, they are beginning to explore the world of imagination and fantasy, exploration that continues through the next few years.

Parents may hear about the "elephant" in the neighbor's backyard, or other tall tales of the child's creative imagination.

The child is not trying to deceive. He is just telling the parent a tall story—perhaps very similar to the one his parents read to him the night before.

What to do? The development of a child's creative imagination should generally be

encouraged rather than frowned upon, as long as the child is not seeking to deliberately deceive the parent.

A parent can enter into the child's fantasy game, yet instill a sense of reality by saying, "Draw me a picture of your imaginary elephant."

Parents can also talk with their children about their "stories", indicating their recognition that this story is not true, without judgment or condemnation.

• **Lying to avoid punishment.** By age four or five, children are beginning to have a better grasp of the difference between reality and fantasy. But they don't yet understand the concept of lying in an adult manner.

When they do something wrong, they consider that action to be more serious than the telling of a lie.

Furthermore, they may believe that if they confess, the parent will think they are a "bad person."

They cannot yet distinguish in their minds the difference between a "bad deed" and a "bad person."

Sometimes children will lie because of an overwhelming fear of what the consequences of their action might be.

Their anxiety will show in their body language, such as shifting from one foot to another, avoiding eye contact, biting their

lips, or blinking their eyes.

What to do: Even though a child's lying, for whatever reason, can greatly upset a parent, it is best to remain calm. Try to figure out why the child may be lying.

Above all, resist the temptation to try to "scare" the truth out of your child with harsh or severe punishment. This will only make the child more fearful.

A child who is afraid of being punished will choose to lie rather than risk arousing a parent's anger.

He will be more truthful if he learns from experience that his honesty will be respected and, indeed, sometimes even rewarded.

• **Lying to gain attention.** Sometimes children lie to gain attention from adults. This sometimes happens in times of transition, such as when a family moves, or a new baby arrives in the home.

At such times, a young child may feel neglected. He may, for example, deliberately pour the entire bottle of bath bubbles down the drain and then deny he did it.

What to do: If the parent already knows about, or has even witnessed, the child's misbehavior, it is best to avoid setting him up for "defensive lying" by asking: "Did you do that?"

Chances are he will deny it or, worse yet, blame his baby brother for doing it!

Children generally respond more positively when parents confront them directly with what they already know: "I saw you doing that. It wasn't a nice thing to do."

To prevent a child's misbehavior or lying as a way to gain attention, it will help if parents can spend a little more time with the child who feels left out, especially during times of transition.

• **Lying to impress.** A child may sometimes tell lies to impress friends or family members.

continued on page 351

continued from page 350

These types of lies are often told in an after-the-fact situation such as when a child wishes he had performed better in a game than he did.

He may report a story based more on what he wishes his skill level had been than on what actually happened. In such reporting, he is more preoccupied with who he wants to be than with who he really is.

What to do: The child who lies to impress others has somehow learned that, in order to be considered a worthwhile person, he must excel in whatever he does.

Rather than focus on the lying behavior, it is more important to determine why the child feels such pressure to excel.

Without intending, parents may sometimes convey the message—in subtle unconscious ways—that winning is everything and that good effort, without success, counts for nothing.

To help a child overcome this pressure—and thereby overcome this type of lying—parents should focus on the child's own good qualities without making comparisons with others.

Helping a child improve the basic skills he wants to develop—if done in a fun-filled manner—will also help him abandon lying as a naive way of trying to impress others.

• **Lying as wishful thinking.** Similar to lying to impress, a young child may sometimes lie due to wishful thinking.

For example, even though he knows his parents are not going to get him the bicycle he wants, he may nevertheless tell his friends: "My parents are getting me a bicycle for my birthday." This helps him feel part of the group, especially if the others already have bicycles.

To dream about getting a bicycle also helps him cope with the fear of not being loved as much as the other children with bicycles are loved by their parents.

What to do: When parents become aware

of such behavior, it doesn't help to call the child a "liar." That would only serve to diminish the child's self-esteem and could eventually become a self-fulfilling prophecy.

It is more effective to use a calm and factual approach: "I know that's not true and you know it's not true. Try to be more accurate in what you say."

If a child persists in lying, the parent can say something like: "It's really important for you to learn to tell the truth, even when it hurts you to do so. Telling the truth lets other people know you can be trusted. On the other hand, a person who tells lies has to tell more lies to cover up the lies he already told. Eventually he won't even believe himself."

• **Lying as imitative behavior.** Some children learn to lie by listening to adults. They may hear parents or other adults telling "little fibs" without understanding the purpose of a "white lie."

To alleviate a child's fear, for example, a dentist may say, "This won't hurt." Or a parent may tell Grandma that her cake was "delicious" after previously telling the child

it really tasted awful.

A young child usually doesn't understand the fine points of polite speech. What he heard was a deliberate lie. So he presumes he too can tell lies.

What to do: Instead of changing the child's behavior, the focus is now on changing the parents' behavior—at the very least, being more sensitive to what is said in the presence of a young child.

Even if you try to explain it, a young child is not likely to understand the distinction between "white lies" and real lies. Furthermore, parents who tell "white lies" to their child frequently create more problems than they solve.

When they are not truthful about a painful event—such as a death or an impending divorce, for example—a young child's fertile imagination can create anxieties far worse than the reality itself.

Parents should serve as good role models of truthfulness for their child. In that way, a child learns that truthfulness—unpleasant as it sometimes may be—is ultimately the best policy.■

A Hopping Game

Your child at this age is developing better control over the large muscles of the body. That is why she enjoys activities that involve running, hopping, or skipping.

Here is an activity that will help develop better large muscle control.

With a piece of chalk draw a row of circles on the sidewalk, one behind the other. Have your child hop from one foot to the other in going from one circle to the next one.

Next, have her go from one circle to the next by hopping on her right foot only. At the end of the row, have her turn around and come back, hopping this time on her left foot only.

When this task becomes too easy, you can make it more difficult by rearranging the circles into more challenging patterns.

By numbering the circles (1, 2, 3, ...) you can help her learn to count by counting aloud as she hops from one circle to another.■

Children and Strangers

Many parents have known the feeling of terror if they have briefly lost sight of their child in a crowded supermarket.

The thought of their child being abducted or sexually abused is one of the worst nightmares any parent can have.

By far the most effective way to prevent abduction is for parents to discuss personal safety with their child in a calm and straightforward manner.

Causes of reluctance

First, we need to consider five reasons why parents are sometimes reluctant to talk with their child about personal safety.

1. *"I don't want to scare my child."* Parents don't want to raise a child who is fearful and suspicious of almost everyone in the world.

But just as parents would talk about the *danger* of playing with fire, which is warm and attractive, so, too, they should be able to discuss personal safety without scaring their child.

2. *"I'm pleased that my child likes to be friends with everybody."* Such a child can be praised for having a positive outlook on life. But sooner or later she will learn that not everybody is "nice" and "kind."

It's best that she learn about that sad aspect of life in the loving warmth of her own home rather than be a potential victim.

3. *"My child is too young to discuss these matters with."* Actually the child may know more about these matters—from television, or friends, for example—than her parents realize.

She will learn better from a parent's calm discussion than from a sensationalized television news story.

4. *"When I was growing up my parents never talked to me about possible abduction or sexual abuse."* There is no doubt that our society has changed.

Experts give a number of reasons—greater family mobility, higher divorce rates, more "latch-key" children—for the increase in child abductions and sexual abuse.

Yesterday's answers are no longer adequate to address the problems of today.

5. *"These things only happen in other people's families. It would never happen to my child."* This is perhaps the most common reason why parents don't discuss personal safety with their child.

True, the chance of a child being abducted by a stranger may be only one in a million. But, if it happens, the consequences are traumatic both for the child and the parent.

How to protect your child

Here are some recommendations that can protect your child from abduction and/or sexual abuse:

1. Generally children under age 12 should not be left alone at home.

2. If they are alone, even for a brief period of time, they should know not to open the door to a stranger.

3. Each family needs to establish rules about whether children should answer the telephone if they are home alone.

If they do answer, they should never reveal that their parents are not home, nor give their name, age, or address.

By installing a telephone answering machine, calls can be monitored by a child when a parent is not at home.

She picks up the receiver only when she is certain it is her parent's voice.

4. Children need to be well- informed about dialing 911 and other emergency procedures, such as where to reach parents or how to contact neighbors.

5. Children under 12 years of age should

never be left unsupervised in any public place, such as a park, playground, or shopping mall.

6. Discuss beforehand what your child should do (where to go, whom to contact) if she should happen to get separated from you or lost in a crowd or in a park.

7. Make sure your child knows her address and telephone number.

8. Discuss with your child what "abductor" means. Some children may think of an abductor, or even stranger, as some type of monster with horns.

They don't realize that it's often a person with a big smile, a warm embrace, and lots of candy.

Or it may be a nice person with a story of a lost kitten or puppy who asks for help finding the pet.

Most incidents of abduction and sexual abuse involve a relative, neighbor, or friend of the family.

9. Role-play some situations with your child so that she can practice how she would deal with it (for example, yelling "No!" or running from danger).

10. If your child is allowed to visit a friend's or neighbor's house, have her call you when she arrives and before she leaves to come home.

11. Make sure she knows in advance who will pick her up after any visit or other event.

12. As much as possible, know where and with whom your child is at all times.

What every child needs to know

These are some personal safety tips that every child should know:

1. Don't stop to talk to someone you don't know.

2. Stay away from anyone who watches

continued on page 353

Kindergarten Journal

you and follows you either on foot or in a car.

3. Never get in a car or take a ride in a car from someone you don't know—even if they tell you, for example, "Your Mommy is very ill, and I'll take you to the hospital to see her."

4. Don't accept candy from someone you don't know. Even at Halloween it can be dangerous to accept candy or fruit from a stranger.

5. Don't go places on your own. It is safer to be with one or two of your friends.

6. Avoid alleys or dark streets—even if they are a shortcut to where you're going.

7. Don't let anyone touch you in the area covered by your bathing suit. And don't touch anyone else in that area, even if they want you to.

8. Don't be afraid to say "No." Yell it loudly, if necessary.

9. Be on your guard when someone tells you to keep something "as a secret" from your parents. You need to TELL your parents at once if this happens.

More information

There are a number of agencies which can provide more information for parents to help prevent abduction and/or sexual abuse of children: These are just a few

1. National Center for Missing and Exploited Children, 2101 Wilson Blvd., Suite 550, Arlington, VA 22201. Website: www.missingkids.com Telephone: 1-800-843-5678.

2. Child Find of America, Inc. Website: www.childfind.org

3. East Bay Agency for Children. Website: www.ebaac.org

4. Office for Victims of Crime. Website: ojp.usdog.gove/ovc/pulications/factshts/cevcjr/htm This website provides additional information and references.■

Whenever your child starts kindergarten, keep a journal with him. Write down noteworthy events:

• What did you wear to school?

• What did you learn today?

• With whom did you play?

• Did you make new friends?

• What did you eat?

• What did you like the most about kindergarten?

• What did your teacher wear today?

In order for this to be a fun experience for both parent and child, keep in mind the following:

• Your child may not give you all the information you expect at the time you ask the question.

So, don't be concerned if he doesn't immediately answer your questions or gives you only short answers.

• You may get answers to your questions at most unlikely times later, such as when doing the dishes or driving in the car.

Just try to remember what you were told so that you can enter it later in the journal.

• As much as possible, report what you hear in your child's own words without corrections, editing, or embellishing. In that way it will serve as a more accurate record for your child.

If you keep these journal entries in a scrapbook, you can add other items, such as a picture, a photo, or your child's artwork, to illustrate happy times.

By keeping a journal you are helping your child in a number of different ways:

1. You are helping your child become more perceptive of the world around him. ("What did your teacher wear today?")

2. You are exercising and training your

child's memory.

3. You are helping your child mentally organize the day's experiences. ("First we did this, then we did … ")

4. Your child is also developing better communication skills by talking to you about the day's events.

5. Your child is learning from you that *writing* can be fun. And *reading* what you wrote can be even more fun.

6. By keeping a journal, you are helping to reinforce what your child learned in school that day.

For example, if he learned a new letter of the alphabet, you can help him find a word in a magazine that begins with that letter.

Then cut out the word and paste it in his journal along with a picture depicting that word.

To learn the letter "c", for example, help him find a picture of a cat, cut out for him the word "cat", and have him paste them both in his journal opposite the letter "c."

7. Lastly, by keeping such a journal you are starting to develop what will become a treasured record both for you and your child—preserving happy memories that might otherwise be lost.■

10 Tips for More Effective Discipline

Parents may sometimes wonder why their child didn't do what he was told to do.

They may instinctively want to blame the child. But the problem may, on the contrary, be more directly related to a parent's use of inappropriate discipline methods.

Some methods of discipline are effective. Others are ineffective.

Here are some tips which parents can use for more effective discipline.

DO:

1. Focus on only one behavior or misbehavior at a time.

2. Make sure your child clearly knows what behavior you expect.

3. Make direct statements ("You spilled sugar on the floor.").

4. Be as specific as you can ("Joe, don't hit your brother.").

5. Be as brief as possible.

6. Focus on what happened here and now.

7. Be consistent in what you say.

8. Keep your emotions under control.

9. Keep the tone of your voice as neutral as possible.

10. Let your child know you love him even when you dislike his misbehavior.

DON'T:

1. Don't use one misbehavior to bring up old grievances.

2. Don't make unclear statements ("Remember, I want you always to be a good boy.").

3. Don't ask questions with no meaningful answer ("Why did you just do that?").

4. Don't give vague directives ("Didn't I just tell you to be nice to your brother?").

5. Don't give long lectures.

6. Don't drag up past history ("Haven't I told you a thousand times before ...?").

7. Don't correct if it's only because you are in a bad mood.

8. Don't explode in anger.

9. Don't yell or scream at your child.

10. Don't use sarcasm and disparaging comments ("You're a dummy.").■

Growing Child™

P. O. Box 2505 • W Lafayette, IN 47996
(800) 927-7289
www.GrowingChild.com

Contributing Authors

Phil Bach, O.D., Ph.D.
Miriam Bender, Ph.D.
Joseph Braga, Ed.D.
Laurie Braga, Ph.D.
George Early, Ph.D.
Carol R. Gestwicki, M.S.
Liam Grimley, Ph.D.
Robert Hannemann, M.D., F.A.A.P.
Sylvia Kottler, M.S.
Bill Peterson, Ph.D.

Making Something Grow

Making something grow will help your child learn about nature, about responsibility and about the need for patience.

Most children are interested in learning about plant care—how to know if the soil needs water; how to decide whether sun or shade is needed.

Many materials are available which are almost cost-free. Some things to plant:

(1) Lemon, grapefruit, or orange seeds. Fill a small pot, which has holes in its bottom, with soil. Push seeds into the soil until they are covered with 1/4 inch of soil. Next, add water. Finally, wait for the seeds to develop.

(2) Grass seed. If you want instant success, sprinkle some seed on a damp sponge. Or let Youngster sow some grass seed in the spring or fall.

Have her water it lightly each day. In a little while the tiny blades of grass will begin to appear.

(3) Lima beans. Line a glass jar with moist paper towels. Then place the beans between the towel and the jar to enable you to watch what's happening. Now cover the jar. Finally, watch and wait for the beans to become plants.

(4) Sweet potato and avocado pit. Place toothpicks around the middle of the potato or pit in order to hold them up.

Place them in a glass jar so the bottom tip is covered with water. Keep the plant out of direct sunlight until it has leaves. Continue to add water because the tip must be covered.

In about six weeks there will be roots. Then you may plant either potato or pit in the soil, keeping the top of the plant soil-free.

What unique and funny- looking plants they turn out to be!■

'But Do You Love Me — Best of All?'

Every parent of two or more children has probably been faced with some variation of this age-old question. Perhaps the question will be phrased differently. "Do you still love me, Mommy? More than Jenny?"

Sometimes the question may take the form of an accusation, such as "You're always picking on me! You don't love me—you only love Debbie!" "You think everything is always my fault. You never pick on him! You love him more than me!"

If you are on the receiving end of such questions or accusations, you may find yourself struggling to answer the question or defend yourself against the accusation.

Often one's first impulse is to respond to accusation with a counterattack:

"How can you say such a thing! Of course I love you as much as I love your brother/sister! That's no way to talk!"

But a counterattack doesn't solve the problem or reassure your child. It can only make him feel worse—more rejected, less worthy.

The anguished quality of your child's voice reflects his pain and his feelings of being pushed aside in favor of another child.

How can you explain to him that you love all of your children equally, that babies and toddlers need more care, that you are proud of his growing independence?

How can you heal his hurt and help him understand and believe you? What can you say or do to make things better?

First, listen to what your child may really be saying: "You don't give me as much attention as I need. I'm afraid that my new sister/brother will take my place. I feel abandoned and alone. I'm too little to be alone. I need you!"

Then reflect some of those unsaid feelings back to your child. Let him know that you understand how he is feeling by putting his feelings into words. "You're feeling sad (angry), aren't you, because Mommy has been so busy with your little brother/sister."

"It's hard, isn't it, to share Daddy's time and attention with someone else?"

As you talk with him about his expressed fears and resentments you might use one of the following approaches.

"Mommy's (Daddy's) love for you is special for you and always will be. I don't have to take away any of my love for you to give love to your little brother/sister. I have a whole lot of new love to give to him/her. This new love is different because you and the baby are different—but it is no bigger and no better—just different.

"I love each (both) of you. I love you just because you are you. I love you as my oldest son. I also love your sister just for being who she is. I love her as my youngest daughter.

"And I love your little sister because she is so tiny and needs me right now.

"So, I love each of you because each of you is so special to me!"

Take time to hug him and reassure him. Bring him into the circle of your attention by making him part of what you're doing. Ask him to hold something for you, or hand you something.

Make a point of spending a "special time" with your hurting child. This special time need not be a long time—perhaps 15-20 minutes, but it must be time spent only with this one child.

It could be during a younger child's nap time or after he is settled for the night. When the time is snatched out of your busy schedule will depend upon your own family's lifestyle.

Always have something planned to do—for example, read a favorite story—but be flexible and give your child time to talk about what he is thinking and feeling.

Cuddle him close to you or on your lap. Relax, and say, "My, but it's nice to be here with you!"

Be a good listener! You may have to "prime the pump" with open questions like, "What made you think that I love Timmy more than you?" or "What do you suppose our dog (or cat) would say if he could talk?" or "What would you do if you could fly like a bird?"

Then listen to him and talk with him. Even five special minutes are worth more to him than a whole day of half-listening attention. ■

Good-bye Baby Teeth

"When will I lose my first tooth?"

Most young children look forward to losing their first tooth. It becomes not only a milestone ("Now the tooth fairy can come visit me."), but also a status symbol of growing up ("How come you haven't lost your first tooth yet?").

As a result, many children will vigorously wiggle a loose tooth to try to speed up the process. Fortunately, gentle wiggling of a loose tooth will generally do no great harm.

When will this landmark event occur? Just as no two children follow the same schedule in learning to walk or talk, so, too, no two children lose their first tooth at exactly the same time.

The timing depends partly on heredity and partly on the child's diet and general health.

Most children lose their first tooth between 5-1/2 and 6-1/2 years of age.

But some may lose it as early as five years, whereas, for others, it may not happen until seven years of age.

Every person normally has two sets of teeth, the temporary teeth which are often referred to as "baby" teeth, and the permanent teeth which begin to appear around this age.

Children are born with the tooth buds for both the temporary and permanent teeth. When a baby tooth becomes loose, it's a sign that a permanent tooth is pushing it out of the way.

The baby teeth that were the first to cut through the gums are usually the first to be pushed out.

A permanent tooth usually goes through a cycle of growth and then rest. As a result, the baby tooth will go through a similar cycle of loosening and tightening before it ultimately comes out.

Between five and 13 years of age, children will generally lose all of their 20 baby teeth

which are then replaced by the stronger permanent teeth. During the teenage years, more molars are added until there are a total of 32 permanent teeth.

Visit to the dentist

Many children have already made their first visit to the dentist. However, if this has not been done, now is a good time to make an appointment. Even baby teeth can develop cavities which need treatment.

Also, beneath the surface of the gums, the permanent teeth are beginning to exert pressure on the roots of the baby teeth.

The dentist can check if a permanent tooth is growing behind or in front of a baby tooth.

Furthermore, whenever a baby tooth falls out, the teeth on either side of it may shift slightly causing the permanent tooth to come in crooked, overlapping the tooth next to it.

The earlier such a problem is detected, the more easily it can be corrected. So, every six months a dentist should inspect what is happening at this important stage of development.

If you have concerns or questions about your child's teeth, be sure to bring them up at the appointment.

For example, the dentist will be glad to reinforce your brushing/flossing procedure and comment on good tooth-care habits.

The dentist will also check if the teeth are coming out in the proper sequence: first the two lower incisors (center teeth), then the two teeth on either side of them or else the two upper front teeth—which, of course, gives all young children a delightful, toothless smile.

Proper food and drink

To prevent tooth decay, it is also important to be aware of the effects on teeth of different foods and drinks.

Certain foods, such as raw carrots, celery, apples, and pears, as well as other raw vegetables and fresh fruits, are called detergent foods. They contain tough fibers which help to clean the teeth and gums.

Other foods, such as candy, cake, and crackers, are called impacting foods.

When they get pressed into the spaces in and between the teeth, they ultimately cause decay unless removed with a toothbrush or by flossing.

Likewise, soft drinks containing sugar will be acted upon by bacteria which are harmful to teeth. That's why brushing after eating or drinking is so important.

And it's also a good idea to limit eating and drinking between meals and at bedtime — especially drinking cola and sugary treats like candy and sweets.

How and when to brush

Five-year-olds need to know how and when to brush their teeth.

• Upper teeth should be brushed downward, away from the gum.

• Lower teeth should be brushed upward in a similar manner.

• The flat, biting surface of the teeth may

continnued on page 357

continued from page 356

Family Album on a Wall

be brushed in a back and forth movement.

Get your child a soft, multi-tufted nylon bristle brush. (If in doubt, consult your dentist.)

Use a toothpaste with a flavor your child likes. The brushing and rinsing are more important than the type of toothpaste used.

Every child should develop the habit of brushing teeth before going to bed. It is during the night when less saliva is produced that bacteria can do the most harm. He will need help from you to floss his teeth.

In the morning, it is more effective to brush teeth after eating breakfast than before. Otherwise powerful bacteria will be at work throughout the day.

The importance of good teeth

There are a number of very good reasons for taking care of one's teeth:

• Good care of teeth helps prevent decay, painful toothaches, and expensive dental treatment.

• A good set of teeth helps to promote good general health.

• A mouth which is free of dental decay helps prevent bad breath.

• A full set of teeth gives better shape to a person's face, especially around the mouth, jaws, and cheeks.

• Good speech is influenced by one's teeth. (Of the 26 letters of the alphabet, 18 require the use of one's teeth for proper pronunciation.)

• Good teeth also help a person to have an attractive smile—an important attribute for one's later social, business, or professional life.

• The best way to protect your child's teeth is to teach good dental care at as young an age as possible.

As a child moves into the preschool years, he becomes more and more aware of time as an important factor governing the organization of the world around him.

As a toddler he was concerned mainly with the daily and weekly routine of his life: getting up, eating breakfast, playtime, and bedtime.

Day and night, waking up time and going to bed time, Daddy and/or Mommy going to work and coming home, these events governed his day.

A little later the routine of the family week was anticipated and words like tomorrow, Saturday, and Sunday had special meaning.

Holidays such as Easter, Fourth of July, Thanksgiving, and Christmas have little meaning until the child is about three years old.

By five years of age children, anticipate all such special events and enter whole-heartedly into the celebration.

They remember what they did yesterday or last week but have little concept of the duration of time.

Yesterday may seem to have been a long time ago while something that happened a month ago may be remembered as having happened yesterday.

Family relationships, especially those spanning generations, remain an unsolvable mystery.

The child has great difficulty seeing Mommy or Daddy as anything but parents.

Grandma is just Grandma. The idea that she is Mommy's mother and that Mommy was once a little girl is almost inconceivable.

Daddy is Daddy. How could he have ever been a little boy with a daddy of his own?

Five-year-olds love to hear stories from their parents that start, "Once when I was a little girl/boy—," and "When you were a baby—."

Grandparents are especially good at stories

not only about Mommy's and Daddy's childhood, but even about when Grandpa was a little boy.

These stories are like fairy tales to the five-year-old and are a great source of information for them. Nevertheless the child is unable to understand the time sequence involved.

Here is where the family album comes in. Your family photographs are probably kept in albums. Your child will love to look at those pictures with you, to hear the names and stories of the people pictured.

However, photograph albums are rarely available for use by the child.

So how about making a family album on a wall where it can be seen and referred to frequently.

Include pictures of yourselves as babies with your parents, and as teenagers.

Also include your wedding pictures, pictures of your child as a baby and of brothers and sisters as babies or as they are now.

You can arrange the pictures in a family tree beginning with your parents and including your brothers and/or sisters as well as yourselves.

Your child can look at the pictures, and talk about them.

In learning about his family, he is also learning about himself.■

Nail Biting and Other Undesirable Habits

Many young children display a variety of undesirable habits such as nail biting, hair twisting, nose picking, or thumbsucking.

Parents often find these behaviors of their child to be embarrassing and exasperating—all the more so when they find that the more they chastise or punish, the worse these behaviors usually get.

Nail biting, which can sometimes cause sore and bloody fingers, is one of the most common of these habits.

About one-third of all children between five and 15 years of age bite their nails. The habit sometimes persists into adulthood.

Among teenagers, nail biting has been found to be one of the most common means of relieving tension and over 25 percent of college students continue to bite their nails.

Overall, it is estimated that nail biting afflicts more than 40 million Americans. So, if your child engages in this behavior, it may be because he is imitating someone among his friends or family.

Hair twisting usually begins as a comfort-seeking behavior in infancy or early childhood. This habit, which is usually unconscious, often eventually results in hair pulling and hair loss.

It is particularly irritating to parents because bald spots on the head—which in extreme cases can be permanent—are so apparent to others.

Masturbation is a common childhood habit and may be used as a form of self-comfort for children.

For children, this may seem no different than picking their nose or hair twisting, so if necessary, explain that this is a private activity, much like toileting and is best limited to the bedroom or bathroom.

It is most often a normal part of childhood development and children should not be punished or shamed for masturbating.

As with other childhood behaviors, don't make a big deal about this, so that you don't reinforce the habit.

Nose picking usually begins at an age when the child doesn't yet know how to blow her nose or use a tissue.

Few childhood habits arouse as much disgust in adults and other children as nose picking. Besides being unhygienic, it can result in a bloody nose and the spreading of germs.

Thumbsucking, which emerges in infancy or early childhood, is related to the sucking reflex with which every normal child is born. In its initial stages, it is a rather harmless way of seeking comfort and pleasure.

If the habit continues as the child grows older—past four years of age—it can cause malocclusion or improper bite due to pushing the permanent teeth out of line.

The extent of the deformity depends on the frequency, intensity, and duration of the thumbsucking.

In addition, if thumbsucking continues to an older age, the child might experience social isolation from other children since he can't play or talk to others when his thumb is in his mouth.

Why do some children develop these undesirable habits? There are no easy answers to that question. But there is ample evidence to indicate that:

• These behaviors are initiated by the child as a way of seeking comfort and pleasure.

• They can eventually become unconscious, compulsive behaviors.

• They are more likely to occur when a child is experiencing anxiety or stress of some kind.

• Children who engage in these behaviors, however, are not necessarily more anxious than others.

• These habits are not an indicator of emotional disturbance.

• Short-term solutions—such as putting an unpleasant tasting substance on the nail or thumb—are generally not effective and may in the long run only increase the child's stress level.

• Nagging, threatening, or punishing a child for self-stimulatory behavior may stop the behavior for a short time, but ultimately may also increase the child's stress level.

The following considerations are important in helping a child overcome an undesirable habit:

• Focus on the whole child rather than on the habit which the parent finds irritating. Think of some of the good things the child does.

This helps the parent keep the irritating behavior in proper perspective.

• Be aware that, for adults as well as children, instant success in breaking an unconscious habit is very rare.

• Success will most likely be achieved when the child—not just the child's parent—wants to break the habit.

• Many children want to overcome these habits when they begin school and interact with peers who draw attention to the undesirable behavior.

• Some habits are easier to break than others. For example, if a child engages in nail biting or thumbsucking simply because of fear of the dark, a nightlight in the bedroom may be sufficient to change the behavior.

Likewise, in the case of nose picking,

continued on pageaa 360

Guidelines for Teaching and Learning

Why does your child learn some new things with ease while others seem so difficult for her?

Why does she seem to be able to stick with some activities for a long time but gets easily frustrated and upset by others?

How can you help her get the most out of each learning opportunity, whether it is a special planned activity or a part of her everyday experience?

One of the most basic rules about learning is that there must be a good match between a child's interest and present abilities, and the skill, material, or experience to be learned.

Following are some guidelines that can help you plan new activities for your child so that they are well-matched to her learning abilities.

By using these guidelines you may simplify an activity that is too difficult in order to make it possible for your child to be successful. Or, if you find the task is too easy for her, you may increase the challenge to help her develop some new skill.

1. It's easier to learn something that presents a slight challenge than something that is very difficult.

A child learns best when a new experience is just a little harder than what she's used to.

A slight challenge, a small "stretch" of physical or mental abilities makes an activity more appealing. If a task is too hard, it's simply frustrating.

Look at what your child does well now and see if there are ways you can help her stretch her abilities—by introducing a slightly more difficult challenge.

If an activity is either too easy or too difficult, it will need to be modified in order to be interesting and educational rather than boring or frustrating.

2. It's easier to learn a new skill that is similar to one that's already mastered

than one that's very different from what is already known.

Your child will learn best when she moves from the known to the unknown. A little novelty is important to sustain interest.

However, if the activity or materials are too different from what she is familiar with, she may become frustrated and lose interest.

3. It's easier to learn new skills when they are related to real-life experiences than when they are taught in isolation.

Your child's daily life is full of potential learning activities. Mealtimes, for example, are excellent opportunities for learning.

As she helps you set the table, she learns to put one glass, one plate, one napkin, and so on, for each person. This is an important beginning math skill called "one-to-one correspondence."

As she pours herself something to drink from a small pitcher, she learns to gauge how much is enough—another math lesson, in quantity.

Pouring, serving herself, and eating with a fork or spoon also improve her coordination with her hands.

Talking about the size of food portions, the colors, shapes, and textures of foods helps her increase her vocabulary and thinking skills. Daily routines are a great source of learning experiences.

4. It's easier to understand a new idea

using real-life objects than using pictures or words.

For example, it could be difficult for your child to understand that the word "orange" stands for the fruit she eats as well as for the color of certain things if you just told her about it or showed her pictures.

But if she touches, smells, peels, and eats an orange and then looks around the house for objects that match the color of the orange peel, the idea will "come alive" for her.

Any time she is having trouble understanding something from a description or picture, try using the real object.

5. It's easier to receive and understand information than to reproduce or express that information.

For example, we all learned to understand language before we could use it.

Your child will learn to recognize words before she can write them. She can understand what she sees before she can draw it. She can recognize a piece of music before she can sing the melody.

6. It's easier to accomplish actions requiring large movements (gross motor abilities) than those requiring smaller, more precise movements (fine motor skills).

The rule for the development of motor skills is that control proceeds from the head downward and from the midline of the body outward to fingers and toes.

Thus, a child learns to reach with her whole arm before she learns to use her hand to grasp large objects, and she learns to do that before she learns to use her fingers and thumb to hold and manipulate small objects.

7. It's easier to use the hand than to use a tool. Your child learned to feed herself well with her fingers before she could use a spoon or fork with similar skill. She can

continued on page 360

continued from page 358   continued from page 359

parents can help a child practice blowing her nose and make sure she has a supply of tissues.

• In general, if a parent believes that a child is engaging in a habit because of stress or anxiety, it would be helpful to determine, if possible, what is causing such stress, and then try to remove the cause.

For example, if a child experiences tension or anxiety when watching certain television programs, then television viewing needs to be more carefully monitored.

• As a child grows older, it is possible to bring an undesirable habit to her awareness, discuss possible reasons for this behavior, and suggest some ways in which to eliminate it.

• Above all, parents should not blame themselves or their child whenever a habit is difficult to break.

Mark Twain once remarked: "Habit is habit and not to be flung out of the window by anyone, but coaxed downstairs one step at a time."

Next month we will discuss how parents can help young children handle stress, which is often the root cause of these undesirable habits.■

tear paper before she can cut with scissors.

It is easier for her to accomplish finger painting than the more precise coordination necessary to paint with a paintbrush.

In learning to use any tool—eating utensils, scissors, pencil, pen, marker or paintbrush—she needs practice in learning to use it before she can use it skillfully for any purpose.

For example, when she was first introduced to a pair of scissors, she had to learn how to hold them and snip with them before she could cut a straight line.

She probably still needs practice cutting on lines before she can use them to cut a shape out of paper with skill.

8. It's easier to learn in a relaxed, accepting atmosphere, than in a tense, "expecting" environment.

Your child will learn most easily when she feels that you accept her, respect her judgment, and allow her to follow her own pace in learning.

On the other hand, if she feels that you expect her to perform in a certain way or that you will be disappointed if she fails to meet your expectations, she will be less

P. O. Box 2505 • W Lafayette, IN 47996
(800) 927-7289
www.GrowingChild.com

Contributing Authors

Phil Bach, O.D., Ph.D.
Miriam Bender, Ph.D.
Joseph Braga, Ed.D.
Laurie Braga, Ph.D.
George Early, Ph.D.
Carol R. Gestwicki, M.S.
Liam Grimley, Ph.D.
Robert Hannemann, M.D., F.A.A.P.
Sylvia Kottler, M.S.
Bill Peterson, Ph.D.

able to learn effectively.

Her anxiety will interfere with her learning. Instead of judging for herself what she can do, she will be more concerned with your judgment of what she can do.

This will undercut her self-confidence and her capacity for self-starting. Try to be more like a helping coach than a concerned instructor in your child's learning.

Be patient and encouraging. Watch the activities she chooses for herself. Observe her level of competence. Use this information to determine her learning abilities, needs, and interests.

This is also a good time to recall Vygotsky's idea (see Month 52) that children's thinking is influenced by interaction with other people.

When getting support from more competent peers or adults, children are enabled by a scaffolding process to use their best thinking or problem solving.

When presented with tasks that are slightly beyond their present mental capability—what Vygotsky called the zone of proximal development—the more knowledgeable parent or sibling asks questions or gives hints to guide the child to move ahead in their thinking.

For example, a child who can solve a 10-piece puzzle is given one with 20 pieces.

Rather than show the child how to do the puzzle, the parent may suggest that the child look for all the pieces with straight sides, or ask the child what color piece would show the bird.

Thus while parents construct a scaffold (or framework) for a child's problem solving and thinking, they do not perform the tasks for them but provide a supportive structure for problem solving, with the actual solution left to the children.

Next month we will offer some more guidelines for teaching and learning that can help you help your child learn.■

Five Years Old

A child's fifth birthday is an exciting and important milestone. It marks the end of the early childhood years.

Five years of age is also the beginning of an important new stage in life. It is at this age that most children will begin their school experience in kindergarten.

At five, children are usually imitative and imaginative, sometimes very noisy and almost always very busy.

But suddenly they may become very tired.

Just as suddenly, they can recover their energy as they go bounding out the door to the next "important activity" on their own busy agenda.

In describing the behaviors of a typical five-year-old child, it is important for parents to remember that not all children are "typical."

Some may be more advanced in one area and less advanced in another.

By knowing some of the characteristics of a typical five-year-old, parents can better appreciate the uniqueness of their own child.

By now most five-year-olds have gained better large muscle control. So they usually enjoy running in a park, climbing a slide, balancing on a beam, swinging on a jungle gym, pulling a little red wagon, or riding a small bicycle.

They also enjoy rough-and-tumble activities, such as rolling down a slope. All these activities help to further develop the large muscles of the body.

Five-year-olds now display a lot more grace and coordination than just one year ago.

They enjoy doing simple dance steps, swinging their legs and arms to the beat of a musical rhythm.

But they will probably still prefer to create their own rhythmical body movements rather than follow the set pattern of an instructor.

Small muscle control, though somewhat less advanced, has also improved during the past year.

Five-year-olds, for example, will now be more skillful when drawing with crayons.

With improved eye-hand coordination, they are also a little more skillful in throwing or catching a ball and in using a small hammer.

They also enjoy working with simple picture puzzles (which, incidentally, are usually available from the children's section of a public library).

They are beginning to show greater concern for accuracy in whatever they do, as well as more persistence and more patience.

When they engage in these activities they want adults to watch what they are doing. They crave adult approval and repeatedly seek praise and encouragement.

They enjoy parental attention even when they are not experiencing any success.

By five years of age, most children have also overcome many of their earlier speech difficulties.

Their language proficiency can sometimes be remarkable. But, frequently, perhaps to the frustration of some parents, they prefer to ask questions than to make statements.

Their questions are now less general and more to the point.

They want to know what things are made for and how they can be used. ("What can I do with this?").

They look for short answers to their questions and won't pay sustained attention to a longer, more detailed response.

They usually understand the meaning of a word in terms of how they themselves relate to it. For example, "horse" would mean "something I can ride."

Their perception of time and space is by now more differentiated and more mature.

For example, they can talk meaningfully about what places they visited, in sequence, yesterday and where they will be going tomorrow.

But they still have difficulty thinking about events in the more distant past or future.

At this age, they seem to learn best when they can relate new learning to their own life and experiences.

Hands-on experiences and trial-and-error approaches are more effective learning strategies for them than any attempt at more formal education.

They also learn well from dramatic play activities. They usually enjoy acting out a familiar part in some favorite book.

They like to role-play as a way of dealing with their emotions.

continued on page 362

continued from page 361

For example, they may be heard "scolding" teddy bear for dropping cookies on the floor—right after Mom corrected them for this same behavior!

Their favorite books are now more likely to include comedy and real-life stories to which they can relate, rather than fantasy and fairy tales, although they still enjoy the latter.

Many five-year-olds are also beginning to develop their own individual sense of humor. And they want *you* to attend to and repeat the things you read or say that make *them* laugh. This makes interaction with them at this age a special delight.

Most five-year-olds have also developed basic socialization skills related to daily living, such as eating, drinking, sleeping, and toilet learning habits. They are also more independent in dressing and taking care of themselves.

They are likely to have their own individual preferences: for particular food and clothing, for example, as well as particular toys, CDs and TV programs.

Also at this stage they begin to show increasingly more interest in activities outside of their own immediate family.

More and more, they enjoy the companionship of other children their own age. And they may by now even have one or more "best friends."

By interacting with other children, five-year-olds learn about sharing, taking turns, and teamwork.

Though their game skills have not yet been well developed, they are beginning to learn the importance of cooperation, compromise, and negotiation—all of which are social skills they will need for the rest of their lives.

They are getting ready to move into the wide world of social experiences—all of which make five years of age such an important and wonderful time for them—and for their parents.∎

Developmental Milestones–5 Years

Social/Emotional Behavior

- Dresses and undresses independently.
- Uses knife and fork competently.
- Washes and dries hands and face well.
- Selects own playmates.
- Is protective of younger children and animals.
- Comprehends simple rules of games and the concept of fair play.
- Demonstrates a sense of humor.
- Understands the necessity for tidiness, but requires frequent reminders.
- Experiences fears involving self—dogs, falling, physical dangers.
- Picks nose, bites nails.
- Sucks thumb before falling asleep or when fatigued.

Language

- Speaks fluently except for a few mispronunciations (s, v, f, th, r).
- Gives full name, age, birthday, address.
- Defines concrete words by their function.
- Asks meaning of abstract words and unfamiliar words and will later use them.
- Loves to recite and chant jingles and rhymes.
- Enjoys being read to or told stories, and acts them out alone later.

Visual-Motor

- Threads a large needle independently and sews real stitches.
- Copies circle, square, cross and capital letters: V T H O X L Y U C A.
- Draws a house with these features: outline, door, windows, chimney and roof.
- Draws a person with these features: head, arms, legs, trunk.
- Draws a variety of other items and names them *before* producing them.
- Uses brush, crayons, and pencil with better control.
- Crayons and colors forms within the lines.
- Matches 10 colors.
- Names at least four primary colors.
- Copies simple block patterns containing as many as 10 blocks.

Gross Motor

- Can walk a narrow line without stepping off.
- Climbs, swings, runs skillfully.
- Moves rhythmically to music.
- Stands on one foot (either foot) with arms folded across chest to a count of 10 seconds.
- Hops two to three yards forward on each foot.
- Enjoys ball play and understands rules, positions, and scoring.
- Bends and touches toes without bending knees.
- Grips strongly with each hand.
- Can run lightly on toes.

More Guidelines for Teaching and Learning

Last month we provided a number of guidelines to use in helping your child get the most out of each learning opportunity.

Those guidelines and the ones to follow can be applied in any situation and at any age.

Anytime your child is engaged in a new learning experience, you can help by simplifying the task so that it contains just the right amount of difficulty and novelty: not too easy, but not too hard; not too familiar, but not too different.

The following guidelines can help you find the right match between your child's abilities and the new skill to be mastered.

1. It's easier to demonstrate how to use an object than to recognize its name. Sometimes your child may know something about an object even though she doesn't recognize its name.

For example, she might not correctly identify a piece of chalk, but she still might know how to use it correctly to draw on a blackboard.

2. It's easier to explain what an object is used for than to describe it. For example, if you ask your child what an umbrella is, she might say "for the rain" rather than describe its appearance.

If you ask her what a car is, she's more likely to answer "to ride in" than to tell you it's something that has a motor and four wheels.

3. It's easier to match two things that are the same than to identify the item by name. For example, if you showed your child these two pictures and asked her to "Point to the triangle," she might not be able to do so.

But if you change the task and ask her to "Find the one that's the same as this one,"

she may do so correctly, even though she doesn't know the name.

4. It's easier to follow an instruction if it's accompanied by a demonstration.

Words often aren't enough for a child to perform an unfamiliar action. She needs to be shown as well as told.

If the activity is complicated, she'll need to be shown slowly, in small steps and given a chance to practice the action herself until she can do it.

This is a good guide for specific learning activities as well as for things you ask her to do around the house, such as tidying her room.

5. It's easier to match things that are the same than to tell the difference between things that aren't the same.

For example, it would be easier for your child to tell you if two sounds you make are the same than to tell you if they were different.

The first of the following tasks would be easier than the second:

a) Show me the one that's just like this (the first) one.

b) Show me the one that's not the same as the others.

The first of the following tasks is easier than the second:

Show me the one that's the same as the first one in each line.

line 1

line 2

6. It's easier to describe something than to classify it. For example, if you ask your child what an apple is, she's more likely to tell you what it looks and tastes like than to tell you it's a fruit.

Describing something involves concrete thinking. But classifying it ("It's a fruit.") involves abstract thinking which is a higher thinking level.

7. It's easier to recognize something than it is to name it. Sometimes your child might not be able to tell you the name of an object when you ask her, "What is this?" But if you put that object in a group and ask her to "Show me the _____," she might be able to point to it.

8. It's easier to name something than it is to define it. If you ask your child, "What is this?" she will probably be able to name most familiar objects ("It's a shoe." "It's a hat."). But she will find it more difficult to answer a definition question, such as "What is a shoe?" "What is a hat?"

We hope these guidelines will help you plan special learning games to play with your child.

We also hope they'll help you to increase your knowledge of what your child can do, particularly in her routine day-to-day experiences. The more you know about her present skill level, the better helpmate you'll be to her in her learning.

The more successes you can help her to have, the more likely she is to succeed in the future and see herself as a successful person. With these kinds of good feelings about herself, she will be able to view occasional failures as challenges rather than as personal shortcomings—an attitude that will be very helpful to her in her adult life. ■

Helping a Young Child Deal with Stress

In bygone days, the preschool years were a carefree time for joyful music, play, and dancing—waiting for the "real" world of school to begin.

In today's fast-paced world, however, even young children are caught up in the pressures of modern life.

What was once intended to be informal, lighthearted enjoyment of music, play, and dance has now become more serious and highly organized music lessons, competitive sports, and dance classes.

Not surprisingly, many young children today show signs of stress due to the pace and pressures of our contemporary world.

Stress may be defined as feelings of anxiety, frustration, or anger that a person experiences in dealing with the demands and pressures of life.

Some children are more prone to stress than others. It's important, therefore, for parents to know the unique characteristics of each of their children.

Within the same family, children react differently to the same situation or event.

For one child, meeting new people at a birthday party is perceived as an enjoyable experience; for another, it is a dreaded and fearful encounter.

A child who considers taking a test or playing a competitive sport as an exciting challenge will likely do better than the one who feels threatened and insecure.

And what may appear to be an exciting schedule of activities to one child, may be seen by another as too demanding and hectic.

Parents can help prevent stress by being sensitive to each child's characteristics and coping abilities.

How young children cope with stress

Children develop their own ways—some good, some not so good—of dealing with the stress they experience in their daily lives.

For example, a child may suddenly run around the playground, skip rope, or kick a football as hard as he can. He may engage in these activities without even being conscious of his stressful feelings.

Creating an imaginary friend can be a helpful way for some children to deal with stress.

Even though parents may be irritated by having to reserve a seat in the car or set an extra place at table for an imaginary companion, research studies have indicated that the companion can often play a helpful role in relieving stress in young children, especially for those who have a vivid imagination, and are intelligent and socially well-adjusted.

Some other coping strategies, such as regression or denial, need to be more carefully monitored by parents.

In regression, the child reverts to an earlier stage of development. For example, the arrival of a newborn baby can be a stressful experience for some young children.

They fear they have lost the love and affection of their parents, and act younger than their years in order to get some of the attention and affection being given to their younger sibling.

Children who use denial act as though the stressful event did not occur. For example, after a favorite pet has died, the child may continue to prepare food for the pet.

These methods enable a child to cope with immediate stress until time eventually helps to heal the stressful situation.

Extreme forms of regression or denial—in which the child, over a period of time, loses contact with reality—may indicate the need for parental or even professional help.

Warning signals

Stress can sometimes build up to the point where a young child is no longer capable of coping on his own. At that point, he needs the help of an adult to deal with

overstress. That's why it's important for parents to be aware of and recognize the warning signals of too much stress.

There are many different physical and psychological symptoms a child may exhibit in reaction to being overstressed.

Some of the most common reactions include: loss of appetite, restless sleep, bedwetting, stuttering, headaches and stomachaches.

When parents have noticed the warning signals of stress in their child, it is helpful to identify and try to deal with the underlying cause.

If a child continues to show signs of extreme stress, parents should consult a pediatrician or child psychologist.

Some possible causes

The causes of stress in young children are not always easy to determine. Some causes are genetic, others are environmental.

From a genetic standpoint, for example, some children are born with a nervous disposition or temperament which causes them to be easily stressed.

But environmental factors—such as poverty, divorce, or death of a close relative—can also lead to stress.

Before trying to help a young child deal with stress, it is important to give some consideration to whether the cause of the stress may be genetic or environmental.

When a young child's stress is due to genetic factors, it is likely to be more deep-rooted and long-lasting.

Rather than trying to change the child's basic temperament, it is generally more helpful to teach the child specific ways of coping effectively with stress. (See "Specific relaxation techniques" below.)

On the other hand, when the cause of stress is mainly environmental, it is more helpful to focus directly on the cause of the stress.

continued on page 365

continued from pagea 364

Environmental factors often have a ripple effect. For example, Jimmy was a five-year-old child who did not have adequate nutrition before going to school and was unable to concentrate on what was being taught.

As a result he routinely performed poorly, and had low self-esteem, all of which caused him considerable stress.

When the specific underlying cause was addressed—his parents made sure he ate a good breakfast—his concentration got better, his work improved, and he developed higher self-esteem, which eventually got rid of his feelings of stress.

A young child's experience of stress is usually related to his age and developmental level.

It is perfectly normal, for example, for all children to experience some degree of fear.

But in a young child, some types of fear can cause particularly great stress:

• Fear of the dark ("The monster might come."), fear of abandonment ("My parents don't love me any more.");

• Fear of the unknown ("What will the doctor do to me?"), or

• Fear of failure ("My parents will be disappointed in me.").

What parents can do

• The most important things parents can do to help a young child deal with stress are:

(a) Become aware of each child's unique characteristics, (b) try to determine the cause of the child's stress, and (c) become more aware of what helps the child to relax and overcome stress.

• Once parents become aware of each child's unique characteristics, it is often possible to do something about an underlying environmental cause of stress.

So, parents respect their child's fear by providing a nightlight in a dark bedroom,

or discussing in a matter-of-fact way what will most likely happen at the doctor's office.

• Teach your child how to appropriately express feelings such as anger.

This can be done either verbally (by talking about the child's reason for being angry) or nonverbally (by providing the child art materials with which he can make big sweeping strokes in vivid colors, or by active outdoor play—running and swinging).

Feelings that are held inside, without being expressed, are a potential source of stress.

• Make sure your child has time for his own unstructured play activities.

Young children can avoid stress by having a variety of activities: (a) some that are enjoyed but require little or no effort; (b) some that are absorbing and more demanding; and (c) a few that are more difficult and truly challenging.

By becoming aware of each child's unique characteristics, parents will readily be aware when an activity becomes too challenging and overly stressful.

• Share a laugh with your child. Humor is a very effective way to dispel tension and overcome stress.

Specific relaxation techniques

• Teach your child breathing techniques for relaxation:

"Breathe in slowly through your nose. Feel your stomach and chest fill with air. Hold in your breath while I count to five. Now, breathe out slowly through your mouth, letting go of all the tension in your body."

• Teach your child muscle relaxation exercises.

Because a young child may not understand the meaning of the words, "Relax your muscles," it will sometimes help for him to have a hard, smooth rock to hold in one hand and a soft sponge ball in the other.

You can then help him relax each of the major muscles of the body by saying, "Make the muscles of your feet and toes hard like a rock. Let's count to 5: 1-2-3-4-5.

Now let go and make those muscles soft like a sponge."

Start at the feet and work your way up the body to the neck and head, tensing and releasing each of the muscles along the way.

• Play soft, soothing music. For many people, music provides an effective form of relaxation which can be used either by itself or as background for the breathing and muscle relaxation exercises.

Lastly, remember that children learn from their parents' behavior. What you do is more important than what you say.

When parents know how to handle stress in their own lives, they are better able to help a young child deal with stress.

For example, since it is easier for parents to handle stress than children, parents may have to modify some of the stressful things in their children's lives.

In divorce situations, parents can work out picking up arrangements between themselves to keep it simple and reduce confusion for the child.

Next month we will discuss some specific ways for parents to deal with their own stress levels.■

Bicycle Safety

Many five-year-olds enjoy riding a bicycle.

When a child has developed reasonably good cycling ability, he sometimes wants to take greater risks. Unfortunately, he may not yet have acquired the good judgment needed for his own safety.

So, it is important for parents to give careful thought to bicycle safety. By doing so, they may help their child avoid a serious accident.

Here are some things to consider:

The bicycle: Make sure the bicycle is the correct size for your child. Sitting on the saddle, he should be able to place both feet on the ground.

The bicycle should be well-maintained, with brakes that function well and with no loose parts. Tires should be inflated properly.

Bikes should be equipped with reflectors on the front and rear, on the wheels, and on the pedals.

The helmet: Everyone who rides a bike should always wear a helmet.

According to the Snell Memorial Foundation, over 5,000 head injuries to bicyclists are treated every year in hospital emergency rooms. The highest rate of injury is for children between five and 15 years of age.

Studies indicate that wearing helmets can prevent 85 percent of head injuries.

The helmet should be made of strong, shock-absorbent material, with crushable internal padding adjustable for proper fit, and with an adjustable chin strap that will stay securely fastened.

The U.S. National Highway Traffic Safety Administration recommends using only helmets with a label of approval from the American National Standards Institute (ANSI) or the Snell Memorial Foundation (SMF).

Clothing: Your child should wear only close-fitting clothes, with no strings, loose shoelaces, belts, or other items that could get caught in the bicycle wheels.

A child needs to see and be seen by others. Wearing white clothing doesn't necessarily work.

Rather, neon, fluorescent or other bright colors are more visible. Also wear something that reflects light, such as reflective tape or markings.

Remember, just because a child can see a driver doesn't mean the driver sees the child.

Some basic safety rules for your child:

• While cycling, keep your mind on what you are doing, always being on the lookout for danger.

• Look left-right-left again before coming out of a driveway.

• Watch for cars coming out of or turning into driveways.

• Watch for hazards in the bike's path such as broken glass, gravel, puddles, holes and dogs.

P. O. Box 2505 • W Lafayette, IN 47996
(800) 927-7289
www.GrowingChild.com

Contributing Authors
Phil Bach, O.D., Ph.D.
Miriam Bender, Ph.D.
Joseph Braga, Ed.D.
Laurie Braga, Ph.D.
George Early, Ph.D.
Carol R. Gestwicki, M.S.
Liam Grimley, Ph.D.
Robert Hannemann, M.D., F.A.A.P.
Sylvia Kottler, M.S.
Bill Peterson, Ph.D.

• Ride in a straight line, not weaving back and forth.

• Stop at corners of sidewalks and streets to look for cars and to make sure the drivers see you before crossing.

•Enter a street at a corner and not between parked cars.

• Ride in single file, on the right side in the same direction as other vehichles. Go with the flow, not against it.

• Never use headphones while riding a bicycle.

• Children under ten years old are better off riding on the sidewalk, not the street and never on a public roadway.

•Check the law in your state or jurisdiction to make sure sidewalk riding is allowed.

•Do not ride at night.

These are some simple precautions that can help your child avoid a serious accident.

For more information on bicycle safety, visit the National Highway Traffic Safety Administration's website:
www.nhtsa.dot.gov

Some information from an article on this site ("Kids and Bicycle Safety") was used in this article.

The U.S. National Highway Traffic Safety Administration uses the term pedalcyclists to include bicyclists and riders of two-wheel nonmotorized vehicles, tricycles and unicycles powered solely by pedals.

In 2009, 63 pedalcyclists were killed and an additional 51,000 were injured in motor vehicle traffic crashes.

The number of pedalcyclist fatalities in 2009 is 12 percent lower than the 718 pedalcyclists fatalities report in 2008.

Help your child learn the rules, practice safe bicycling and avoid becoming one of these statistics.■

Growing Child

Helping Your Child Feel Good About Himself

One of the most important things a child learns in his early years is how he feels about himself. He learns this from the experiences he has with people and things.

If his experiences are generally positive, he develops good feelings about himself. He comes to think of himself as a competent, worthwhile, and likeable person.

In contrast, if his experiences with the people and things in his life are generally negative, he develops doubts and fears about his ability to be successful. He comes to see himself as a person who is not likeable or capable.

We've talked about these ideas before and they bear repeating because they are important to your child.

How he feels about himself affects his whole life. His "self-concept" affects how he views the world, how he acts, and how others react to him.

His confidence in himself, or his lack of it, becomes a self-fulfilling prophecy. If he expects to be successful, chances are he will be.

If he expects to fail, he probably will. If he expects people to like him, his attitude toward himself will tend to make him likeable.

If he doubts people will like him, his feelings of discomfort will often produce negative feelings in others, and they will find him unpleasant to be around.

Thus, a cycle is formed which confirms his original feelings about himself.

A child's "world-view" is a reflection of his feelings about himself.

A self-confident child sees the world as a generally interesting, inviting, and rewarding place to be. He finds his relationships generally satisfying and approaches new people and experiences with hopeful anticipation.

In contrast, a child who lacks confidence in himself also lacks confidence in the world. He feels alone, abandoned, neglected, and disappointed by people.

He finds the world to be a cold, punishing, and frightening place. He approaches new people and experiences with fear, apprehension, and hesitation.

Most people—children and adults—have had a mix of experiences in their lives, some of which helped build their self-confidence and others which helped destroy it.

Consequently, they feel good about

themselves in some ways, and harbor doubts about themselves in other areas of their lives.

Few people are completely without positive feelings about themselves, and no one—however confident they may appear—is entirely without self-doubt.

But too many people are handicapped in their relationships with others and/or in their personal development by a lack of confidence in their ability to be successful.

Your child's experiences during the early years become the building blocks for the rest of his life.

Since he came into the world, he has been gathering information which he has used to build an idea of who he is and what his place is in the world.

By now he already sees the world through his own personal set of "I-glasses." He will tend to interpret the experiences he has now and in the future in terms of the feelings he has about himself and the world.

As the most important force in his life right now, you, as a parent, can have a fundamental influence on his "self-concept."

Whatever his present self- and world-view, you can help him gain a more secure and stable sense of himself as a person who can meet life with ultimate confidence in his ability to be successful and find satisfaction.

continued on page 368

continued from page 367

Here are some guidlines to help you fulfill this responsibility.

1. Have confidence in yourself. We recognize that this is easier said than done. It is natural for you to worry if you are doing all you should for your child.

After all, this is the most important job in your life, and no one has provided you with specific training for it.

Sometimes the advice of "experts" may only create confusion and doubt in your mind. And you may not agree with the way your parents raised you or the way you were treated as a child.

Nevertheless, you do have within you the necessary resources to help your child grow to be a happy, healthy, responsible adult.

Just try to remember how it felt to be a child, and try to treat your own child as you would have liked to have been treated. Be as kind, understanding, patient, and supportive as you can.

You'll make mistakes; that's a part of being human. But the more relaxed you are about yourself, the more you'll be able to learn from your mistakes, and the more successful parent you'll be able to become.

Your own confidence in yourself will, in turn, have a positive impact on your child.

2. Have confidence in your child. Trust him to learn from his mistakes and to outgrow any aggravating habits he may pick up as he's growing.

Pay more attention to his strengths than to his "shortcomings." You'll find you'll see more of whichever one you focus on more.

Be alert to and encourage his natural talents. Have patience with him in the areas in which he doesn't excel.

Have faith in his willingness and desire to do things because he loves you and wants to please you rather than because he's afraid of displeasing you or being punished.

Try to give him the benefit of the doubt when you find your confidence in him lacking.

3. Encourage your child to demonstrate confidence in himself. Help him learn to reflect positively on his own accomplishments and good qualities.

Self-pride is essential to self-confidence. If he's doing a good job at something, make a point of asking him how he feels about what he's doing.

Be specific in your feedback. For example, let him know that you think he should feel proud of himself "for working so hard on that puzzle", "for helping out his little sister", "for sticking with such a hard job."

Have a particular time every day, for example, at dinner, when each of your children can report on something that they did or that happened to them that helped them feel good about themselves.

4. Provide opportunities for your child to be successful. In order for your child to develop feelings of confidence in his ability to be successful, he needs repeated experience at being successful.

Observe his present interests and skills. Then, introduce him to activities which will spark his interest and stretch his

skills, challenging him while assuring success.

Encourage him to stick with an activity until he has accomplished what he set out to do. Perseverance is an important part of success. If he meets with difficulty, encourage him to "just try."

If you can suggest a way of simplifying the task, do so without undermining his own efforts. But resist the temptation to take over and show him how by doing it for him.

That's a subtle way of conveying a message to him that he is incapable of doing it himself, which would undermine his confidence in his own ability.

5. Encourage your child to assume responsibilities. Expect him to take responsibilities around the house for jobs he can do.

Learn to accept his less-than-perfect performance rather than doing it yourself which might be easier and faster. Enlist his help whenever you're doing something he could assist with.

When you're teaching him a new job, break it down into small steps at which he can be successful, one at a time, while he's learning.

Try to be patient, and try not to push him beyond his present capabilities. But give him the chance to learn to do for himself.

Follow the old Chinese dictum: "When you give me a fish, I eat for a day. When you teach me to fish, I can eat for a lifetime."

6. Learn to give your child constructive feedback. Whether your child has done a good job or has failed, try to focus on what it is he has done rather than on him personally.

For example, if he remembers to wipe his feet before coming in the house, thank him for wiping his feet rather than simply telling him he's "a good boy."

continued on page 369

continued from page 368

Personal Characteristics

Merely telling him he's "a good boy" doesn't help build his self-confidence. It makes him dependent on your judgment.

The other side of this example is that if he were to forget to wipe his feet before coming in the house, tell him you're upset when he does that because then you have to clean it up.

Don't tell him he's "a thoughtless, sloppy person." Such generalized blame and criticism only causes generalized feelings of guilt. It destroys self-confidence. It doesn't teach better behavior.

If you learn to say what you mean and mean what you say, you'll help your child learn from his mistakes and at the same time feel good about himself rather than feeling he's a bad person for making mistakes.

Helping your child feel good about himself is one of the most important jobs you have as a parent.

Don't worry if you sometimes do things that you don't feel are helpful in building your child's self-confidence. What's important is the overall consistency of your behavior.

If you're usually helpful and supportive, you are not likely to do any permanent damage if you occasionally do something that makes him feel bad.

In fact, you can use these occasions as opportunities to talk to him later about his feelings, thus becoming more attuned to his needs and perceptions.

Your example of turning your mistakes into opportunities for learning will teach him to do the same.

Your confidence in yourself will give him confidence not only in you, but in himself as well.

By your example you will teach him to accept and learn from his mistakes, to strive to be the best he can be, and to expect to be successful in whatever he seeks to achieve.■

Many parents want their children to be well-accepted, to be "popular" in school.

It must be recognized that it is not possible to produce a perfect child in the way it is possible to produce a perfect loaf of bread. Children cannot be molded like dough—if we could, there would be many identical children.

Some children are, by nature, outgoing, aggressive, or sensitive while others are quiet, compliant, or passive.

Parents should not reproach themselves nor their children if their children's personalities or characteristics are not similar to their own or those they wish to foster.

In fact, a characteristic which may be perceived as a weakness in early life can be a virtue later on. For example, the serious, quiet kindergartner may be the scientist or scholar of the future.

On the other hand, what may appear as an asset in the early years can in fact interfere with effective maturation.

This is something often observed in children who are great in Little League because of a competitive nature, competitive parents and/or physical strength but who are unable to overcome their stardom in order to become productive adolescents or adults.

Since there is no way to predict how and which parental characteristics will be most influential, the best thing that parents can do is feel secure that they have been good parents.

Then they can relax and allow their child to feel the effects of their relaxation.

The opposite is to experience stress which emerges when children are unable to meet particular standards set by parents who want their children to excel academically, socially, athletically, or in other ways.

Surely the most enduring social characteristics are good manners exhibited in respect for other individuals and respect for the environment.

Most importantly, children should have freedom to enjoy being themselves—each with unique personal characteristics.■

Familiar Associations

This activity will teach your child to make associations. Using pieces of cardboard, paste on pictures of familiar objects. Then have your child make associations with the pictures, such as:

1. Comb—brush
2. Sock—shoe
3. Knife—fork
4. Mitten—cap
5. Cup—saucer
6. Coat—hat
7. Table—chair
8. Pencil—paper
9. Bed—pillow
10. Toothpaste—brush

More complex associations:

1. Nose—face
2. Door—doorknob
3. Vegetables (raw)—salad
4. Meat—stew
5. Cow—milk
6. Chalk—blackboard ■

Dealing with Parental Stress

The reality of stress. Five-year-olds are generally highly active and emotionally volatile. They like to run and jump, to talk and ask questions. They may be happy one minute, sad the next.

They may go quietly to bed one night and engage in a drawn-out bedtime battle the next night, all of which can eventually cause stress for the child's parents.

Stress is an unavoidable aspect of modern life. It affects everyone at some time. It can build up gradually or it may erupt suddenly without warning.

Most parents today live stress-filled lives. Their minds go a mile a minute, thinking of all they have to do. Modern technology (with faster highways, all kinds of computers, microwave ovens, cell phones, to name a few) improves some aspects of life but also increases the pace of life.

Even some modern high speed recreational activities (such as car racing or speed boat racing) increase tension rather than relaxing the body.

To deal effectively with stress in your life you need to be able to recognize its symptoms and know what to do about it.

Untreated or unmanaged stress can lead to headaches, indigestion, and insomnia, as well as high blood pressure and ulcers.

Signs of stress. It is important to be able to recognize the subtle signs of too much stress in your life. These include:

• Being easily irritated by things that normally wouldn't bother you.

• Becoming angry about things over which you have no control, such as the weather or being stuck in rush-hour traffic.

• Feeling rushed and pressured to get things done in less time than is realistic.

• Feeling frustrated or helpless because you are unable to keep up with the pace of your life.

• Feeling tightness in your neck muscles, shoulders, or back.

• Finding yourself frequently clenching your jaws or grinding your teeth.

• Feeling constantly tired even before you start a task.

• Having a headache frequently during or at the end of the day.

Long-term strategies. In dealing with stress, which affects the lives of all of us, there are both long-term and short-term techniques. Here are some long-term strategies:

Develop the habit of making a list of things you have to do. An unspecific, vague sense of "having lots to do" can be very debilitating.

Make a list of what needs to be done immediately. Be realistic. Trying to accomplish everything at the same time is unrealistic and can be overwhelming.

Check off tasks as you finish them. A sense of accomplishment—even in getting small jobs done—can give a person renewed energy.

Give yourself more time than you think each task will take. Being rushed creates unnecessary pressure which ultimately saps your energy.

Make time for yourself. This includes planning to take regular breaks and to look after your own interests.

Keep notes on whatever helps you the most to de-stress. For some people listen-ing to music or looking at a particular scene can be relaxing.

For others, a mental sound or picture—such as the sound of waves breaking on the seashore—is more effective.

Exercise regularly. Build some exercise program—even short, brisk walks—into your overall daily schedule. Treat regular exercise as a duty to yourself and others, rather than as an optional daily activity.

Find a long-term friend with whom you can share the cause of your stress. This person must be a good listener whom you trust to protect your confidentiality.

If your stress is long-lasting and becomes more serious, it would be wise to seek professional help.

Short-term strategies. You also need some short-term strategies for dealing with stress.

How do you deal with stress, for example, if your four-year-old spills tomato juice on the tablecloth five minutes before your guests are due to arrive?

There is no time to go for a long walk or listen to soothing music! Here are some short-term strategies:

Breathe deeply five or six times. Breathe in slowly through your nose. Then breathe out slowly through your mouth.

When you concentrate on your breathing— even for a few minutes—it takes your mind off what caused your stress.

Gaze out a window or relax for a moment in a comfortable chair. Focus on some point of interest and continue to breathe deeply.

Tense and relax the muscles of your body. Take in a deep breath. Hold it while you squeeze both hands into tight fists.

Then release the tension in your hands as you breathe out slowly. Repeat this action several times.

continued on page 371

Building a Better Concept of Time

Time is something which cannot be seen or felt. Its passing is measured artificially by clocks and calendars.

Early mankind measured time only in the natural cycles of day and night and the rhythmic occurrence of the seasons.

A journey was a three-day walk; an event took place during the last full moon.

Time during the day was measured by the passage of the sun. Longer periods were measured from new moon to new moon, from season to season.

Now, when many of us live in cities, the cycle of seasons is less apparent. We use calendars instead of moon phases to measure off the months and use clocks to measure off days.

Five-year-olds measure their time by the events of their days which begin at waking-up time and end with bedtime.

Their day extends from waking until it is time to go to bed, rather than the hours measured by a clock.

To expand your child's concept of time, let's begin with answering the question

---

continued from page 370

Stretch your arms and/or roll your head. As you stretch your arms and/or roll your head, you become aware of the parts of your body that are tense.

Feel the tension leave your body as you begin to relax with these slow movements.

Tell someone you love that you need a brief hug. A warm, loving hug can get your mind off your stress and calm you down.

Have a good laugh about whatever it was that upset you. Laughter helps our spirits rise. Laughter also helps to keep upsetting events in perspective.

Keeping troubling events in their proper perspective is a most effective way of relieving stress. ∎

"How long until it will be Thanksgiving?"

For this a large calendar is necessary. Place the calendar within easy reach.

Circle the date of the holiday (in this case Thanksgiving), visit, or special event which is anticipated. Each night before she goes to bed, mark off the day.

As you do this you are teaching her duration of time over periods longer than one day. She can begin to learn the concept of how time progresses in steady, measured segments.

Making a "Time Line" can be a fun way to learn about the sequential events of a single day.

A "Time Line" can be made from a long strip of adding machine tape, 3-4 inches wide. This can be marked off in twenty-four (24) equal segments of 4 inches each.

You will need an eight-foot length of paper tape. Each segment will represent one hour. You may mark them off yourself with a black marker or crayon.

Your child can do it herself if you give her a sturdy piece of cardboard a little wider than the tape and the length of each hourly segment.

Number the segments from one to 12 and repeat to cover the nighttime hours. Put the numbers at the center top of each segment, making each number about 1 inch high, then draw a box around the number.

This project is not meant to be done at one sitting. Depending upon your child's interest in measuring, coloring, cutting and pasting, it can be completed within a few days or may be spread out over several weeks.

Once the 24-hour tape is marked off, you begin to fill in the major events of the child's day.

When does she usually get up? Find a picture of a child getting up, or draw a picture of the rising sun—anything to indicate that the child's waking day is beginning.

Let your child cut out the picture and paste it in the right place.

Proceed through such events as breakfast, playtime or nursery school, snack, lunch, rest, playtime, dinner, story time, and bedtime.

Illustrate each waking hour with a drawing or picture to indicate what the child is most likely to be doing at that time.

Now have the child use dark blue to color all hourly segments between bedtime and waking-up time.

Finally tape the ends of the "Time Line" together. The paper circle can be placed on a table or on the floor.

The child can now walk around the whole 24 hour day and see for herself how one day begins as another day ends.

Concepts of morning, noon and afternoon can be visualized and talked about.

The sequence of events can be pointed out: "What do you do first? What comes next? What's the last thing you will do before you go to bed?"

A "Time Line" is an open-ended experience which leads toward increasingly precise concepts of time.

It's an excellent preparation for the later skill of telling time on a clock. ∎

Eye-hand Coordination

Your child is now developing better eye-hand coordination. Good eye-hand coordination skills are obviously needed to be successful in sports.

They are also essential for school-related tasks, such as reading, writing, and using the computer.

You can help her improve her eye-hand coordination by playing some simple motor activity games.

At first she may not experience much success. With practice she will eventually develop better skills. Let her have lots of fun in playing these games, encouraging her for her efforts. Here is an example of a simple motor activity game to improve eye-hand coordination:

Start with a piece of chalk and a beanbag. On a flat surface, such as a floor or driveway, draw a circle. About three feet in front of the circle, draw a straight line that will be the "throw line."

Give your child a beanbag, saying: "I want you to throw this beanbag into the circle." If this task seems too difficult, you can make it easier by making the circle larger.

Once your child is able to throw the beanbag into the circle, you can draw another circle behind the first one, numbering them one and two.

Now give your child the beanbag saying: "I want you to throw this beanbag into circle number two (point to the circle)." If your child is successful with this task, you can continue to add additional circles: three, four, five ... (see diagram). If this task is too easy, you make it more difficult by making the circles smaller or by increasing the distance between them.

—————throw line

As your child develops better eye-hand coordination, she can try to throw a ball (instead of the beanbag) into a row of wastebaskets (instead of circles).

Just remember that every great basketball star was once a young child who had to learn to develop eye-hand coordination. Likewise, every good reader, writer, and computer whiz also had to develop these skills using simple motor activity games such as the one we have just described!■

A Positive Attitude

A positive attitude can lead to better parenting. In life, two people can look at the same glass: while one sees it as "half full" the other sees it as "half empty." It's just a matter of positive versus negative attitude.

An attitude is something we can work on changing. If I perceive that my attitudes on life are more negative than positive, I can deliberately make a greater effort to focus on the positive (versus negative) aspects of each situation.

Here are some good reasons to develop and maintain a more positive attitude:

1. My attitude helps to determine how I perceive my child's behavior. For example, if my child has recently developed the habit of saying "No!" I can perceive that as either (a) "My child is developing a healthy sense of autonomy and independence" (a positive attitude) or (b) "My kid is becoming a little monster" (a negative attitude).

Growing Child™

P. O. Box 2505 • W Lafayette, IN 47996
(800) 927-7289
www.GrowingChild.com

Contributing Authors
Phil Bach, O.D., Ph.D.
Miriam Bender, Ph.D.
Joseph Braga, Ed.D.
Laurie Braga, Ph.D.
George Early, Ph.D.
Carol R. Gestwicki, M.S.
Liam Grimley, Ph.D.
Robert Hannemann, M.D., F.A.A.P.
Sylvia Kottler, M.S.
Bill Peterson, Ph.D.

2. My attitude helps to determine how I will react. If I perceive my child's behavior in a positive manner ("He's learning to develop a sense of autonomy and independence"), I'm more likely to react to his behavior in a positive way. (For example, by showing him more love and affection to reassure him that it's natural and okay for him to want to demonstrate greater independence as he gets older.)

On the other hand, if I perceive the same behavior in a negative manner, I'm more likely to respond in a negative way ("You'll get a good spanking from me if you keep saying that!")

3. My attitude will affect how my child will respond. When a parent can exhibit a positive attitude toward a child's behavior, the child will more likely develop a positive attitude toward life. Giving him the reassurance that he is loved unconditionally will help him to be more in tune with his world and, therefore, behave more positively.

On the contrary, when a child feels threatened and unloved because of a parent's negative attitude, he is more likely to develop negative feelings toward himself, which ultimately will lead to worse misbehavior.

It's important to note, however that having a positive attitude toward a child's behavior ("I think my child is terrific") is not the same as spoiling a child ("My child can do no wrong").

Whereas a spoiled child will eventually exhibit misbehavior increasingly more demanding of parents, the child who is treated by parents with a positive—yet realistic—attitude will more likely develop a similar, more positive outlook on life.■

How Do You Tell Your Child You Love Her?

Every day ... and in many ways ... your child needs to know how much you love her and what a special treasure she is to you.

Love is more than a feeling; it is a way of being with the person you love that makes her feel safe, comfortable, important, understood, and wanted. We all like to have these feelings.

Don't assume your child knows you love her just because you know that you do. Many adults complain that they did not feel loved as children even though their parents felt they were treating them lovingly.

Here are some guidelines to help you express your love to your child in a way that helps her know of the love you have for her.

1. What you say to your child and how you treat her are both important.

Your words and your actions should deliver the same message.

For example, you may tell her that she is more important to you than anything you have. But if you react very harshly when she breaks one of your possessions, she may have doubts that she's really more important.

2. Point out the qualities that you love and admire in her.

Let her know often how much you love her and how glad you are that she's yours.

Tell her how special you think she is. Notice the things she does well. Compliment

her on how thoughtful or helpful she is.

Let her know when you are proud of her. Make sure that she knows that you always love her, no matter what.

3. Show her through your actions how much you love her.

Touch her gently and often. Hug her, put your arm around her, hold her hand, put your hand on her back.

A child who is used to being touched in love learns to use touch lovingly.

As often as you can, get down to her level so you can look into her eyes, especially when she's talking to you.

Even when you have to talk to her about something she's done that you don't like, look her in the eyes as you explain your feelings.

Try to keep your voice calm and firm. You'll communicate better when the sound of your voice makes her feel safe rather than anxious or afraid.

Be aware too of what your facial expression communicates.

No matter what mistakes she makes, you'll help her improve if you can stay calm and deal with the problem in a loving and supportive manner.

4. Let your child know that you trust her through your words and actions.

Give her room to make mistakes. That's how she'll learn.

Taking responsibility for herself in any area of her life requires practice. Assume a helpful "let-it-be" attitude, offering guidance without taking over for her.

Give her the benefit of the doubt when you are tempted not to believe in her. If she feels you trust and believe in her, she'll want to be honest with you and live up to your trust.

You will be teaching her, by your example and by your treatment of her, to trust you.

5. Treat your child in a way that respects her needs, rights, and feelings as a human being.

Being a small child, she has much growing to do. There is much that she doesn't know or understand.

It is your job to help her, while always showing respect for her judgment.

Treat her as you would wish to be treated yourself. Remember that she will learn

continued on page 374

continued from page 373

and grow best when you are patient, supportive, kind, and understanding.

Try not to rush her or to impose unrealistic expectations. Listen to what she is telling you by her words and through her actions.

Use these messages as you guide her, one step at a time, toward becoming an adult who can respect herself and others.

6. Give of yourself to your child.

All the toys and special learning activities in the world are not as important to her as your time, your attention, your love.

Your life is probably very full and busy. You don't have as much time as you'd like to spend with your child, so try to make the best possible use of the time you do have together.

For example, before breakfast, take a moment to be with her. Look into her eyes and squeeze her hand. Tell her "good morning."

Let her know how glad you are to see her. It doesn't really take that long to let her know you care.

Thirty seconds here and there throughout the day to share a few moments of love and conversation can make the rest of her day and yours more rewarding.

7. Don't "smother" your child with love and attention.

It's not easy to be a parent. Sometimes all the advice from "experts" can make you worry that you're not doing enough.

Guilt can make you overprotective and over-directive of your child.

Try to be alert to how your behavior affects her without becoming anxious about it. If you make mistakes, try to learn from them. Then let them go.

The wonderful thing about young children is that you get a new chance with them each moment; they don't hold resentments for long.

Don't assume your child knows you love her just because you know that you do. Many adults complain that they did not feel loved as children even though their parents felt they were treating them lovingly.

Give your child a chance to be her own person. Don't do things for her that she can do for herself or protect her from the natural consequences of her own mistakes.

Let her have her own life and friends.

Expect her to take responsibilities for herself of which she is capable. Let her do some things her way, without your telling her what to do, what not to do, when to do what she does, and how well she's done it.

She needs to start now to learn some independence from you.

8. Treat your own child with at least as much concern as you do the children of friends, relatives, and strangers.

Without thinking, we may sometimes treat those we love with less consideration than we give complete strangers.

It is easy to get caught in the trap of worrying about what others will think and to take for granted the love and loyalty of our own family members.

It's much better to risk the disapproval of a stranger or even someone you know well

than to choose their needs over your child's needs.

Show your child that she's more important than anyone outside the family. Stick up for her, even if you think she's wrong. You can talk to her later in private, but don't embarrass her in front of others.

Don't compare her with other children. Never tell her you wish she were like some other child. Show her how precious she is to you.

9. Be honest and direct with your child in asserting your own feelings, needs, and expectations.

In trying to be aware of and concerned about her needs and feelings, don't neglect your own.

You'll be better able to care for her if you care for yourself. Too much self-sacrifice almost always leaves one feeling exhausted, drained, perhaps even resentful.

You need time for yourself. Don't hesitate to tell her so. If you don't wait until you're at the end of your rope, you can express your needs to her as kindly as you want her to do if the situation were reversed.

As you assert your own feelings, you're actually helping your child become less self-centered and more responsive to others.

Sometimes it may seem that all the suggestions we make are calling for a superhuman effort which is more than you can make.

Remember that we're only suggesting guidelines. Strive to do the best you can, but be patient with yourself.

Each experience you have is an opportunity for growth. Try not to be too critical of your "shortcomings."

You'll teach your child a very valuable lesson of life by showing her that making mistakes is a positive part of life because it gives you a chance to learn.

Treat yourself with the same care, consideration and love that you give to your child.■

Locomotor Activities

At five years of age, your child is capable of engaging in locomotor activities which make use of his newly acquired physical skills.

Some of the following activities will also challenge his imaginative and creative mental abilities.

1. Walking

Procedures: Find a large area—back yard, gym, playground—which is free of obstacles.

Offer these challenges: "How many different ways can you walk?"

a) Rapidly

b) Very slowly

c) In a circle

d) Taking big steps

e) Taking tiny steps

f) Walking on tiptoes

g) Walking on heels

h) Walking backwards

2. Jumping

Materials: three bicycle tires, a box, and a mat. The mat must be secured to the floor.

Procedures: This is a sequential obstacle course for jumping.

1. "Jump from the box and land in the center of this tire."

2. "Jump from the box, land on the mat and jump into a tire."

Modifications: Color code the tires by taping a color to each: red, blue, green.

1. "Jump from the box into the red tire and then into the blue tire."

2. Rearrange the order of the tires.

3. Adjust the distance of the box, mat, and tires as your child's jumping skills increase.

3. Balancing

Here are a variety of challenges:

a) "Can you stand on one foot? The other foot?"

b) "Can you do it again while I count to 10?"

c) "Can you stand on your toes with your legs apart? With your legs close together?"

d) "Can you walk heel-to-toe on a line taped to the floor?"

e) "Can you walk backwards on the line?"

f) "Can you stand on one foot and hold the other ankle?"

Each time you offer a challenge, your child makes an auditory to motor translation (He hears what you say and then does it. This is an essential skill for academic achievement.

Therefore, avoid demonstrating the challenge. If he fails to perform, make it simpler with fewer words or fewer steps.

4. Managing a ball

Materials: one ball and one tire.

Area: Large and free of interference.

The challenges:

a) "Can you throw the ball into the tire?"

b) "Can you roll the ball to the tire?"

c) "Can you dribble (bounce) the ball while I count to five?"

d) "Can you kick a ball to the tire?"

e) "Can you throw the ball underhand?"

f) "Can you throw it overhand?"

g) "Can you catch a ball from various distances?"

Obviously, your child will have to be familiar with the terms, "overhand" and "underhand" in order to respond effectively.

5. Exploring essential movement

All the previous movements can be integrated into a new variety of challenges:

Slide, gallop, turn and twist, push and pull, bend.

a) "Can you pretend to be an airplane? A snowflake in a storm?"

b) "Show me how you would rake leaves, shovel snow, mow the lawn."

c) "How would you pick a precious flower?"

d) "Can you glide (slide) sideways to the door?"

e) "How would a bunny rabbit get from here to the street corner?"

f) "Can you walk like a toy soldier? A hippopotamus? A rag doll?"

You will observe that there are no "right" ways to carry out these activities. They are generated in the child's own head.

Although there may be similarities, each child's response will be different.

All of these motor activities can be carried out in a group where children of different abilities feel comfortable expressing their own creative movements.■

Family Problem-Solving Skills

Now that your five-year-old is becoming more independent, it is inevitable that family problems will arise.

Such problems may involve sibling disagreements, or how to keep the house more tidy, or deciding who is responsible for various chores.

Family problems provide a wonderful opportunity to teach a young child problem-solving skills.

These skills are important for understanding oneself, getting along with others and, in general, becoming a more mature and responsible person.

Before we consider how to teach specific problem-solving skills, we need to discuss two different styles of parenting which are not conducive to the development of good problem-solving skills, namely, authoritarian and permissive styles.

The authoritarian style of parenting combines a high degree of parental control and demand with relatively low levels of warmth and affection.

Parents make all the decisions without any input from or consideration of other family members' opinions.

Research studies indicate that children who grow up in authoritarian families, while displaying outward signs of conformity and obedience, typically have lower self-esteem, are less skillful in interacting with peers, and usually perform less well later in school.

By contrast, the permissive style of parenting uses a relatively low level of control and demand, combined with a high level of nurturance.

Children who grow up in a permissive-type family are less likely to develop initiative and responsibility and are more likely to exhibit immaturity with their peers and in their schoolwork.

Research studies also indicate that the most positive outcomes for children are in families where parents consistently

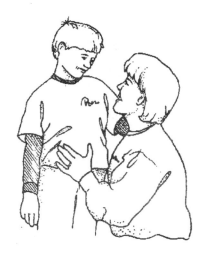

combine high levels of both control and affection toward their children.

In other words, these parents consistently set clear limits for acceptable/unacceptable behavior while at the same time, responding in a caring and loving manner to each child's individual needs.

One of the most effective ways for parents to combine high levels of control with high levels of caring is by using family problem-solving methods.

These are the steps involved in effective family problem-solving:

1. Clearly define the problem. Whenever two members of a family have a disagreement, for example, it is likely that each of them may define the problem in somewhat different terms.

An impartial third party can more easily identify the major issues without accusing or blaming either one of those involved.

2. Establish guidelines for resolving the problem. The problem-solving process must not be perceived by either party as a win/lose competition. On the contrary, successful resolution involves a give-and-take process that leads to consensus.

All must agree beforehand, however, to abide by the ultimate decision and solution of the problem.

3. Listen carefully to both sides. All involved must feel free to express their

opinion without being interrupted. This also implies not passing judgment until all sides have had an adequate opportunity to speak their piece.

4. Generate possible solutions. Make a list of all suggestions for resolving the problem. This helps broaden young children's minds by exposing them to viewpoints not previously considered.

It is often helpful to invite the persons involved to take the opposite side: "If you were in Joe's shoes, what would you consider to be a reasonable solution?"

This helps a young child to develop what psychologists term "perspective-taking skills," by having the child consider a situation from another person's vantage point.

It is important at this stage to avoid any form of criticism which would inhibit brainstorming. Just write down all the solutions suggested without any evaluation of their merits.

5. Examine the pros and cons of each suggested solution.

After all the suggested solutions have been written down, ask each person to comment on each one of the ideas presented: "What do you think are the advantages of that solution? What are the disadvantages?"

This process helps a young child become more reflective and develop better judgment. Instead of impulsively jumping to a conclusion, he learns to carefully weigh each option.

6. Try to reach consensus in resolving a problem. It is important that everyone feel a sense of ownership for the final solution. For that reason it is best to avoid vote-taking, as this usually creates winners and losers.

In compromise, on the other hand, each person must give a little to arrive at the solution which will ultimately be the most reasonable for all concerned.

continued on page 377

Traffic Safety

Although the numbers continue to decline, traffic accidents are the major cause of death among four- and five-year-old children.

According to the National Safety Council, more than 11,000 children under six years of age are killed or injured in traffic accidents every year.

Accidents involving young children have been analyzed by the National Highway Traffic Safety Administration, and a profile has been developed of the different types of accidents most likely to occur at different ages.

The most common accidents involving four- and five-year-olds occur when a child darts into the roadway from between parked cars or other obstacles.

This type of accident accounts for almost two-thirds of all traffic accidents of four- and five-year-old children.

Studies of accidents indicate that the child is usually not trying to cross the street, but darts into the roadway while chasing a ball, for example, or being chased by another child.

Most of these accidents occur near the child's own home, often on the same street where his family lives.

The accidents occur most commonly between 3 and 5 p.m. on warm, sunny days. And more than twice as many boys as girls are involved.

continued from page 376

Teaching young children good problem-solving skills can have lifelong benefits. It teaches them to be more reflective in decision-making.

It also helps them become less egocentric by making them more aware of how other people think and feel.

Most of all, it teaches them that conflicts can be resolved in a fair, reasonable, and nonviolent manner.■

In most cases neither the driver of the car, nor the child who was hit, saw one another until it was too late.

This is also true of accidents while backing a car, when the driver could not see the child and the child was not aware that the car was moving.

Fortunately, backing accidents are not too common, accounting for only two percent of accidents involving four- and five-year-old children.

It is interesting to note that young children all over the world appear to be prone to these types of accidents. Similar findings have been reported in studies of traffic accidents in England, Germany, Scandinavia, Japan, and New South Wales.

There appears to be a number of reasons why four- and five-year-old children are involved in so many traffic accidents.

First, being small in stature, they cannot see over cars or other obstacles and for the same reason, they cannot be seen easily by motorists.

Second, their minds tend to focus on only one thing at a time (for example, chasing the ball that rolled into the street).

Third, their high emotional states, impulsivity, and inability to make good judgments (such as accurately estimat-ing speed and distance) combine to make them prone to traffic accidents.

Here are some recommendations to help reduce the chances of your child becoming a traffic accident statistic:

• Make sure your child is accompanied by an adult whenever he is near traffic in a street.

• Before crossing a street, take your child's hand in yours. If he resists, explain to him that this is not an appropriate time to express his independence. In a calm but firm manner, guide him by the hand across the street.

• If, while walking with your child on the street, you see older children playing on or near the roadway, you can explain that older children are usually more mature and are more familiar with the rules of the road.

If they are doing something such as crossing the road alone, you can explain that older children have shown they can be trusted and have earned that independence.

• In your home, talk with your child about the importance of road safety. Use appropriate books, newspaper articles, and photographs to illustrate the dangers. Avoid overdramatization and grisly details.

After you have finished, ask your child to repeat what he remembered you saying. In that way you can correct any misperceptions.

You may find he did not understand some words or concepts you used. It may take a while for him to remember everything you want to teach him.

• If possible, use a safely fenced play area for your child, either in your own back yard or in a nearby public park or playground.

In a few months we will discuss teaching your child to stop, look, and listen, and other basics of road safety appropriate for older children.■

Developing Better Thinking Skills

Many parents would like to help their child develop better thinking skills. One of the best ways to develop such skills is through the art of questioning.

Research studies indicate that there are different levels of questioning. Likewise, there are different levels of responding by the child.

It has been found that lower level questions merely elicit lower level responses.

Higher level questioning, on the other hand, tends to elicit higher level thinking responses.

We shall discuss some of the differences between lower level and higher level questions and responses.

The lowest level of responding is that of *locating* specific objects or people.

For example, while reading a book aloud, a parent might ask: "Can you show me where the picture of a cow is on this page?" A child can respond to such a question merely by pointing.

The next level of questioning is *remembering*. This means that the child is asked to recall specific factual information. For example, "What was the lady in the story wearing on her head?"

The next higher level is *organizing*. This type of questioning requires the child not only to remember but also, in his own words, to organize events in sequence.

For example, "What was the first thing that happened in this story? What happened next? What came after that?"

The next level is *predicting*. This requires the child to consider the known elements of the story and predict some unknown element.

For example, "What do you think will happen next?"

The highest level of questioning is *evaluating*. This requires the child to weigh alternatives.

For example, "Would you have acted in the same way as the boy in that story? Why? Why not?"

Storybook time provides many opportunities to develop better thinking skills.

To stimulate a child's thinking, it is important to ask open-ended questions for further elaboration (such as the ones below), rather than mere factual questions to which a child can give a "yes" or "no" answer.

And remember that, generally speaking, the higher the level of questioning by the

Growing Child™

P. O. Box 2505 • W Lafayette, IN 47996
(800) 927-7289
www.GrowingChild.com

Contributing Authors

Phil Bach, O.D., Ph.D.
Miriam Bender, Ph.D.
Joseph Braga, Ed.D.
Laurie Braga, Ph.D.
George Early, Ph.D.
Carol R. Gestwicki, M.S.
Liam Grimley, Ph.D.
Robert Hannemann, M.D., F.A.A.P.
Sylvia Kottler, M.S.
Bill Peterson, Ph.D.

parent, the higher the level of thinking response by the child.

Here are some different types of open-ended questions that will elicit higher and higher level thinking responses:

1. Ask the child which character in the story she likes best. What are some of the things she likes about that character? Does the character remind her of someone she knows? In what ways?

2. Ask the child to tell what happened in the story in her own words.

3. At some point(s) during the story, pause to ask her to predict what she thinks might happen next. Ask for her reasons.

4. At the end of the story, ask her to suggest a different way (or ways) for the story to end. Why might her ending be better?

5. Ask her to describe any experience(s) of her own that might relate to what happened in the story.

Actively involving the child in the reading of the story, and personalizing the outcomes, will help to make storybook time more enjoyable.

Giving her an opportunity to react to the story as an active participant not only will add to her enjoyment but will also help her to develop higher level thinking skills. ■

Getting Along With Others

The pattern for a child's relationships with other people is learned in his early years.

He learns how to treat others from the ways he is treated. These patterns are carried into adult life.

You can help him learn to get along with others more happily and effectively by setting a good example for him.

Give him the opportunities, support, and encouragement he needs to work out satisfying relationships with other people.

Here are some guidelines that will help him learn how to get along with others:

1. Your child needs to learn a balance between expressing his own needs and being concerned for others.

You can help him learn to respect the feelings, needs, and rights of others, without sacrificing his own feelings, needs, and rights.

The place to start is with your own relationship to him.

Be honest with him when he has done something that made you angry. Do not hesitate to say "no" when he asks you to do something for him when you really don't want to do what he has asked.

Well-meaning sacrifice of your own needs to his is unfair to both you and him. You don't give him a chance to learn to respect your needs when you don't let him know what they are.

Being either overly demanding of other people or overly sacrificing of one's own needs usually creates problems in relationships.

If your child is in kindergarten or in a preschool program, make sure he is getting some time each day to be involved in activities that the children themselves structure.

The continuous sacrifice of one's own needs creates negative feelings inside oneself.

They may boil beneath the surface, causing one to begin to resent things one used to do with pleasure.

Or, they may eventually explode in anger over an apparently unimportant matter.

It's important that you treat your child in ways that encourage him to express his needs and feelings.

It's equally important that you be honest with him about your own needs and feelings.

2. Your child gets his first lessons in how to relate to other people from your example.

He learns how to get along with others from the ways you and he relate to each other. He also learns from seeing how you get along with other people.

There are several ways in which he learns how to treat others and be treated by others in return:

• how you treat him
• how he sees you treat others
• how you allow him to treat you and others
• how others allow him to treat them

You'll see some of the effects of your "teaching by example" now.

Other patterns, the seeds of which are laid down now, may not appear in his relationships until he's older.

He will learn ways to act with you now to try to please you, and avoid your anger or disappointment.

He will pick up from you different ways to act with others, who are more or less powerful than he is, which he will use when he's in conflict situations.

From observing you he will learn patterns of behavior which he will carry into adult relationships, such as how to treat a spouse and one's own children.

3. Your child needs experiences with other children in order to put into practice what he has learned from you about getting along with others.

He learns how to act with others from family members. But he needs to try out these ideas with other children in order to gain competence and self-confidence.

continued on page 380

continued from page 379

With other children, he can work out different ways of acting and reacting that he probably wouldn't risk trying with you or other adults.

He can get practice being the boss as well as being bossed by another. He can be a leader as well as a follower, a teacher as well as a learner, a caregiver as well as the one receiving care.

With you, he is limited to certain behaviors that are appropriate because he is a child. With other children, his options are more open.

Further, just as you need time away from a child-centered life, he needs to get away from the adult-oriented world.

He needs to be with other people whose view of the world and orientation toward life are similar to his own.

Through his relationships with them, he can learn to cooperate, compromise, and strike bargains.

He needs to be able to work out satisfying relationships with other children in his own way, at his own pace, in terms of his own needs.

This is why "free play" time or recess can be the most important part of a school day.

If your child is in kindergarten or in a preschool program, make sure he is getting some time each day to be involved in activities that the children themselves structure.

Also, try to work out an arrangement with other parents to get your children together on a regular basis, to play or go on outings.

Allow your child to work out his own relationships with a minimum of interference from you. Explain clearly what your expectations and limits are. Then let him be, other than staying alert for problems that require your attention.

Remember to respect your child's needs and preferences about whom he wants to spend time with and in what way.

Don't make plans for him without consulting him. But do give him opportunities to be with other children.

4. Your child can increase the success of his relationships by using "make-believe" activities to practice them.

You can use puppets, stuffed animals, small plastic dolls, paper masks, or cardboard figures drawn and cut out by your child to represent people with whom he has relationships.

You can simply suggest to him that he be one person and you another. Let him take the lead in pretending.

Sometimes he can be himself and sometimes someone else, thus giving him a chance to "try on" different roles.

At other times you can suggest using make-believe to act out specific interactions that are of concern to him.

For example, if he is nervous about an upcoming visit to the dentist, the two of you could act it out beforehand, allowing him to take turns playing himself, the dentist, and you.

This would help him work through some anxieties as well as let you know what are some of his concerns and expectations.

You can also make up stories: "What

would you do if ...?" for him to complete. He can act them out or simply respond to them in his own words.

Such stories can give him a chance to practice typical situations with other people and discover those ways of behaving which make him most comfortable.

You can write up stories that you know would help him with the relationships in his own life.

Here's an example: "Tommy was playing at his friend's house. He accidentally broke one of his friend's toys. What do you think his friend would do? How do you think he would feel?

"What do you think Tommy would do? How do you think he would feel? What would you have done if you were Tommy? If you were Tommy's friend?"

This kind of activity is good for him to play with siblings or friends, also. It could help them begin to understand each other's point of view better, a very important part of getting along with each other.

Also check with your local library about good children's books that talk about friends, sharing, getting along with others.

5. Your child will be more successful in his relationships when he feels comfortable than when he is self-conscious.

If he feels comfortable, his confidence will tend to make those around him feel comfortable too.

Feeling relaxed and comfortable is a key to good relationships.

You can help him feel comfortable with himself and others by being supportive and encouraging rather than critical or discouraging. Here are some dos and don'ts to guide you:

DON'T suggest that he has trouble getting along with others, for example, saying: "Nobody really likes you." "People only like you because you do things for them."

DO give him positive feedback for get-

continued on page 384

Privacy Needs of Children

People of all ages need some privacy in their lives. We all need some time alone to relax and feel free of responsibilities.

Children, too, experience a need for privacy. At about five or six years of age they begin to express more explicitly their need for privacy.

For example, they may request their own room or be in their room with the door shut.

A child's home is a busy and often times crowded place. Sometimes several children must share a room with a sibling. The privacy needs of children can still be met even in the busiest of homes.

When siblings are bunked in the same room, for example, parents can designate areas of the room that are shared and other areas that provide private space for each child.

Children are usually also good at finding their own places of escape such as in a basement, an attic, or under a staircase.

When a young child starts expressing a greater need for privacy, parents may sometimes worry about his wanting to be alone.

It may help parents, therefore, to be aware of some of the reason's for a child's growing need for privacy:

1. Children need "cool-down" time to relax and sort through in their minds their day's experiences.

2. They need some private space to deal with their feelings without the embarrassment of having other people watching over them.

3. They need time alone to learn to think for themselves.

4. They also need time just to daydream and exercise imagination in their own private space.

5. Wanting to be alone can also be a healthy expression of a child's growing sense of independence.

At this developmental stage, it is not unusual for children to request to bathe alone or dress without any help from parents.

Even if the child doesn't do a very good job of selecting and matching clothes appropriately, it is good to let him experience independence and develop self-confidence.

By the time children reach school age, they also begin to see themselves as having a separate identity from their families.

Until this time, they had looked on their parents as all-knowing "superheroes" who knew how to satisfy all their needs and desires. But now, on their own at school, they have to deal with situations without any help from parents.

At this age children realize that their thoughts can be private.

When a child comes home from school, for example, he may answer a parent's question about what he did in school with a single word, "Nothing!"

The child has learned that by keeping his thoughts private, he can control what his parents may know or not know about his daily activities.

It is good, therefore, to give a child "cool-down" time after coming home from school before questioning him about the day's events.

A child will most often be willing to share this information after he has had a chance to relax in private.

Just because a child requests more privacy for himself does not mean that he understands the privacy needs of others. He still needs to learn some basic human courtesies toward others.

The best way for parents to teach these courtesies is by modeling appropriate behavior.

For example, parents should not only teach a child to knock on their bedroom door before entering, but they also need to set an example by providing this same courtesy to their child.

As a child and his parents learn to respect each other's needs for privacy, they are setting a foundation for better communication in their future relationships.

As a child's needs for privacy and independence develop, parents sometimes feel abandoned.

There are, however, ways in which parents can spend time with their child while still respecting his need for privacy.

For example, parents can sometimes arrange to be in the same room as their child but be engaged in separate activities.

This gives the child the satisfaction of being alone while at the same time enjoying the security of togetherness.

Parents need to be aware that even though a child may demand privacy at one moment, the next moment he may no longer want to be alone if, for example, there is thunder and lightning or if he feels frightened or insecure for some other reason.

If parents consider a child's request for privacy to be harmful to family togetherness, they can make family outings more attractive by allowing him to bring along a friend.

This enables all family members to spend time together while allowing the child to have private time either alone or with his friends.

In the hustle and bustle of modern living, children today do not have the opportunities for privacy afforded to those who grew up in a slower-paced era.

For that reason it is all the more important for parents to be aware of their child's privacy needs.

By accommodating those needs, parents are promoting their child's essential development of independence and self-understanding.■

More Thoughts on Discipline

Discipline wears many faces. To some it means punishment. To others it means teaching right from wrong. To still others it means setting clear behavioral limits, making certain that the child knows and respects these limits.

But really all of these meanings imply that discipline is the process by which we "civilize" our children and teach them to live within society's constraints.

There has been a lot written about the dos and don'ts of how to discipline children but this is a subject about which it is very difficult to generalize.

Children's personalities differ widely—what works with one child may be a complete failure with another.

As an individual child grows and develops, her responses change, and the method of disciplining or "civilizing" must also change, if it is to be effective.

Parents who have more than one child usually become aware very early of the different personalities of each of their children.

The shy sensitive child will usually respond to verbal correction or even to a stern look, and, because of a strong desire to please, may need comfort and reassurance instead of punishment.

On the other hand, with a vigorously active and impulsive child, the verbal correction will go in one ear and out the other.

The correction must be reinforced by isolation, loss of privilege, or a vigorous reprimand, before the child can be brought to realize that the specific behavior will not be tolerated.

Such a child must be strongly motivated before she will teach herself to control her impulsive behavior.

And don't think that girls will always respond to verbal correction and explanation, while boys always require sterner measures.

The personality, and not the gender of the individual child is the key to successful discipline.

The age and developmental level of a child is equally important. Behavior which would be considered normal in a two-year-old might be unacceptable in a 10-year-old.

For instance, a very young child has few ways of expressing anger.

It is a rare two-year-old who has not bitten another child who took a favorite toy or interfered with some ongoing play activity.

Undesirable behavior? Yes, but not an earth-shaking calamity.

Correct the behavior—but recognize that these are very normal ways for a two-year-old to express anger, frustration, or aggression.

The same behavior in an eight- or 10-year-old child would be cause for considerable concern because such behavior is not appropriate for that age.

Parents who wish to discipline their child in the most significant yet supportive way need to learn as much as possible about the normal impulses and reactions during the various stages of growing up.

Most five-year-olds are apt, at some time or other, to take something that doesn't belong to them. Does this mean that the child is headed for a life of crime? Or that you have a kleptomaniac on your hands?

Not at all. The five-year-old is impulsive and often a collector of things. She has not yet established a strong sense of "mine and thine."

Although she has been encouraged to share with others, she is still at an egocentric stage of development and has strong feelings about what belongs to her.

Discipline here should be firm but designed to make the child understand that what she takes, someone else loses.

No five-year-old needs to suffer strong pangs of guilt for one-time offenses or infrequent lapses from desirable behavior.

No child should ever be made to feel unworthy of love or that she is a bad person who is beyond redemption.

Rather make it clear that immature impulses in children are what parents are needed for. Parents are here to help the child develop her own controls.

When parents are aware of the impulses and pitfalls which are reasonably normal at each stage of growth, they can act with wisdom and without overreaction.

Finally, we should look to our own goals as parents. We should ask ourselves, "What kind of a person do I want my child to be?"

It follows that we should try as hard as we can to be that kind of person, to serve as a model for our children.

Eda Leshan has said that "the goal of productive and life-enhancing discipline is helping a child to value herself as a human being, safe in the knowledge that the stronger adults who love her will help her deal with impulses she may have which are dangerous to herself or others."

Discipline is not about punishment, but about education—education in the art of being human, of helping a child to understand that falls from grace are part of growing up and not a sign of being a bad or worthless person.■

How Five-year-olds Learn

Have you ever noticed how much your five-year-old wants to learn about the world around him?

Five-year-olds are, by nature, inquisitive and investigative. They want to know how things work and how they are put together.

The years from five to eight are truly wonder years for children's learning.

Wanting to know about the world, they may sometimes tire adults with their questions.

As a parent, you'd better get used to those questions—which will usually be followed by more questions!

Instead of discouraging them, try to encourage them no matter how silly or repetitious they may, at first, appear.

Five-year-olds are beyond the stage of accepting the type of simple answers that would satisfy most three- and four-year-olds. They want to know more. They want to know how—and why.

Their attention span is greater now than it was a year ago. So they can stay focused longer to explore how something works.

For example, when playing with blocks, they are now more likely to experiment with different ways to build a wall or a bridge—whereas a year ago they would have been happy to build anything just for the pleasure of knocking it down!

Although their attention span has increased, it will be some years before they will have developed the type of sustained attention required for formal academic learning.

It would be a mistake, therefore, to try to force development of the academic skills that will be acquired more easily and more naturally in later years.

At five years of age, parents can witness children's first use of simple scientific methods: observing, predicting, experimenting, then arriving at a result. For example, when playing with blocks of different sizes, five-year-olds will observe their different lengths, make a prediction in choosing the right block, then test to see if it works.

If the prediction was incorrect, they can go back and make a different prediction.

When they find their prediction was correct, they will repeat the same procedures over and over, obviously relishing the joy of their new-found learning success.

In the past few decades there has been a remarkable break-through in what is known about how young children learn.

This knowledge has important implications for how to help stimulate a five-year-old's learning, including the following considerations:

• It is important to recognize that every five-year-old is a learner. If a child isn't learning, it's probably because the task is inappropriate or too difficult.

• Play is a child's work. Five-year-olds learn best through play.

• It's possible to capitalize on a young child's natural inclination to learn by providing stimulating materials and experiences.

• A child's enjoyment of an activity enhances learning and, likewise, new learning leads to new enjoyment.

• Children who are between the ages of five and eight must be taught differently and evaluated differently than older children.

• Between these ages, children develop at different rates. Even for children of normal intelligence, there is a wide range of abilities because cognitive development—just like physical growth—takes place in spurts.

• Five-year-olds learn more easily and more quickly when they have hands-on experiences with concrete objects.

For example, they will gain their first understanding of addition and subtraction when they deal with real objects rather than memorizing tables or listening to formal instruction.

• As indicated earlier, most five-year-olds are not ready for formal academic tasks such as reading, writing, spelling, or workbook math problems.

Demanding too much too soon will only lead to feelings of frustration, inferiority, and failure.

• While they are learning, they need to have freedom to move about the room.

The part of the brain which controls a child's energy level is not yet well developed. Hence if they are required to sit still, they will get tired more quickly than if they have freedom of movement.

• Five-year-olds are not yet capable of distinguishing between effort and ability. If they fail after giving their best effort, they may conclude that they will never be able to accomplish a particular task.

• They need to be praised for what they can do, rather than corrected or scolded for what they can't do. Even if a young child's artwork, for example, seems messy to an adult, the child will take great pride in seeing the artwork displayed.

• At five years of age, children's social development is as important as their academic endeavors.

By interacting in groups they begin to learn important lifelong lessons about human interaction and cooperation. These social skills are acquired by learning from their own experiences rather than by direct instruction.

• Children who don't learn to get along with others usually dislike school, often fall behind academically and, in later years, have a higher incidence of dropping out of school.

• In summary, five-year-olds learn best when they are free to raise questions and use investigative discovery methods to seek knowledge about the "real" world.■

A Visit to the Classroom

continued from page 380

Most good schools encourage parents to be actively involved in their child's education. They welcome parents to visit their five-year-old's kindergarten classroom.

In evaluating your child's learning environment, it is wise not to compare it to your own school experiences.

It would be better to use your knowledge about how five-year-olds learn in addressing the following issues:

• Does this kindergarten classroom reflect an atmosphere of active discovery learning on the part of the children?

• Do the children appear to enjoy what they are learning?

• Does the teacher make good use of the children's spontaneous desire to discover for themselves?

• Do the children appear to be personally engaged in what they are doing?

• Does the teacher take into consideration the different developmental levels of the children?

• If some children are tired, are there opportunities provided for rest—sometimes even for sleep?

• Are children praised and rewarded for good effort, not just for successful performance?

• Do the children have lots of hands-on experiences, such as building with blocks and free-form artwork?

• Are there appropriate play materials available to spark the children's inquisitive and investigative minds?

• Does the teacher provide a variety of learning activities?

For example, in addition to hands-on experiences, do the children have access to picture books and puzzles, as well as teacher-guided group activities such as listening to the reading of a storybook?

• Are the children free to move about the room in an appropriate manner?

Or, on the contrary, are they either allowed constantly to run wildly about the room or required to sit still at their desks for long periods of time—both of which would be inappropriate?

• Are opportunities provided for the children to participate in group activities which promote social interaction?

Many parents not only visit their children's kindergarten classroom, but also volunteer, whenever possible, to be a teacher's assistant.

This is an excellent way for parents to become more actively involved in their young child's exciting new learning experiences.■

P. O. Box 2505 • W Lafayette, IN 47996
(800) 927-7289
www.GrowingChild.com

Contributing Authors

Phil Bach, O.D., Ph.D.
Miriam Bender, Ph.D.
Joseph Braga, Ed.D.
Laurie Braga, Ph.D.
George Early, Ph.D.
Carol R. Gestwicki, M.S.
Liam Grimley, Ph.D.
Robert Hannemann, M.D., F.A.A.P.
Sylvia Kottler, M.S.
Bill Peterson, Ph.D.

ting along well with others. For example, praise him for playing cooperatively, doing something thoughtful for someone, being concerned about another's feelings.

Be specific in your feedback:"I really like it when I see you helping Joey put on his shoes."

DON'T force him into uncomfortable positions with other people. For example, don't make him approach a group of strange children.

Don't insist he "make-up" with someone with whom he's still angry. Don't force him to play with someone he doesn't like or whom he feels doesn't like him.

DO respect his wishes about how and with whom he wants to spend time. Some children are very social. Others prefer spending more time by themselves.

DON'T compare him with other children. "Why can't you be like your cousin Charlie?" "Susan is much sweeter to her little brother than you are to yours."

DO allow him to work out his own relationships with a minimum of interference from you.

Explain clearly what your expectations and limits are. Then let him be, other than staying alert for problems that require your attention.

DON'T make him feel that you lack confidence in him. "Now when we go to Grandma's, don't upset her with all your monkey business like you usually do."

DO stand up for him, especially with adults. If he's done something you don't like, let him know later, in private.

But don't apologize for his behavior, criticize him to another, or allow someone to criticize him to you.

Everyone wants someone he can depend on, no matter what. Be that someone for your own child.■

Your Child's Emotional Intelligence

Parents may sometimes be concerned about their child's IQ (intelligence quotient). The IQ test has been perceived for many years as the best predictor of a child's success in later life.

New research studies indicate, however, that emotional intelligence—sometimes referred to as "EQ"—may be an even more important factor in determining the course of one's life.

This is not to say that IQ is unimportant. In the words of one scholar: "IQ may help a person get a job, but EQ will be needed to be promoted."

Emotional intelligence is what enables some people to remain upbeat and optimistic under circumstances that would drown a less buoyant soul.

It explains why the brightest student in high school is not always the most successful in later life.

It has been found that people with good emotional intelligence are likeable and self-confident. They possess good social poise and have an ability to put others at ease.

When engaged in conversation, they have an ability to make the other person somehow feel that he or she is the most important person in the world.

Emotional intelligence has been found to have an important influence not only on a person's career success, but also on one's marriage and family life, one's ability to care for and get along with others, as well as on one's own sense of self-fulfillment.

Awareness of one's own emotional states is the foundation on which emotional intelligence is built. A person who is aware of inner feelings is better able to handle those feelings appropriately.

Emotional intelligence also involves an ability to recognize the emotional cues of others—being sensitive to how another person may be feeling—and then responding appropriately.

Recent brain research has helped scientists develop a better understanding of the relationship between emotions and behavior.

Deep inside the limbic system of the brain is the amygdala, a walnut-shaped structure which encircles the brainstem.

It has been found that a signal in the brain can go straight to the amygdala without passing through the brain's thinking part, namely, the neocortex.

That's what happens, for example, when we react before we think. ("I was so

scared, I couldn't think clearly!") Worrying provides another example of how feelings can block thinking. Excessive worry about failing only increases the likelihood of failure, for example.

While we usually don't have any control over what emotions we experience, we can learn to control what we do about our emotions.

It has been found, for example, that the prefrontal circuitry in the brain, which regulates the relationship between behavior and feelings, probably does not mature until mid-adolescence.

This provides a window of opportunity for parents and teachers to help young children develop better emotional intelligence during the preschool and early school years.

In a study of four-year-olds, each child was shown a marshmallow on a table.

The children were told that they could either eat the marshmallow immediately, or, by waiting until the experimenter had run an errand, they could have two marshmallows.

It was found that about one-third of the children in this study ate the one marshmallow immediately.

Another one-third were able to wait for a short time, but eventually gave in and ate the marshmallow.

The remaining one-third waited until the experimenter returned to the room to

continued on page 386

continued from page 385

give them the two marshmallows.

While it is interesting to note that only one-third of the four-year-olds in this study were able to delay gratification, the results of a follow-up study are even more revealing.

When these same children were tracked down several years later in high school, it was found that those who could not control the impulse to eat the one marshmallow immediately were more likely to be stubborn, lonely, and easily frustrated.

They preferred to avoid challenges and buckled easily under stress.

In contrast, those who had shown greater emotional control by waiting were found to be more confident, adventurous, popular, and dependable.

On average they also scored 210 points higher on the SAT.

These findings would suggest that the ability to bring emotions under the control of the reasoning brain can have significant impact on a person's life.

Here are some things parents can do to help their five-year-old child develop better emotional intelligence:

• Be a good role model for your child by keeping your own emotions under control. For example, instead of an emotional outburst, try counting slowly from one to ten.

• Pay attention to what your child may be feeling, not just what she is doing. For example, try to find out if she is angry, lonely, or frustrated.

• Use your own reasoning ability to help your child better understand, cope with, and control her emotional life.

For example, if she is crying over a broken toy, you might say: "I know you are sad because one of your favorite toys is broken. But there are lots of other toys that you like. Let's pick one to play with right now."

• Act as your child's tutor or coach in helping her to improve her emotional intelligence. For example, encourage and help her to think about and evaluate consequences before she acts.

In summary, helping your child in these ways can have many beneficial effects.

Children with good emotional intelligence usually develop better self-confidence and higher self-esteem.

They get along better with their parents, and are better liked by their peers. They are also more likely to be selected for leadership roles.■

Children and the Environment

Concern for the environment is not just the responsibility of adults. Five-year-olds, too, can learn to become caretakers of the earth.

Wise guidance from parents and teachers can help young children develop greater appreciation for the natural world.

The more they learn about nature, the richer their lives will become.

Good environmental education involves four stages:

1. Building on a young child's curiosity about the wonders of the world around us.

2. Acquiring knowledge about the natural world: birds, wild-flowers, trees, the stars, the seasons.

3. Developing a caring and responsible attitude toward nature.

4. Implementing a proactive approach for conserving the earth's resources and deal-ing with environmental problems. Let's look at each stage more closely:

1. Building on a young child's curiosity. The starting point for environmental education is curiosity.

The best way to promote a young child's curiosity is to have him experience nature firsthand, rather than using a formal teaching approach.

It's a good idea for parents to plan frequent walks in the outdoors to stimulate this curiosity.

In our society, children often spend too much time indoors (watching TV, for example) and not enough time outdoors, exploring the wonders of nature.

Because of his small stature and his still-developing cognitive abilities, a young child perceives the world differently than an older child.

A child who doesn't explore a forest until his later years, for example, will have missed the more awesome and exciting experience it would have been at five years of age when trees seem so much bigger.

Encourage a young child to experience nature with all five senses: seeing, hearing, touching, smelling, but not tasting unless adults are sure it is something safe to eat.

Being outdoors also enables a young child's imagination to develop.

For example, a single beautiful flower can represent, in a young child's mind, a perfect wedding bouquet; a hill can become a fortress or a castle, while a row of tall trees can be transformed into an advancing army of giants.

Later, a child's outdoor experiences can be enhanced indoors. Books, art, music, and dance can all be used to expand outdoor environmental learning.

continued on page 387

continued from page 386

2. Acquiring knowledge. Once a child's curiosity has been stimulated, there is much knowledge that can be acquired in the outdoors: about the force of the wind, for example, the heat of the sun, or the length of one's shadow.

In acquiring this type of knowledge, young children do not respond well to a formal learning approach ("What's the name of this flower?").

They learn best at this age by sharing their thoughts and feelings about what interests them in nature.

Parents can build on this natural curiosity and interest by pointing out, for example, the beauty of the four seasons: leaf buds in spring, summer flowers, autumn leaves, or the serene splendor of a winter landscape.

Fortunate is the child whose parents open his eyes to the wonders of the natural world!

Through the use of library books, parents can further build on their child's interest in nature. ("Let's look in this book for a picture of that beautiful leaf you brought home.")

3. Developing a caring and responsible attitude. Gardening, such as growing vegetables or flowers from seed is a great way for a young child to develop a caring and responsible attitude toward nature.

The child will soon learn that good intentions alone are not sufficient for a plant to grow.

It is essential to learn about the plant's needs and to be vigilant in caring for it, such as by watering it regularly and removing any weeds that grow around it.

Caring for a plant is thus an excellent way to help a child progress from being self-centered to being other-centered.

It will help stimulate the child's interest if the parents take photographs at different stages of the growth process: (a) when the soil has been prepared and the seed sown; (b) when the new growth first appears through the soil; and (c) when it is fully grown.

4. Implementing a proactive approach. Five-year-olds can be taught to conserve the earth's resources and deal with environmental problems.

They can learn to conserve energy, for example, by turning off lights which are not being used. They can be reminded to use both sides of a sheet of paper.

In teaching them to avoid wasting food, they can be made aware of the many children throughout the world who go to bed hungry because of a lack of food.

Parents can set a good example by recycling what is sometimes referred to as "beautiful junk"; an empty egg carton, for example, can be used for sorting buttons or an empty jam jar can be used to store small objects.

Five-year-olds can also learn to sort objects—such as aluminum cans, bottles, newspapers—to be taken to a recycling center.

They can also participate in litter clean-ups. Seeing the ugly effects of litter on the environment will serve to remind them not to throw paper wrappers, for example, out of a car window.

By becoming involved in the beautification of the environment, rather than its destruction, young children learn to be more responsible for the world in which they live.

It also helps them become more aware of healthy lifestyle habits for themselves, such as keeping their own bodies clean, eating healthy foods, and getting sufficient sleep at night.

Thus, as young children learn to respect nature, they also learn what is best for themselves and others.

In summary, there is much that parents can do to help a young child become a more responsible caretaker of the earth.

Developing a child's sense of responsibility for our world is not only good for nature but is also very beneficial for the child.

Here are some books with lots of environmental activities for young children:

Carson, R. (1998) The Sense of Wonder. HarperCollins Reprint.

Cornell, Joseph. (1998) Sharing Nature with Children: The Classic Parents' and Teachers' Nature Awareness Guide. Dawn Publishers, CA.

Herman, H.L., Passineau, J.F., Schimpf, A.L., & Treuer, P. (1991). Teaching Kids To Love The Earth. Duluth, MN: Pfeifer-Hamilton.

Kasperson, J., Lachecki M., and Holman, K. (1994) More Teaching Kids to Love the Earth. Pfeifer-Hamilton.

Louv, R. (2006)Last Child in the Woods: Saving Our Children from Nature-Deficit Disorder. Algonquin Books.

Milord, S. (1996 Revised). The Kid's Nature Book. Charlotte, VT: Williamson.

Petrash, C. (1991). Earthways: Simple Environmental Activities For Young Children. Mt. Rainier, MD: Gryphon House.

Potter, J. (1995) Nature in a Nutshell for Kids: Over 100 Activities. Jossey-Bass

Rockwell, R.E., Sherwood, E.A. & Williams, R.A. (1986). Hug A Tree And Other Things To Do Outdoors with Children. Mt. Rainier, MD: Gryphon House.

Sheehan, K. & Waldner, M. (1991).Earth Child: Games, Stories, Activities, Experiments And Ideas About Living Lightly On Planet Earth. Tulsa, OK: Council Oak.■

Putting Thoughts and Feelings into Words

Do you find it difficult sometimes to let other people know what's on your mind?

Do you sometimes get the impression that no one knows how you really feel?

Do you think that others sometimes misinterpret the things you say, that they misunderstand you?

These are thoughts and feelings shared by many people. They reflect the difficulties that can occur in people's communication with one another.

Faulty patterns of communication begin in childhood. You can begin now to help your child learn to communicate her own thoughts and feelings.

If you do, you will be saving her many problems and misunderstandings in the future.

At the same time, you may learn some things that can increase the effectiveness of your own communication with others.

Communication is a skill. Like any skill, it is taught through a combination of example and practice.

You teach your child how to communicate by communicating with her and giving her a chance to practice communicating with you.

You may find it difficult to change some patterns of communication you use now, even though they are not satisfying. It takes a while to replace an old habit with a new habit.

Have patience and try not to get discouraged when you don't feel you've responded to your child in the way you wanted.

Use your successes and your failures as opportunities for learning. Just try to communicate with her as you would like her to communicate with you if your positions were reversed.

By trying, you will succeed.

Here are some guidelines to help your child develop the ability to communicate better with you and others.

1. Encourage your child to express her needs, desires, feelings and opinions.

How often do you ask her what she thinks of something, what she'd like, how she feels about something?

Without thinking, adults often forget to treat children as human beings with their own valid opinions. Children are often left out of decision-making that affects them.

It's not fair to you, to the rest of the family, or to your child to allow her to rule situations, as can happen when parents are hesitant to set limits.

But it is fair to all concerned to allow each family member, including your five-year-old, to have a say in matters that concern them.

Take into consideration your child's unique personality characteristics.

For example, if she is very shy and quiet, encouraging her to tell you some foods she'd enjoy having for meals and snacks can be an important step in helping her begin to express herself.

If she's more verbal, asking her a question such as what she thinks about adults who talk to you about her as if she weren't there ("How old is she now?") can further open the lines of communication between you.

Make use of opportunities in your daily routine to encourage her to offer her point of view.

Set aside time for just the two of you to talk about things that are on her mind.

Encourage her to share positive feelings about herself, joys, and accomplishments as well as worries, fears, and anxieties.

If she isn't used to expressing her thoughts and feelings in words, be patient. You will help her learn to share more of her needs, desires, feelings and opinions by showing her that you really are interested.

2. Be accepting of what your child says even when you don't agree with her.

This rule applies, for example, to not correcting her speech or not making her feel embarrassed about an opinion she offers.

If she comes breathlessly into the house and announces, "Susie ain't got no father," this could be a chance for you to strengthen your relationship as she shares a puzzling and perhaps disturbing discovery with you.

If you were to respond by correcting her speech, you might discourage her from talking to you about her concerns.

If, instead, you were to say back to her. "Susie doesn't have a father?" you would be encouraging her to continue the conversation.

At the same time, by your example, you would be teaching her the correct way to say what she had said.

3. Help your child discover and explore her own thoughts and feelings.

When you and your child are talking, try not to dominate the conversation.

Even when she asks you a question, try to guide her to discover what she really wants to know rather than telling her what you think she wants to know. Listen for the questions behind the questions she asks.

For example, suppose she asks you if you and Mommy (Daddy) will ever get a divorce.

Chances are she's seen what's happened to a playmate whose parents are separating, and she's worried whether it could happen to her.

By saying something to her such as,

continued on page 389

continued from page 388

"You're worried that Mommy (Daddy) and I might stop loving each other?" you'd be giving her a chance to begin to explore just what it is that she's concerned about.

Once she's gotten the chance to express her thoughts and feelings, you can help by giving her whatever assurances and straightforward, honest information you can.

At this point your contribution to the conversation will be guided by your understanding of her concerns.

Thus, you'll be much better able to communicate with her than if you'd simply tried to answer her opening question.

You can help her in this way to explore the fears and anxieties that are often at the root of her "What if...?" questions.

By helping her look at her fears, you'll help her learn to face problems with confidence rather than fear.

4. Be careful not to put words and thoughts into your child's mind that do not reflect her true feelings.

In order for her to come to know her own mind and take responsibility for her thoughts, feelings, and actions, she has to be encouraged to express her own point of view.

Many adults spend their lives holding others responsible for how they feel, what they think and what they do. Statements such as, "Well, I just did it because you made me so angry" are common.

If you want your child to learn to be in charge of her own mind, you have to allow her to be so now.

For example, suppose she is beginning to get impatient with herself after working hard on an art project.

You might be tempted to tell her something encouraging, for example, that you think it's good or that she should be proud of herself for working so hard.

You could be more helpful, however, if instead you helped her explore her own thoughts and feelings about what she's doing. "Looks like it's not going the way you want it to go," for example, might be a good opener to get her to start talking.

In this way you may lead her to the conclusion that she really does feel good about the work she's doing.

With your guidance she may find out how to make it go the way she wants. But, wherever the discussion leads, she'll be taking the responsibility for her own thoughts and feelings about the situation.

5. Learn to use problem situations as opportunities for meaningful communication between you and your child.

Sometimes you may respond to her in ways that you don't feel good about afterwards.

For example, suppose she tracks dirt into the house for the fifth time in one day. You lose your patience and explode: "You are so messy. Haven't I told you a thousand times not to track dirt into the house? You ought to be ashamed of yourself."

Your anger would have caused a different message to be delivered than you intended.

Instead of talking about your feelings about a specific action on her part, you would have told her how she should feel about herself and what kind of person she is.

Repeated messages of this kind, if not discussed and remedied, can cause her to lose faith in herself. She will come to trust your judgment of her more than her own, thus giving up responsibility for herself.

However, you can turn such a problem into a chance for learning. You could let her know that you did not mean to explode.

You do feel angry when she keeps tracking dirt into the house but you don't think she's a messy person, and you don't want her to be ashamed of herself.

You just want her to try to remember to wipe off her feet. Then ask her to share with you how she felt when you reacted the way you did.

Together you can explore how you both feel in such situations and figure out how to handle them in a more satisfying way for both of you in the future.

This kind of approach to problems will help her learn to communicate her thoughts and feelings honestly and effectively.

continued on page 390

Fractions

continued from page 389

Every day your child hears about fractions and encounters their use in ordinary experiences: "Half a slice of bread," "quarter slice of pizza."

Why not allow him to manipulate these concepts in practical and fun experiences?

Materials:

1. Seven round cardboard discs (sold at pizza parlors).

2. Forty-two cup hooks or knobs.

Procedures:

1. Divide each disc into sections so you have one disc containing each of the following: 1/2, 1/4, 1/6, 1/8, 1/10, 1/12.

2. Attach a hook or knob to each section. (This is designed to make the pieces easy to pick up.)

3. Start with only the first three discs—whole, halves, quarters.

Offer challenges, don't teach. "Can two half pieces make a whole?" "Does it look like the uncut disc?"

A more difficult challenge: "Can quarters make a whole?" "Is it possible to make a whole with a half piece and two quarters?"

It may take a while to reach the harder puzzles. The objective is for your child to experiment and as a consequence perceive relationships of parts-to-wholes.

Customarily fractions are not taught until third grade. Then they are taught abstractly in workbooks with pencil and paper.

Some children have difficulty learning fractions because they do not relate them to experiences in the real world.

Hopefully your child will enter school with all the necessary readiness skills because fractions for him will already be functional and understandable.

Variations:

1. Color each disc a different color. This makes the "trade-offs" more vivid.

2. Introduce new discs with more complex trade-offs. "Can two one-eighth pieces fit into the space of a quarter piece?" ■

'I Love You'

Parents may sometimes too easily presume that their child knows she is loved and appreciated. Studies of children indicate, however, that in order to develop a positive self-concept, they need to be reminded repeatedly that they are loved by the most important adults in their lives.

There are many ways to communicate your love for your child throughout the day. Here are some suggestions:

• You're terrific. • You're a very good listener. • I like you just the way you are. • Good job. • You're very special to me. • Thanks for putting away your toys. • Your hair looks really nice today. • I'm very proud of you. • You're my big helper. • I'm very glad we are such good friends. • You are very thoughtful. • Have I told you lately how much I love you? • I want to give you a great big hug. • I love you. ■

P. O. Box 2505 • W Lafayette, IN 47996
(800) 927-7289
www.GrowingChild.com
© 2012 Growing Child, Inc.

Contributing Authors

Phil Bach, O.D., Ph.D.
Miriam Bender, Ph.D.
Joseph Braga, Ed.D.
Laurie Braga, Ph.D.
George Early, Ph.D.
Carol R. Gestwicki, M.S.
Liam Grimley, Ph.D.
Robert Hannemann, M.D., F.A.A.P.
Sylvia Kottler, M.S.
Bill Peterson, Ph.D.

-It will also reinforce her feelings of trust in you so that she will feel able in the future to share what's on her mind without fear or hesitation.

6. Develop the art of "responsive listening" with your child.

The reason most people feel that others don't really understand them is that they don't. Many people spend more time in a conversation "rehearsing" what they will say next than listening to the person who is talking.

Real communication requires that each member of the conversation try to hear the other person's point of view. You can only do this if you're really listening.

You can teach your child how to listen, and thus how to communicate, by your example.

At the same time, she will be coming to know her own mind as she speaks it. From this she'll learn to say what she means and mean what she says, a rare and valuable asset.

The thread that weaves itself through many of the guidelines suggested above is a technique called "responsive listening."

It involves "saying back" to your child what you think she's said. That way you give her feedback that you have heard her and that you understand her.

If you have heard her correctly, your repeating what she had said lets her hear her own thoughts and feelings more clearly.

This gives her a chance to evaluate if that's really how she feels or thinks. It helps her discover, explore, and clarify her own thoughts and feelings.

If you have misunderstood her, your feedback gives her a chance to let you know that.

You can give your child no greater gift than the ability to know and express her own mind. ■

Growing Child

Learning to Control One's Behavior

Self-control takes a lifetime to learn. The most important first steps toward self-control, however, can be learned during the first six years of life.

An infant as young as four months who is hungry can be observed trying to suppress a cry when being held lovingly by his parents.

Likewise, a nine-month-old child may be observed sucking vigorously on his knuckle or thumb as he tries to hold back tears.

In general, however, the first two years of life are more a time of external control with only occasional evidence of any self-regulation of behavior.

As a young child acquires language, around two years of age, he may be heard to repeat to himself an adult's command or prohibition ("No, no!") if he starts to move toward a forbidden object.

More self-regulating speech may be heard during the third and fourth years.

By five or six years of age, most children have developed more numerous and more complex self-control strategies.

Research studies indicate that a child's transition from external control by adults to internalized self-control is guided primarily by the development of private speech.

Private speech is a term used to describe the self-talk which preschoolers use, for example, while working on a task.

Children begin to use certain key words

(sometimes called "telegraphic speech") from their parents' prohibitions ("Don't touch—hot!") to guide their own behavior.

Adults also use private speech when learning a new skill such as a good golf swing. It begins with audible self-statements ("Proper stance. Eye on the ball.")

After a while it takes the form of whispering to oneself. Then it becomes an inaudible self-statement. Ultimately it becomes automatic thinking to direct and control one's behavior.

Researchers have found that children are more likely to use private speech when they are trying to begin a new task or when they encounter a challenging problem.

Gradually as a child masters a task, there is less need for self-talk as the routine becomes more automatic. It should be noted that some children learn self-regulation skills more easily than others.

There is evidence that children are born with different personality characteristics. Easygoing, happy children, for example, learn self-control skills more readily than difficult-to-raise children.

It has also been found that children who are inattentive and impulsive often have not developed the self-talk skills that would enable them to better control their behavior.

Likewise, it should be noted that although children go through the same developmental stages, they do not develop at the same rate.

This is as true with regard to the development of private speech and self-control skills as it is for physical, intellectual, social, and emotional development.

Parental behaviors can also affect a child's development of self-control skills.

Parents who are too authoritarian, for example, make demands on their child that are overly severe. As a result, the child's emotions may be bottled up, which might eventually give rise to a sudden outburst of anger.

Permissive parents, on the other hand, who fail to provide clear and consistent rules of social behavior, are likely to have a child with poor self-esteem who may lash out aggressively at the slightest provocation.

The good news is that there is much that parents can do to teach their child better self-control skills.

continued on page 392

continued from page 391

Here are some ways to teach a child better self-control skills:

• The first step is for parents to monitor their own behavior.

By being good role models of self-control, parents become a child's most important and effective teachers of self-regulated behavior.

• It's important to be aware that young children are more likely to react to the emotional tone of a parent's command than to its verbal content.

Thus, shouting impulsively at a young child ("Don't touch the stove!") may actually increase the likelihood of the child carrying out the dangerous act which the parent intended to prevent.

• It's a good idea for parents to let their child hear them thinking aloud. ("I'm going to look to the right and then to the left before I cross the street.")

This helps a young child understand the connection between *thought* and *behavior*.

• It's also wise to rehearse a particular scenario with your child.

For example, "I'm going to take you with me to the store, but you must stay with me at all times. If you run up and down the aisles, as you did the last time, I will not be able to take you with me the next time."

In this way the child learns to *think* about his behavior and to *predict* future outcomes, rather than reacting impulsively on the spur of the moment.

• It's important to give your child an understandable explanation of any rules you make rather than relying on commands, threats, or punishment.

If the reason you give is: "Just because I said so", this explanation leaves behind no information on which the child can build self-control.

Research studies indicate that giving children a good reason for obeying a com-

Teaching self-control skills to a young child is not an easy task for parents. It's one that must begin early in a child's life.

mand ("Be careful with that toy because it will break easily.") is a more effective way to get them to obey the command than giving the command alone ("Be careful with that toy.").

• If a child misbehaves, it is better to ask him questions about his misbehavior ("What rule did you just break? What is the consequence for breaking that rule?") than to issue a stern correction ("I told you not to misbehave.").

In this way, the child learns to assume responsibility for his own behavior, rather than perceiving himself unduly controlled by adults.

• A child will learn more self-control skills from calm review of his misbehavior than from an adult's angry outburst.

From such a review a child can learn that there were other options available which he hadn't considered.

He can, therefore, think about how he might behave differently in a similar situation in the future.

• Reading children's books in which an animal or storybook character has to deal with a problem situation is a very effective way to help a child learn how to deal with a similar situation, such as how one can maintain self-control while being teased by others.

• Likewise, from a storybook, a young child can learn how to behave when faced with temptation as well as what to say to himself ("If I just wait, I'll get a lot more candy later.").

• Pictures can be used as helpful reminders in exercising self-control. If a child has difficulty sitting still at the dinner table, for example, a picture of a turtle in his place at the table can help to remind him to slow down and behave appropriately.

• In helping a child to develop better self-control skills, it is more effective to focus on one or two major problem behaviors, (for example, not interrupting other people while they are talking), while, as far as possible, ignoring other problem behaviors.

In summary, teaching self-control skills to a young child is not an easy task for parents. It's one that must begin early in a child's life.

Research studies indicate that children who have not developed fundamental self-regulation skills early in their lives often have attentional and impulsive behavior problems in school.

On the other hand, it was found that preschoolers who had developed good self-control skills displayed more positive characteristics later in their lives.

As adolescents, they were rated by their parents as having above average academic and social skills.

They were also better able to cope with stress in their lives and were better liked by their peers.

Developing good self-control skills helps a child become a more reflective, more relaxed, and happier human being.■

More About Traffic Safety or "Stop-Look-Listen"

Motor vehicle accidents are the leading cause of death among children under nine years of age.

These accidents are most likely to occur: (1) near the child's own home; (2) on warm, sunny days; (3) between 3 and 5 p.m., and (4) without the motorist seeing the child or the child seeing the automobile in time.

What can be done to prevent such accidents? If the child is old enough to be allowed near traffic, it is recommended that parents teach the **"STOP-LOOK-LISTEN"** routine.

It's a simple method that can help a child remember what to do near traffic or when crossing a road.

1. "STOP." The most effective way to teach a child to stop is to have the child act as the guide for an adult. It is the child's responsibility to say "stop" whenever there is danger.

At first the adult may have to prompt the child ("You were supposed to say 'stop' whenever there was possible danger.")

Board games or pictures with streets may also be used to teach this concept. Eventually the child will get better at predicting and recognizing possible danger.

2. "LOOK." Children must learn to look to each side, left and right, for approaching traffic.

They must learn that they may cross the road only when there are no vehicles in sight.

They must also learn to look for traffic signs and signals—and know what they mean ("red," "yellow," "green," "walk," "don't walk," "stop").

At home they can be shown pictures which illustrate traffic signs and then look for similar signs when out walking with an adult.

3. "LISTEN." As adults we are used to differentiating traffic sounds. By listening carefully we can tell the difference between oncoming vs. departing traffic, starting vs. stopping sounds, fast- vs. slow-moving vehicles.

A young child has to learn to listen for such sounds and then correctly identify what the sounds mean.

He has to learn, for example, that the sound of an approaching car gets louder and departing traffic becomes quieter. Eventually he will learn to estimate both speed and distance from the sounds he hears.

Never violate the safety rules you are trying to teach your child—even if it means arriving late. You must serve as a good role model for traffic safety.

You will then be doing your part to prevent your child from becoming an accident statistic.

The **"STOP-LOOK-LISTEN"** skills which you teach your child need constant review and practice. Even though a child is capable of demonstrating these skills, he must learn to apply them *every* time he is near traffic.

That's why it's important to give your child many opportunities to be your traffic-safety guide, *stopping, looking, and listening* whenever you go for a walk together.■

Help for Serious Problems

There are often times when your children have problems that you can't seem to handle all by yourself.

Growing Child usually suggests that you call your doctor for advice.

But not every doctor is equally interested in every kind of problem.

There may be times when you feel that your doctor isn't paying enough attention to your worries, complaints or fears about your children.

When that happens there are several things you can do. You can make it clear to your doctor that you aren't satisfied with the answers you have been given.

Sometimes, when doctors are busy they don't realize they haven't really answered the question in a way you can understand. Telling them so may help get a better answer.

If it doesn't, you might ask your doctor to refer you to someone else for that problem or you might start looking elsewhere on your own.

Most parts of the country now have children's agencies, clinics, or groups of parents or other citizens which exist just to answer the kinds of questions which you may have.

The important thing is for you not to give up if you are not satisfied with the answers you receive. Whether your fears are real or not, your child will probably not do well until you get more information.

So, whether it is your child or you who needs advice or help, you should keep trying until you get answers that make sense to you.

If you think you or your child needs help, keep looking until you find the help you need.■

How to Handle Negative Feelings

Do you sometimes feel guilty after being angry? Do you become impatient with yourself for feeling unhappy?

Many people have difficulty dealing constructively with negative feelings such as anger or unhappiness.

Negative feelings often foster more negative feelings like guilt and impatience.

For some people it may come as a surprise to learn that negative feelings can be handled in a positive and constructive manner.

Now is a good time to help your child learn how to deal constructively with negative feelings.

Before you can help your child, however, you must first examine your own attitudes toward your negative feelings.

You probably have some contradictory attitudes toward negative feelings which make it hard for you to deal with them.

First, you need to remind yourself that no one can be happy, uplifted, and clearheaded all the time.

When you feel lonely, anxious, afraid, angry, frustrated, or just low, these are normal messages from your mind that something is bothering you—just as physical pain is a message from your body that something is wrong.

You need to listen to these messages in order to resolve the problems that cause you discomfort.

Second, negative feelings won't go away by trying to avoid them. Unless you deal with them, you can't do anything about them.

Third, it doesn't help to dwell morosely on them because then you never get beyond the immediate feelings to begin to explore different ways of looking at the problem and possible solutions to it.

What is needed is a balanced attitude and approach.

Here are some ways you can help your child learn to deal constructively with negative feelings:

1. Be accepting of your child's negative feelings.

Take them seriously, even when they don't seem important to you. They are important to her.

She will feel that you understand and care about her feelings if you treat them with the same seriousness you would want someone to treat your feelings.

In trying to help her feel better, don't try to talk her out of her feelings. You can help most by letting her know, by your words and actions, that you understand how she feels and that it's all right to feel that way.

For example, suppose she is afraid of going in the water at a lake or pool. You might be tempted to try to convince her that there's nothing for her to be afraid of and try to talk her into going in with you.

You could help much more by acknowledging her feelings: "You're not sure you want to go into the water just yet? That's fine. That may be because you're not used to it. If you decide you'd like to try it later, I'll stay with you and make sure nothing happens to you."

Then, let her approach the feared situation at her own pace, without pushing or urging.

2. Help your child learn to express her negative feelings in words.

Often, when parents discourage their children's negative feelings, they mean to discourage their behavioral expression rather than the feelings themselves.

At this age, your child has good enough control of her actions and good enough language to learn to substitute words for actions when she feels angry, frustrated, or upset. But she needs your help.

For example, suppose her little brother scribbles in the pages of her favorite book. She has a right to be angry, but she doesn't have a right to hit or yell at him.

You can help her learn to express her feelings in an acceptable way by (a) the way you respond to her when she expresses her anger, and (b) your putting into words for her how you think she probably feels. "Are you mad because Joey scribbled in your book? Feel like talking about it?"

When she sees you correcting Joey in a firm but calm manner, she learns that it was more effective for her to express her feelings to you in words than to start a fight with Joey.

3. Help your child explore and discover what's causing her to feel bad.

Sometimes when she is upset, there's a specific cause.

For example, she might feel hurt because someone said something unkind to her. Other times it may be hard to pinpoint the reason for her unhappiness.

For example, she might feel a little blue without knowing why when her older brother starts school and she's left at home with you.

At other times she may be a little whiny, clingy, or cranky for no apparent reason. She may be overtired, hungry, sick, or just going through too many changes in her life. Anything that drains energy can make her feel low.

Whatever the problem is, you can help her feel better by helping her explore her feelings.

If you know what the problem is, you can start the conversation by trying to put what you think her feelings are into words: "Your feelings are hurt because Dana called you a baby. Is that true?"

If you have only a general idea, you might say: "It's tough for you to have to stay at home with me when Tommy goes to school."

When you really don't have any idea what the problem is, you might say: "You seem a little sad (angry, upset, confused). Can

continued on page 395

continued from page 394

I help? Do you want to talk about what's making you feel sad?"

You may get a little resistance at first. Be patient and don't push her to talk if she's not ready.

Let her know that you're willing to listen if she wants to share her feelings with you.

Later in the day—sometimes at a most unexpected moment—she may unload how she is feeling.

Once she has started talking, use the "responsive listening" technique to help her continue to explore her feelings. In other words, say back to her what you think she has said.

Try to resist giving advice or telling her how she should feel. Just listen and accept what she says. Help her express what's on her mind by showing her that you understand and care.

4. Help her try to resolve the problem that's causing her discomfort.

Often just in talking aloud about what's on her mind, she will feel better about whatever is bothering her.

For example, as she talks about her jealousy over the time and attention you give her baby brother, she, herself, will probably conclude that the baby really needs the special care, and she is grown up enough to take care of herself in many ways.

With this kind of problem, you can help most by being alert to her moods.

Look for openings to help her talk about what's bothering her: "Sometimes the baby takes so much time, you and I don't have enough time together, do we?"

This is especially important in situations in which she probably isn't sure herself why she has negative feelings.

Once she's gotten her feelings off her chest, you can help her find a solution by suggesting different ways of looking at the situation.

For example: "I sure could use some help

with the baby. Can you help me get him dressed?"

Be specific about ways she really could help. Let her know there will be a reward for good behavior: "The more you help me, the sooner we'll get done—and the more time you and I can spend together, just the two of us."

5. Help her generate and examine alternative ways to handle negative feelings.

Children—and adults too—sometimes get in the habit of repeatedly dealing with a negative feeling in the same manner—always losing one's temper, for example, whenever one is angry—without realizing that there are other possible alternatives.

These alternative solutions often provide a more positive way to handle negative feelings.

Telling her a story about another child's feelings is a good way to help her generate and examine alternative solutions.

For example, if the story was about a little girl who got angry with her brother, have her think of different ways in which the little girl might deal with her anger:

(a) She might yell at her brother; (b) she might hit him; (c) she might just tell him she was angry, then say no more; (d) she might wait until her anger was under control before deciding what to do; or (e) she might tell her parents and ask them what

she should do.

It could then be pointed out to her that (a) and (b) are not really good ways for the little girl to deal with her anger.

There are other more positive ways, such as (c), (d), or (e), for dealing with those feelings.

6. Help her look for something positive to learn from problems for which there is no solution.

Many times in life we have problems for which there really is no solution. It still helps to talk about our feelings.

Sometimes the only way we can reach some feeling of peace is by looking for something in the situation from which we can learn.

For example, suppose your child's cat has disappeared, and you've done everything you can to find it without success.

This is upsetting, both because of the loss of a loved pet and because of the uncertainty of the situation.

You could help her talk about her feelings by saying: "You must be pretty upset about your cat." Help her explore the positive possibilities as well as her concerns.

Ask her, for example, if she can think of anything good about all this. She may reassure herself by a hope that someone has found her cat who will love him like she does or will ask around about the owner.

Encourage her to look for something in the situation from which she can learn.

She might decide, for example, that the next cat she has should wear a collar with her name, address and telephone number. Or she might decide that she doesn't want any more pets for now.

She may conclude that when we love something, even thought it's hard to lose it, it's still worth the pain.

continued on page 396

A Sorting Game

Sorting by category, which involves making comparisons and drawing conclusions, is a necessary skill for later school achievement.

This skill can be developed through activities such as "A Sorting Game."

In this activity, items are to be sorted into one of three categories, "water," "land," or "air."

For example, animals have particular habitats: a seal lives in water, a rabbit on land, and a bird in the air.

Likewise clothing fits categories—swimsuit in water, spacesuit in the air, snowsuit on land.

Other objects can be sorted—lawn mower on land, parachute in the air, boat in water.

Materials:

1. Pictures of animals, clothing, and other objects, such as vehicles or transportation items, to be sorted under the appropriate category.

Virtually any picture from magazines or merchandise catalogs can be adapted for use.

2. A 9" x 12" piece of cardboard. Cut the cardboard into three equal pieces.

On one piece prepare the cue or signal, waves, for "in water," and below it print the words: "in water."

Next prepare a sheet for "on land." Cues, such as a landscape with tree and house would be appropriate.

Again, below it print the words: "on land."

Finally, prepare the third sheet, "in the air," the cue being cotton balls for clouds, for example, pasted on the paper.

Below it write the words: "in the air."

Procedure:

Your child sorts the pictures by placing each one under the appropriate category.

It may be necessary to give some clues by asking pertinent questions: "If the animal lives mostly in the air, where will the picture go?"

"Show me the animals you don't recognize so that I can help you decide if they go on land, air, or water."■

P. O. Box 2505 • W Lafayette, IN 47996
(800) 927-7289
www.GrowingChild.com
© 2012 Growing Child, Inc.

Contributing Authors

Phil Bach, O.D., Ph.D.
Miriam Bender, Ph.D.
Joseph Braga, Ed.D.
Laurie Braga, Ph.D.
George Early, Ph.D.
Carol R. Gestwicki, M.S.
Liam Grimley, Ph.D.
Robert Hannemann, M.D., F.A.A.P.
Sylvia Kottler, M.S.
Bill Peterson, Ph.D.

Allowances

Just about every kindergartner appreciates the value of money. An allowance is a particular amount of money that parents decide to give their children on a regular basis and with no strings attached.

This sharing of family resources says to the child, "You are an important member of the family and we want to share our trust, love, respect and wealth with you."

It represents a share in the family treasury, a sign that the child is a member of the family circle.

An allowance should not be confused with wages. A child doesn't have to produce or perform in any particular way to receive an allowance.

Wages are a reward for productivity—mowing the lawn, taking out the garbage, making the beds.

The amount of an allowance should be decided by parents in terms of their own financial status and community standards. Too much is as bad as too little money.

If you want to teach thriftiness, give the child a small sum of money to deposit in the bank.■

continued from page 395

So we should appreciate what we have when we have it.

Remember to help her find her own positive perspectives on the situation, if she can, rather than trying to get her to accept your viewpoint.

If you allow her to express her feelings of anger, sadness, loneliness, and other negative feelings, you'll also help her find something positive, even from a difficult situation.

Learning to deal constructively with negative feelings is not easy. It is the task of a lifetime. With your help, your child can lead a happier life as she learns to handle negative feelings in a positive manner.■

Growing Child

Five and a Half Years Old

Five-and-a-half-year-olds are generally delightful. Although still egocentric in their thinking, they have achieved a level of socialization and independence that makes them a joy to be around.

The typical five-and-a-half-year-old has been developing abilities in several different areas, including gross motor skills.

By now he can walk a two-inch-wide line easily for a distance of about 10 feet.

He no longer runs flat footedly but runs lightly on his toes.

He thoroughly enjoys playground equipment and is active and skillful in climbing, sliding, and swinging.

Five-and-a-half-year-old girls usually learn to skip while boys are more apt to gallop but may learn to skip in kindergarten.

Both girls and boys enjoy doing various "stunts"— somersaults, swinging on a jungle gym, jumping from heights of two to three feet, or climbing up a slide.

Five-and-a-half-year-olds enjoy moving to music and keep time reasonably well. This age is the time when dancing and gymnastics are enjoyed and during which children show real progress in these areas.

They have the control to stand on one foot — either foot — for about 8-10 seconds. Many can stand on the preferred foot with arms folded for the same length of time.

Other one-foot skills include hopping forward eight to 10 feet on each foot separately.

From a standing start on both feet they

can broad jump a distance of three and a half to four feet.

They have learned to catch, throw, and kick well enough to play a variety of ball games with their peers.

Most five-and-a-half-year-olds have learned to recognize many letters and can print a few spontaneously.

Language and speech development have kept pace with general body control and eye-hand coordination.

Their speech has become fluent and grammatically correct. They can use plurals, pronouns, and tenses correctly and in well-constructed sentences.

Usually they have a few remaining sound confusions: these are most often confusions of the s, f, and th group.

They love to recite or sing rhymes and jingles. Television commercials, cartoon music, jingles, and the like, are often favorites.

Kindergarten and Sunday school songs are performed both with and without

encouragement.

They love to be read to or to be told stories.

They often have favorites that they have heard so often that they can "read" them aloud to themselves from memory. They may act them out in detail either alone or with friends.

Most five-and-a-half-year-olds can give their full name, age, and address when asked. Some may also know their birth date.

With regard to using other people's names, they haven't yet learned the finer distinctions of whom to greet by title rather than by first name.

Thus they may greet their neighbor, Mr. Jones, by saying in an adult-like tone of voice, "Good morning, Bob."

While it may startle Mr. Jones to be greeted in this manner, they would merely be proudly repeating what they have previously heard an adult say.

They will usually define concrete nouns by their uses, as: Water is for drinking, a bicycle is for riding, a ball is for throwing.

They are interested in new words, especially abstract ones, and are constantly asking their meaning.

They will pick a word out of a conversation, repeat it correctly and ask, "What does that mean?"

They ask questions for information and their questions are now more challenging!

continued on page 398

continued from page 397

They can use a knife and fork with reasonable competence.

They can dress and undress alone, managing buttons and ties except those they cannot see. They can close or tie their shoes although perhaps not as tightly as they should be.

They can wash and dry their face and hands but need help or supervision for bathing.

In general, their behavior is more sensible, controlled, and independent than it was a year ago.

They are beginning to understand the importance of order and tidiness but may need constant reminders.

Their play is now much more complicated. Some constructive or dramatic play may be continued alone or with playmates from day to day.

Their floor games can become quite complicated—whole neighborhoods or towns may be laid out on the floor.

Imaginative play may turn a picnic table into a big ship, some boxes can become a bus. They know what they want to build and go about it industriously.

Friends are now chosen, not just accepted because they happen to be present. At the same time they are usually tender and protective toward younger children and pets. They will most likely comfort a playmate who has been hurt or is unhappy.

They have also learned to share and take turns. They are cooperative with playmates most of the time and understand the need for rules and fair play.

Of course, their flexible ideas about rules are sometimes startling but, all in all, their playtime is generally free of friction.

Most five-and-a-half-year-olds have become skillful on a tricycle. Having nearly outgrown that vehicle, they are ready to learn to ride a small bicycle.

Before they become six years old, they will have mastered getting on, starting, balancing and stopping on the "two-wheeler."

These general body skills have provided the background of coordination needed for learning the finer eye-hand skills that will prepare them for writing.

They can now hold a pencil or crayon in an essentially adult grasp between the thumb and first two fingers. They can copy a circle, cross, square, and a triangle in recognizable form. They can draw a recognizable "person" with head, trunk, legs, arms, and features.

The "house" that they draw will probably have a door, windows, and a chimney. Most importantly, they can announce beforehand what they are going to draw.

They can usually count the fingers of one hand with the index finger of the other.

They can color pictures neatly, staying pretty well within the outlines. Their color choices may be bizarre: a purple dog and a yellow tree would not be unusual!

They know what colors the objects are — but just happen to like purple or yellow. Or they may just wonder what objects would look like in a different color!

Many five-and-a-half-year-olds can name the four primary colors or more and can match up to 10 or 12 colors.

This is a time when parents can detect if their child is color-blind, a phenomenon found more frequently in boys than girls.

At this age they are busy getting "ready" for the structured learning of the classroom.

Allowed the independence to grow and the opportunities to learn self-sufficiency, they will move comfortably and successfully into the school years.∎

Preparing for Success in School

There are many things a parent can do in the home that can help to prepare a child for success in school.

Here are six things your child will be expected to do in a classroom setting, and what you can do to help him get ready:

1. Follow simple directions precisely. ("I want you to go to your room and bring me your red sweater.")

2. Wait a reasonable length of time. ("After I have finished washing these dishes, I will read you a story.")

3. Listen to a story and respond to simple questions. ("Listen carefully because I will ask you some questions about the story I'm going to read to you.")

4. Be able to complete a task. ("Pick up all your toys and put them in the toy box.")

5. Raise a hand. ("It's important not to interrupt me when I'm talking to someone else. When you raise your hand, you know I will attend to your questions or your needs as soon as I can.")

6. Take turns. ("I will ask each of you a question: first Mary, then Jim, and then Joe.")

Children who develop these six skills in the home will more easily adjust to the classroom setting.

As a result, they will more likely enjoy their school experiences. ∎

More About Classroom Visits

Some months ago we encouraged parents to become more involved in their child's education by visiting the kindergarten classroom, if possible.

What should parents look for if they make a visit to the classroom? Here are a few important clues:

1. Teacher enthusiasm for what he or she is teaching.

If your presence appears to distract the children from the ongoing lesson, it may be that they find you more stimulating than the teacher.

2. Teacher concern for individualizing instruction.

Individualization allows each pupil to work independently and at his or her own speed.

Bright children can progress rapidly while the "average" learner takes the time necessary to understand, without being penalized for lack of speed.

With individualized education, every student is an achiever!

3. Teacher encouragement of learning partnerships — experiences where children can work cooperatively to seek answers to questions they generate.

Even in kindergarten children discover the scientific principles of gravity and balance, for example, as they join together in construction of unit blocks.

4. Teacher approval of a variety of approaches to learning — intellectual as well as practical.

Some young children must be convinced about the need to learn something difficult or theoretical.

However, abstract learning can be effectively related to meaningful, everyday, interesting experiences.

5. Teacher commitment to the regular observation of each child during learning and play.

Teachers who are good observers try to observe objectively and use the information gained from the observation to better teach and serve each child.

Developing observational skills is not easy because human behavior is complex and any given act may have many different causes.

Teachers who are good observers are neither subjective nor speculative; they refrain from making interpretations or hasty conclusions about the behaviors they observe.

Instead they try to observe objectively — separating interpretation from fact — and use the information gained from the observation to better teach and serve each child.

Regrettably there are some teachers who interpret behavior: "Bill can't concentrate today; he's too tired;" "Amy is such an aggressive girl;" "Jane becomes hysterical when she's frustrated."

How much better it would be if teachers described overt behaviors that any observer can verify: "Billy has been yawning all morning and he sits at his desk without starting one assignment."

"Amy, without asking, grabs and runs away with the toys that other children

have been playing with."

"Jane throws herself on the floor, crying and kicking her feet when she is asked to count out loud from one to ten."

In other words, good teachers observe their pupils individually and in groups, specify the performance of behaviors that they feel are important and keep in mind the context in which they occur without placing a label of interpretation first.

6. Teacher confidence that children can accept and assume responsibility for some of what they learn.

Even in kindergarten and the early grades, children should be expected to make choices about what they learn.

Teacher-constructed activity centers that are pleasant, intellectually challenging, and contain stimulating materials provide children with sufficient alternatives from which to choose and to decide what to do with certain materials and how to use them.

This suggestion does not mean that the teacher is abdicating her role nor that the basic skills are neglected.

But, by offering children opportunities to select what is within their ability and control and within teacher-established limits, they can experiment, use trial and error techniques without penalty, and demonstrate some really productive thinking.

7. Teacher insights into how to help children think creatively.

Listen for how often the teacher employs "open-ended" kinds of questions such as: "How would you do it?" "Can you think of another way?"

"This is what I think; what do you think?" "What is your opinion?" "Tell me what you plan to do." "Why would you do it that way?" ■

More About Coping With Stress

In order for your child to learn to deal effectively with stressful situations, he needs practice facing them now when he has your help and support.

Many people have difficulty dealing with stress because they didn't get enough opportunity to learn about coping when they were young.

Children are often shielded from problems because adults feel they can't handle them. In protecting children from being hurt or upset by stressful life-events, often more harm is done than good.

One of the best guarantees that your child will deal successfully with his problems, now and in the future, is in his feeling confident that he can handle them to his satisfaction.

In coping with stress, as with any skill, competence and confidence are achieved through practice.

Learning to deal constructively with the major and minor challenges that confront a person every day is an important part of becoming a competent and happy human being.

Life is filled with problems, large and small. How they affect you, and how well you cope with them—regardless of whether you solve them or not—sets the tone for much of the rest of your life. People deal with stress in different ways and with differing degrees of success.

The way that you deal with the major crises of your life, as well as with the minor annoyances and irritations of your day-to-day existence, will teach your child attitudes and approaches to his own problems.

By your example, and by giving him opportunities to learn to deal with stress in his early years, you can help him develop problem-solving skills he can use in many ways.

He can adapt these skills to the many large and small stressful situations he will have in his life.

Here are some guidelines for helping your child cope with the various predictable and unexpected stressful life-events that can occur in his life:

1. Your behavior in stressful situations will affect your child's reactions.

If you are able to remain calm, despite feeling upset, this will give him a feeling of security.

This feeling is especially important in very frightening situations, such as a car accident or a natural disaster.

It is also important in the case of more routine problems such as when he has made a mistake and is afraid of disappointing or angering you.

Naturally, you will have your own feelings to contend with, and you should be honest with him about them.

Let him know, for example, that you feel frightened, too, in a bad winter storm, or that you feel sad about leaving behind friends and favorite things when you move.

This knowledge helps him feel more comfortable about such feelings in himself.

Try to teach him by your example to put these feelings into words rather than becoming immobilized by them.

He depends on you for comfort, reassurance, and stability, especially in times of stress.

2. Honest and straightforward information helps your child cope better with stressful situations.

The unknown is much harder to deal with than the known.

For example, if your child knows what to expect in situations holding major changes for his life, then he's better able to handle the changes as they come.

Because he's had time to prepare himself, he feels more confident. Even though he may have little control over the situation,

his knowledge gives him control of his own reactions.

This control is extremely important in highly upsetting life-experiences, such as the long-term illness and expected death of a loved one.

You would not, and could not, tell him when his loved one is expected to die. But you should let him know that she or he is very sick and may not get well.

Explain simply what is wrong and what is being done. Answer any questions he has and encourage him to share his feelings.

Give him all the reassurances you can. Don't give him false hopes but don't leave him without hope, either.

If he, himself, is seriously ill or in danger of dying, then it's even more important that you be open and honest with him so he can share his feelings and finish his "unfinished business" with you.

3. Major changes in your child's life — whether positive or negative — create stress because they require adjustment.

You can help your child make the required adjustment with the least amount of stress by preparing him for the anticipated changes.

Whatever the expected changes—moving to a new home, the arrival of a new baby, a relative coming to live with you, your going out of town without him, family separation or divorce—let him know what to expect.

Involve him in any ways possible in the planning and preparation.

Try to provide as much stability and predictability in other areas of his life as you can.

For example, if you are moving, try to take him to see the new home and neighborhood ahead of time.

Let him know when you'll be leaving, what the actual move will be like, and

continued on page 401

continued from page 400

whatever you know about the new place.

Try to have him meet children in the area before you move so he can look forward to seeing his new friends.

Give him jobs to do during the move such as packing some of his own clothes and toys. Be sure he keeps out at least one special toy, pillow, or other possession to have with him during the transition.

Give him time to say good-bye to friends and favorite places, and ask him if there are any special things he wants to do before he leaves. Be understanding of his feelings. It's tough to uproot and reestablish in a new area.

4. In any stressful situation, your child is likely to behave like a younger child.

This is true in such simple situations as being overtired or hungry, as well as in more obviously stressful situations such as his getting lost or hurting himself.

It's something you should certainly keep in mind in a highly stressful life-event such as a family separation.

For example, if you are going through a divorce, your child may begin to behave in ways similar to how he acts when he's not feeling well.

He may be whiny, clingy, and demanding. He may tire easily and be generally slowed from his usual pace. And, he may have trouble concentrating as well or for as long a time as he can normally.

The stress of the situation drains energy and doesn't leave him enough to cope as well as he usually would.

Understanding this will help you be more patient and supportive with him.

When you are undergoing marital problems in your own life, it's hard to find the reserve energy to give your child, especially when his needs for your attention increase just when you've barely got enough for yourself. But it's important that you

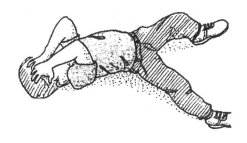

and your mate take the time to sit down together with him to let him know what's going on.

Reassure him that *it is not his fault,* and that both of you still love him. Try to find special time for you and him to spend together.

Encourage him to talk about his feelings and ask you any questions he might have.

Try to let him know how this will change his life as well as what things will stay the same.

Be aware that his needs for love and reassurance, from both of you, are very strong at a time like this.

Don't make him take sides or let any of the negative feelings you may have for each other spill over to him.

It's especially important at such a disruptive time that you provide as much stability in his life as possible.

5. The little frustrations, disappointments, and misunderstandings in your child's life can sometimes be as big a problem for him as more serious problems.

Try to see his problems from his point of view and to take them seriously even when they don't seem important to you.

You'll be better able to help him put them in their proper place if he feels you understand.

There are many adults who are able to rise to the occasion in emergencies, but who

are unable to cope effectively with the small day-to-day irritations that plague us all.

You can help him cope with both large and small problems by your example.

Patiently help him examine and seek solutions to situations that cause him stress. Even if he can't solve a problem, he will grow simply by making the effort.

The kinds of situations that might upset your child include such things as someone hurting his feelings, something not going the way he expected, and breaking or losing a prized possession.

In such situations, the real problem is how he feels about the situation rather than the situation itself.

Once you've really listened to his feelings and allowed him to express his point of view, you can often help him feel better about whatever is causing him stress.

You can help him look at the situation from other points of view, perhaps finding some bright side or some learning for now or the future.

Take a look again at last month's article on "How to Handle Negative Feelings" for more detail on how to help him work through and learn from these feelings.

Here are two resources you might find useful in helping your child cope with stressful life-events.

The Bookfinder is a guide that tells you about children's books dealing with subjects related to the needs and problems common to children, aged two to 15.

It summarizes and categorizes current children's books according to psychological and developmental themes, such as divorce, going to the hospital, fear, sex, death, fighting, nightmares, and running away.

A to Zoo (Carolyn W. Lima and Rebecca L. Thomas, 2010) provides subject access to children's picture books. Both books are available in most library reference centers.■

A Positive Attitude

A positive attitude can lead to better parenting.

In life, two people can look at the same glass: while one sees it as "half full" the other sees it as "help empty." It's just a matter of positive versus negative attitude.

An attitude is something we can work on changing.

If I perceive that my attitudes on life are more negative than positive, I can deliberately make a greater effort to focus on the positive (versus negative) aspects of each situation.

Here are three good reasons for seeking to develop and maintain a more positive attitude as a parent:

1. My attitude helps to determine how I perceive my child's behavior.

For example, if my two-year-old has recently developed the habit of saying "No!" I can perceive that as either:

(a) "My child is developing a healthy sense of autonomy and independence" (a positive attitude) or (b) "My kid is becoming a little monster" (a negative attitude).

2. My attitude helps to determine how I will react.

If I perceive my child's behavior in a positive manner ("He's learning to develop a sense of autonomy and independence"), I'm more likely to react to his behavior in a positive way.

For example, I can show him more love and affection to reassure him that it's natural and okay for him to want to demonstrate greater independence as he gets older.

On the other hand, if I perceive the same behavior in a negative manner, I'm more likely to respond in a negative way ("You'll get a good talking-to from me if you keep saying that!")

3. My attitude will affect how my child will respond.

When a parent can exhibit a positive attitude toward a child's behavior, the child will more likely develop a positive attitude toward life.

Giving him the reassurance that he is loved unconditionally will help him to be more in tune with his world and, therefore, behave more positively.

On the contrary, when a child feels threatened and unloved because of a parent's negative attitude, he is more likely to develop negative feelings toward himself, which ultimately will lead to worse misbehavior.

It's important to note, however that having a positive attitude toward a child's behavior ("I think my child is terrific") is not the same as spoiling a child ("My child can do no wrong").

Whereas a spoiled child will eventually exhibit misbehavior increasingly more demanding of parents, the child who is treated by parents with a positive—yet realistic—attitude will more likely develop a similar, more positive outlook on life.■

Growing Child™

P. O. Box 2505 • W Lafayette, IN 47996
(800) 927-7289
www.GrowingChild.com
© 2012 Growing Child, Inc.

Contributing Authors

Phil Bach, O.D., Ph.D.
Miriam Bender, Ph.D.
Joseph Braga, Ed.D.
Laurie Braga, Ph.D.
George Early, Ph.D.
Carol R. Gestwicki, M.S.
Liam Grimley, Ph.D.
Robert Hannemann, M.D., F.A.A.P.
Sylvia Kottler, M.S.
Bill Peterson, Ph.D.

Simple Science

Here are some activities related to wind and water that will challenge your child's thinking skills.

Wind

In which direction will an object move? When children blow on a tissue, a ping-pong ball or another light object, they will discover that they are unable to blow anything toward themselves.

Thus things move in the direction of the wind.

From which direction does the wind come? Wet a finger and hold it in the air.

Children will determine the wind's direction from the fact that the wind comes from the direction of the side of the finger which dries faster and feels colder.

What else can you do in your everyday observations to find out what else the wind does?

You can see that it holds things up — kites, planes, birds. It also can blow things away — paper, clothes, leaves.

Water

How will objects glide through water? Which ones will move the easiest and the fastest?

To explore speed, direction and movement in water, assemble a variety of items to float— air-filled plastic bottles, coffee cans, wood cubes, corks, and foam.

Do size or shape influence the ease and speed of movement? What happens when you make waves?

Process of Learning

Simple activities such as these stimulate your child's curiosity, which, in turn, stimulates his thinking.

You will increase his learning and fun if you ask him to predict what will happen each time and then discuss with him what did happen and why.■

Family Chores: A Good Way to Develop Responsibility

How can you help your child develop a better sense of responsibility as early in life as possible?

By now you have undoubtedly become aware that responsibility is not an inborn natural trait of young children!

It is learned slowly, often painstakingly, over a long period of time.

Family chores—routine jobs around the house and yard—can be an excellent way to help a child develop responsibility.

The primary purpose is to give the child an opportunity to grow and mature as a responsible human being.

It must be stressed that reducing the parents' workload is not the purpose of involving a young child in family chores.

Most parents can attest that assigning family chores to a young child seldom, if ever, reduces their own workload.

On the contrary, it usually results in more work for the parent!

Unfortunately, in many homes today, children are not helping with family chores as much as they once did. There are a number of reasons for this change.

For one thing, children today have more choices and distractions—television, video games, and computers, for example—with which to occupy their time.

Also, in homes where both parents are working, there is little time to assign and supervise family chores.

Furthermore, with so few opportunities for parent-child interactions, parents

don't want to spend that time in nagging and scolding. Hence they don't require their child to engage in family chores.

By not being involved in family chores, however, these children are deprived of a most effective way to develop responsibility.

There are other parents who, on the contrary, impose a rigid, regimented schedule of chores for each child, only to discover that this becomes a source of great disillusionment and disappointment for the parents and a source of deep resentment and frustration for the child.

Parents soon learn that assigning chores to a child does not automatically, magically, teach responsibility.

Expecting too much maturity from a young child can be counterproductive.

The child who is overwhelmed will quickly develop feelings of helplessness and inferiority. ("I will never measure up to what my parents expect from me.")

When constantly told that he is behaving

irresponsibly, that message will eventually become a self-fulfilling prophecy.

Responsibility is best learned in a happy home environment in which parents have realistic expectations based on their child's developmental level.

Family chores should be a normal part of every child's home life.

Here are some constructive ways in which family chores can be used to help a child develop responsibility:

1. Choose tasks which are developmentally appropriate for your child.

A five-year-old, for example, may enjoy sweeping the floor with a small broom because it enables him to use his newly-acquired motor coordination skills.

He also enjoys being assigned to do something he previously thought only adults could do.

2. Develop a system for assigning chores.

One way of assigning chores is for the parents to make a list of all the chores that need to be performed.

Then rotate assignments provided they are appropriate for each person's age and skill level.

Another way is for the family as a whole to develop the list of chores together.

The chores can then be ranked and assigned by the group according to skill level and amount of time involved.

continued on page 404

continued from page 403

3. Involve each individual as much as possible in the decision-making.

Whatever method of assignment is used, children generally feel more positively about doing chores when they have input into the process.

A child with good organizational skills, for example, may volunteer to help sort the laundry, set the table, or unpack the groceries.

Another child, who prefers outdoor jobs, may volunteer to wash the car or clean the doghouse.

A task that is unpleasant to one child may not be unpleasant to another—if his interests are taken into consideration.

4. Be a good role model.

The most effective way to develop responsibility in a young child is for parents to be good role models of responsible behavior.

Furthermore, children are happier doing their assigned chores when they see that all family members are expected to help.

5. Give guidance when it is needed.

Assigning chores to develop responsibility does not mean you have to let the child sink or swim on his own.

Parents need to provide some guidance and support, especially for younger children.

If necessary, give a demonstration—but don't take over the whole task even though you know it would be done better and more quickly if you did it yourself!

It may be necessary to break a task into several parts. For example, a five-year-old cannot fully comprehend the assignment, "Tidy your room." But he can understand a more specific directive, such as: "Pick up your dirty clothes and put them in the hamper."

6. Give reminders.

Young children do not have the same attention span as adults. They are more easily distracted.

Distractions are often what makes an otherwise boring job fun and interesting for a child. Hence little reminders to get back on task may be needed from time to time.

It is usually best to express a reminder in the form of a question. ("What is it that you are supposed to be doing right now?") Avoid nagging as it will elicit a negative reaction in your child.

7. Provide variety in assignments.

Children enjoy variety in their lives. A child may not want to be assigned the same task, such as taking out the trash, week after week.

Young children usually prefer some form of rotation of jobs. Furthermore, they often like to explore different ways to perform the same task.

8. Be generous with praise and encouragement.

Giving praise and encouragement helps a child develop a sense of competence and enhances self-esteem.

A five-year-old doesn't judge "quality work" the same way an adult would. His idea of "excellence" is different from that of his parents.

So don't expect or demand perfection. Instead, praise the child's effort.

Focus on the process, not just the end product. ("I see you're working very hard at your job.")

9. Make family chores a positive experience for your child.

It's a good idea if everyone works at the same time, such as Saturday morning.

More will be learned by your child when family chores are perceived as a positive experience rather than a negative one.

For that reason it is best, as far as possible, to avoid criticism. Imperfections should be ignored until your child has gained a certain level of confidence in doing a job.

Correction is best provided in the form of help and encouragement. ("Would you like me to show you how I would do that?" rather than "That's not the right way to do that.")

10. Build family team spirit.

Young children generally do not like to be alone when given a job to do. They prefer to be part of a group project.

For that reason it's a good idea to assemble the whole family for the assignment of chores. In that way all are made to feel they are part of a team effort in which each one must do his or her full share.

After all the work is done, the whole family can also participate in the "tour of inspection" to admire the collective effort of all involved.

Each child's self-esteem will be enhanced when the child is praised in the presence of other family members.

Furthermore, with a team approach, family solidarity and cohesiveness will be greatly strengthened.

In summary, family chores can play a significant role in a young child's development.

Parents need to choose tasks that are realistic for their child's ability level, adjust their expectations to that level, and praise their child's effort even when it is short of perfection.

When used in this manner, family chores become an enjoyable way for a young child to learn to become a more responsible person.■

Ten Roadblocks to Communication

Here are some roadblocks which can interfere with parent-child interaction and communication:

• Overdramatizing: "That's the worst thing I ever saw."

• Providing criticism instead of feedback: "You didn't do a very good job."

• Being too vague rather than specific: "You're acting immaturely."

• Implying motives: "I know you did that because you're ...."

• Belittling: "Look here, little smarty baby."

• Diagnosing: "What's wrong with you is ..."

• Using sarcasm: "Why don't you burn down the house while you're at it?"

• Bringing up past history: "You're behaving just like your older brother did."

• Giving broken-record messages: "I've told you a thousand times not to do that."

• Giving a double message: "You did a good job BUT ..."

Do you find that you have used some of these types of roadblocks? It's not easy to avoid them.

Being aware of what some of them are is a first step toward improving communication.

After awareness, the second step is to try to avoid using roadblocks altogether.

The third step is to communicate with your child in a positive manner.

That will be better for your child and will more likely accomplish what you desire.

Next month we will discuss ten ways to enhance communication with your child.■

On Being a Good Parent

Nobody ever said that parenting would be easy. Being a good parent is even more difficult!

Here are six guidelines to help you put into practice some principles of good parenting that you probably already know but for which you may need an occasional reminder:

1. Be consistent in your enforcement of rules.

Be certain that your rules have these characteristics: They must be clearly defined, reasonable, and enforceable.

Rules in the home help children feel more secure and comfortable when they are faced later in life with rules in school and community.

A seven-year study done by the National Institute of Mental Health indicates that self-confident children who succeeded in their undertakings usually came from homes in which there were rules that were reasonable, consistent, and enforced with affection.

2. Permit children to make mistakes and even fail sometimes.

Children learn by doing, rather than by

passively absorbing the experiences of others.

Making mistakes is one basis for future independence, self-direction, and intelligent decision-making.

3. Keep promises.

When children know that they can anticipate consequences, they are being helped to develop an understanding of cause-effect relationships.

4. Resist the temptation to over-organize.

Don't over-structure a child's whole day

with lessons, sports, and other activities. Children need time to be leisurely and to enjoy unstructured play.

5. Maintain a sense of humor.

When something interferes with the daily routine, try to see a funny side of the situation.

For example, when there are toys, clothes, or other things left about randomly, gather them into a locked box and charge a "fee" (such as a kiss on your cheek!) for later retrieval of an item.

If the bathroom becomes a mess, then draw a sad face on the mirror.

Ah, but when things look improved, don't forget to reinforce with a happy smile!

6. Take care of yourself.

It's important for parents to take care of their own health and psychological needs.

A parent who is overworked or overstressed will less likely be able to implement the above recommendations.

Hence, taking care of oneself—with adequate rest, leisure time, and proper nutrition—is also an important part of being a good parent.■

Getting Ready for Mathematics

How high can your child count? To five? To ten? Higher?

Most five-year-olds learn to say numbers up to about 13. But this doesn't necessarily improve their understanding of numbers. It's as though they were reading words in a language that they don't understand. They know the symbol but not its meaning.

Children under the age of seven usually have limited understanding of mathematical concepts.

This is because their minds aren't ready yet to process information in an abstract form. They think only in terms of what they actually experience with their senses.

You can help your child get ready for mathematics through some simple, real-life experiences.

Mathematics is an important part of our day-to-day lives. For example, something as ordinary as getting dressed or setting the table involves math.

Matching a foot to a sock and a shoe, or putting the right number of place settings for the number of people to be served, requires an understanding that one item of one kind can only be matched with the same number of another kind: You don't put two feet in one sock, two shoes on one foot, or set two forks for three people.

This point seems obvious, but this simple rule, called "one-to-one correspondence," is the basis of much more complex mathematical relationships.

By becoming aware of the many opportunities your daily life offers for using math, you can help your child learn the basics she will need to get her ready for arithmetic and other kinds of mathematics in school.

Here are some guidelines to help you:

1. Give your child practice counting real objects.

Unlike mere recital of numbers, counting real objects teaches a child about the meaning of numbers. You can count

anything, anywhere, any time.

For example, while you're waiting in the grocery line, you and your child can count the number of people waiting in front or behind you, the number of cans you're buying, the number of people with babies, and so on.

Typically, most four-year-olds can count at least three things correctly. Most five-year-olds can count at least five. This means they can match up the numbers with the objects.

Beyond a certain number, they simply recite the numbers they know without specific reference to the actual number of objects.

A good way to help your child practice counting correctly so that she understands the meaning of the numbers is to have her use objects she can touch, having her put her finger on each object as she says the number.

2. Give your child practice connecting numbers with the quantities they specify.

Take any opportunity you see in your daily life to ask her to show you one of this, two of that, three of this one, and so on.

Don't expect her to be able to correctly identify more than three to five items. For example:

• Hold up your fingers, and ask her how many she sees.

• Ask her how many eyes, ears, arms, and legs her doll has. Have her count to check.

• Get her a set of Cuisenaire rods, or make a set out of cardboard.

Cut ten pieces. The one piece should be one inch square, the two piece the size of two ones, the three piece the size of three ones, and so on up to ten.

Have her color, and print the correct number on each piece. Give them to her to play with, showing her that if she puts two ones together, she would have a two, and so on.

As she gets older, you can make up more of the smaller pieces to help her understand about adding and subtracting. For now, they will give her a concrete idea of what numbers "look like" and what they stand for.

3. Give your child practice using number, size, and quantity words such as "one half," "big," and "more."

Make a point of using them yourself. Ask your child questions so that she has to use these words in her answers. For example:

• At mealtime, ask her if she wants a lot or a little, less than this or more than this, and so on.

Cut an apple in half and say, "Here's one half for you and one half for me." Ask her how many pieces she wants, if she wants a big piece or a little piece.

• When she's helping you around the house, ask her to bring you three pieces of paper, put the can on the shelf that's got the most room, use a little more soap on the dishes, and so on.

• Give her a choice of three groups of pennies to take shopping: One with one, one with three, and one with six pennies.

Ask, "Which one do you want?" "Can you buy more with this?" "Can you buy as much with this as with this?" "Which one can you buy the most with?"

continued on page 407

continued from page 406

• Show her a picture of herself and others. Ask her, "Who is the tallest?" "Who is the shortest?" "Are you as tall as ... ?" "Is ... shorter than you?"

• Let her help you cook: Show her how to measure out two tablespoons, mix in one-half cup, and so on.

Give her the measuring cups and spoons and a pan of dried beans to experiment with — to see how many teaspoons in a tablespoon, how many half cups in a cup, and so on.

4. Give your child practice learning about the relationship between volume and quantity.

How many times have you chosen a container for leftovers only to find that it's the wrong size?

This task is just one practical application of an important mathematical concept: the relationship between the capacity of a container (volume) and the amount that will fill that container (quantity).

Many adults have trouble estimating what amount different sized and shaped containers will hold. It's a skill, like any other, that requires practice.

You can help your child develop this skill using items you have around the house:

• Give her several different shaped containers that hold the same amount — a pan, a jar, and a plastic container which each hold a quart. Ask her which is the biggest, which one will hold more.

Then give her some macaroni, dried beans, or similar material to put in the containers. Have her fill one container. Then ask her what she thinks will happen when she puts its contents into one of the other containers. Let her try it.

• Encourage her to repeat this game of filling, emptying, and comparing, using different materials and different sized/shaped containers.

For example, use sand or water in clear containers so she can see how far an amount that fills a short, wide container will go in a tall, thin one. (The bathtub or outdoors is a good place for this.)

Also, try using blocks or some other uniform-sized item so she can count how many go in one container compared with another.

• Let her help you with jobs that require estimation of how much will fit in a particular space: Choosing a container for leftovers, putting cans away in a small amount of shelf space, finding the right sized box to hold a present for someone, and the like.

Don't expect the "right answers," even when the evidence is right before her eyes. She needs both practice and maturation before she'll fully understand the relationship between volume and quantity.

5. Give your child practice comparing sizes. There are many experiences in your daily life that you can use to help her learn to compare size. For example:

• When you're doing the laundry, ask her whose clothes are bigger, hers or yours.

Get her help in putting all the big towels in one pile and the small ones in another, or in separating all the baby's small clothes from her larger ones.

• When you're shopping, ask her to hand you the larger of two boxes or the smaller of two cans of a certain brand.

• When you unpack and put away the groceries, let her estimate if an item is too big, too small, or just right for a shelf before trying it.

• When putting her toys away on a shelf, have her try lining them up from the smallest to the largest or put all the small ones on one shelf and the big ones on another in order of their size.

• Introduce her to the words and ideas of "long" and "short," "thick" and "thin," "heavy" and "light," and so on as more specific ways of looking at big and little, large and small.

6. Give your child practice comparing quantity. An important part of understanding numbers is learning to see differences in amount.

At first she will be able to distinguish between one and many or between a small amount and a large amount.

With time and practice, she'll learn to put things in order from the least amount to the most. This kind of distinguishing is the conceptual basis of counting.

Give her a snack of raisins. Divide it into two piles, one with just a few, the other with noticeably more.

Ask her which has more, which has less. Add some from the large pile to the small one and ask again.

Try spreading the ones in the small pile out in a line while keeping the large pile all bunched together in a smaller space. Now ask her which has more. Her answer may surprise you.

Her thinking at this age is based on how things look to her. So she may answer that the one that's spread out has more, since that's how it appears.

Have her count each group; give her help if she needs it. Ask again which group has more.

It will take maturation and practice with this and other kinds of experiences using different quantities of materials arranged in different ways for her to learn that an amount stays the same even when it looks different. Try to find ways in your day-to-day life to give her more practice in comparing different quantities.

Each day is full of situations in which mathematics plays a part. Understanding and using mathematics is necessary to cope with day-to-day life. Learn to notice and use these opportunities to help your child get ready for mathematics in school.

Helping her to develop a positive attitude while learning basic math concepts will benefit her later classroom learning.■

Developing Visual-spatial Abilities

You can help your child develop her visual-spatial abilities with the following simple exercises:

1. Tracing lines that are vertical, horizontal, diagonal, as well as curved:

2. Recognizing a sequence and replicating it:

Form pattern:

▲●◼▲●◼

Space pattern:

●● ● ●● ●

3. Recognizing her own first name in print or writing:

Nancy

4. Copying patterns (such as form and space patterns in #2 above), as well as copying letters (such as the letters in her own first name) and numbers:

A B C D E F

1 2 3 4 5

5. Printing or writing her first name from memory:

All of these skills will be useful for later learning in school.◼

The Family Table

The family table is where people come together to share a meal.

It is also a meeting place where children learn to communicate—to talk, to behave, take turns, to be polite, not interrupt. These are all good lessons for life.

A body of research supports the conclusion that families who have a family table and eat there together on a regular basis have children who do better in school and are less likely to smoke, drink or take drugs.

One study shows that eating meals with their family was a stronger predictor of academic success than whether children lived with one or both parents.

Families may not have money, education or a spouse but they do have it in their power to eat with their kids.

Some families do not have a table on which they eat. Instead they eat in front of the television, and often family members eat at different times.

For other families, their meals feature different formats but have several things in common.

They talk, share joys, achievements and disappointments. Each person—children included—is expected to participate and contribute.

At one family table, if the child had nothing to say, he was expected to go to the encyclopedia and bring back a point of interest.

In time, the children came to the table prepared. Their bit of information added to the conversation.

These are the habits our children will take with them and most likely merge with other traditions as they marry, have children, and eat together around their family table.

Mealtime used to be so important in some homes that the doorbell and the telephone went unanswered.

Today this would mean no TV, cell phones or other distractions during mealtime. The family dinner is an eyeball-to-eyeball, ear-to-ear, heart-to-heart event.

Laughter is the best dinnertime music, and the atmosphere at a family table should be that laughter is welcome.

Everyone at the table should feel free to talk, to contribute to the conversation, and encouraged to listen.

This is also a good time to pass on those family traditions and stories from your childhood.

When the meal is over and the table cleared, use it for games and puzzles. This is your chance to be a role model for your children. Let them learn from you.

Each child wants to share his or her days with the most important people in their lives—their parents—other relatives and adults.

They want to be seen and to be heard. They want to be rewarded for their success by sharing their experiences with their family.

Begin having conversation and dinner together around your family table. Give your children the gift of growing up as a child in a family that cares.◼

Growing Child™

P. O. Box 2505 • W Lafayette, IN 47996
(800) 927-7289
www.GrowingChild.com
© 2012 Growing Child, Inc.

Contributing Authors
Phil Bach, O.D., Ph.D.
Miriam Bender, Ph.D.
Joseph Braga, Ed.D.
Laurie Braga, Ph.D.
George Early, Ph.D.
Carol R. Gestwicki, M.S.
Liam Grimley, Ph.D.
Robert Hannemann, M.D., F.A.A.P.
Sylvia Kottler, M.S.
Bill Peterson, Ph.D.

Almost Six Years Old

Now that your child is almost six years old, it's a good time to review some of the developmental characteristics for this age.

(1) Most children of this age show an intense interest in what is happening HERE and NOW.

Questions are practical and persistent: "How does it work?" "What do you do that for?" "Why is it like this?" The child is involved in solving issues of the real world.

Essentially most play activities help generate new knowledge. For example, pretend play is now conducted with serious duplication of people and life, unlike earlier pretend play that assumed a quality of magic or invention.

(2) The desire to make something "real" can be seen in the child's play with water, textures, clay and blocks.

All products must be useful—water is for washing; textures are sorted for placemats, potholders, or napkins; clay is modeled for dishes, pots, or vases; blocks are used for villages containing tunnels, tracks, buildings, or streets.

The love of woodworking can be seen in boys and girls who can handle simple tools efficiently when taught.

(3) Gross motor development is sufficiently mature at this age to allow children to enjoy activities that are airborne—climbing ropes and rope ladders, using stilts, jungle gym and trapeze bar.

At the same time activities that are close to the ground are also enjoyed—roller skating, although not thoroughly coordinated, is one example. Box scooters, coaster wagons and even full size scooters are favorites.

(4) Fine motor development is refined enough to provide pleasure from painting, drawing, lacing, stringing, coloring, cutting and pasting.

Again the desire for realism is apparent in the child's product that must be completed in a reasonable time. It also has value in showing off to others.

While handedness is fairly well established, there are times when the use of the preferred hand is not yet consistent.

Sitting still for extended periods of time may produce a lot of movement or scratching, stretching, wriggling, and pulling on clothing.

(5) Social growth is reflected in the imitation of adult models. Praise is often sought by the child. Criticism, even when deserved, can be devastating.

The attraction of television and computers is strong. Children at this age particularly want every item they see advertised.

Family spirit is strong. An almost six-year-old enjoys such things as helping in the kitchen or planning a trip.

Sometimes the people with whom the activity is enjoyed are more important than the "how" or "where." Favorite trips generally begin with the child's interests—the fire or police station, dairy farm, railroad station, state parks.

(6) Enthusiasm for academic learning can be seen in the child's interest in numbers and the alphabet. Clocks and calendars are captivating.

While the four-year-old wanted you to print his name for him, a five-year-old wants to print his own name.

Copying intricate patterns requires enormous eye-hand control that is not always present. Nevertheless the effort of a five-year-old to achieve and make a good copy is generally deliberate.■

An Indoor Ecology Garden

Now is a good time to teach your child about the wonders of nature by helping him grow some plants from seed. You will need a non-porous plastic egg carton, fine gravel, potting soil, seeds.
1. First, sprinkle a small amount of fine gravel in the bottom of each section of the egg carton.
2. Fill each section about 3/4 full of potting soil and sprinkle a little water in each one.
3. Have your child make a hole in the soil with his finger and then place a seed in the hole. Cover the hole and sprinkle more water into each section.
4. Place the egg carton in a sunny place.
5. Water when the soil feels or looks dry.
6. In a few days watch for signs of the plant growing.■

The stages of parenthood

I live in the part of the country that was ravaged by hurricanes one summer.

My granddaughter Lila was well aware of the damage when she visited, murmuring, "Poor trees," when we drove down roads now spoiled by the devastation.

Later in a conversation, she heard me refer to "Charley." "Who's Charley?" she asked. "Oh, Charley is the name of the hurricane," I replied.

A look of total horror crossed her little face. "Why would anybody name a hurricane?" she asked, looking alarmed at such adult nonsense in giving a friendly name to something so unlike a pet.

I laughed, and explained, of course. But later it got me thinking about the different roles played by adults in children's lives. As they develop, children need such different things from their parents.

Often we are so busy considering our children's development that we do not reflect on the stages of parent development that we experience.

Those stages are largely responsive, arriving as we perceive the varying needs of our children as they grow.

Ellen Galinsky wrote a book titled <u>The Six Stages of Parenthood</u> in which she outlined a six-stage model to describe parent development.

Let me describe these six stages of parenthood briefly, and encourage you to consider the changes you have already embraced, and those that lie ahead.

The six stages of parenthood include:

1. The Image-making stage or the prenatal period. This is the time when parents begin to consider who they will be as parents, and what the parent-child relationship will be like.

2. The Nurturing stage during the first two years, a period of attachment and questioning of the realities of parenthood, vs. that earlier image.

This is the stage when parents almost lose sight of life beyond the parent-child pair.

3. The Authority stage when the child is between two and four-five years, and parents decide what kind of authority to be. Decisions made here will affect the course of future parent and child relationships.

4. The Interpretive stage from the child's preschool years to the approach of adolescence, where parents are interpreting the world to their children.

This was the stage of development drawn forth by Lila's question about the hurricane.

5. The Interdependent stage during the teen years, where parents form new relationships with "almost-adult" children. Parents' roles must change as their children assume more control of their decisions.

6. The Departure stage when children leave home and parents evaluate the whole of their parenting experience. Why is it important to consider the idea of stages of parenthood?

One reason is to realize that your life as a parent will be at least as dynamic and changing as the lives of your growing children. Learning new skills and emphasizing different roles will be a part of this life you have chosen.

Just as with children's development, earlier stages lay the foundations for what will follow for parents.

The focus of those of you with youngest children is the loving attachment that will allow them to accept the limits that come with the Authority stage.

The security of those limits will direct them to you as the Interpreter, and give you both the guidance and trust needed for negotiating the last two stages successfully.

What a grand journey you are on, together with your children.

Read more about these six stages in Ellen Galinsky's <u>The Six Stages of Parenthood.</u> (1987)∎

Ten Ways to Enhance Communication

In previous generations, people didn't have to worry about good communication skills because they had plenty of time to talk to one another.

With so many changes in today's fast-paced world—such as greater mobility, television, radio, computers—many things can interfere with good interaction between parent and child.

Here are some ways to enhance communication with your child.

• **Be an attentive listener.** When your child has something important to tell you, give her your full undivided attention, maintaining good eye contact.

Even if the topic seems trivial to you, it may be very important to your child.

• **Be patient.** Even though you may want to interject an immediate automatic response to what your child is telling you, it is best to be patient and let her first finish what she has to say.

Otherwise you may inhibit any further elaboration on her part.

• **Paraphrase.** It's helpful to repeat to your child, in your own words, what you think you heard her say.

This will avoid unnecessary misunderstanding and will give your child an opportunity to clarify what she wants to tell you.

• **Be sensitive to your child's body language.** Attend not only to your child's words, but also to her body language, such as nervous behavior, facial expression, or other signs of her inner feelings.

• **Focus on one topic.** When you have something important to say to your child, focus on only one issue at a time.

It's better to convey a clear message on one topic than to confuse your child by addressing several issues at one time.

• **Be brief.** Keep your message as short as possible because young children have a rather limited attention span.

• **Keep your message simple.** Use simple words—one or two syllable words—which your child understands. Use no more than 9 or 10 words in a sentence.

• **Be positive.** Even when your child says or does something that greatly displeases you, try not to focus on the negative behavior. Focus instead on its opposite, positive behavior that you wish to instill in your child.

• Deal with the here and now. The concepts of time which children have are different from those of adults.

Children tend to live in the present rather than in the past or future. Re-opening old wounds from the past will only get in the way of what you want to communicate right now.

• **Be aware of your own body language.** When talking to your child, be aware of the nonverbal messages your body may be communicating.

With good eye contact, for example, your message will be conveyed more effectively.

Young children attend more to your facial expression and to the emotional tone of your voice than to the actual words you use.

Good communication between parent and child becomes very important at this stage of a young child's life.■

Form Perception

As children deal with their spatial world, they are constantly dealing with figure-ground relationships, that is, a central figure against a background.

To focus on the figure in the figure-ground relationship, the child must be able to change attention from figure to ground and back again without losing the relationship.

For most of us this process is so automatic we cannot imagine it ever being a problem.

However, when our perception of form is deliberately interfered with, we may have some hesitation before discerning the figure.

For example, it may take a few minutes before the parts of the figure in this article are sufficiently integrated for you to perceive a teddy bear.

The child entering school is expected to perform essentially the same operations for the recognition of letters, numbers, and graphics.

The child is required to hold in mind the parts of the figure while integrating the total form.

Customarily adults do not attend to each and every element of a letter or word. Rather we use a few cues for word recognition.

We do this efficiently and effortlessly because we have learned how to do it automatically. For young children, it's a skill that is developed gradually.■

The Three Rs of Childrearing

Although we're familiar with the 3 R's from school, there are three different R's that are useful ideas for parents of young children.

Let's begin by considering the importance of routine in the lives of young children and their parents.

If someone asked you what comes to mind when you hear the word "routine," you might associate some less positive words: unvaried, tedious, boring, everyday work.

Routine often implies for us some of the less attractive aspects of daily life.

You might be surprised to consider that routine means very different things to young children. For our children, routine means predictability, security, consistency, and certainty.

Life from the perspective of a baby or young child must often be enormously confusing.

People appear and disappear in some random way, and children's activities are interrupted, often without warning.

If there is a pattern to living in this world, the little ones are often hard pressed to discover it.

Think about living in this chaotic way. Surely it would increase apprehension and uncertainty if we never were sure what would happen next.

One of the most important components to personality development in the first year is a sense of trust, believing that the world is a good place, with helpful people.

Babies develop this sense of trust as they experience the rhythmic pattern of expressing a need, such as hunger, and having that need satisfied.

As needs are met reliably and predictably, babies come to believe they will be cared for. Studies show that babies who have received consistent responses cry less and less, believing that help will come.

In teaching desirable behaviors to young children, we know that repetition is an important factor. When the morning pattern involves some time to snuggle in bed, then getting dressed, eating breakfast, and tooth brushing, for example, children develop habits of behaving.

They know what to do without having to be told, and proceed with confidence and without opposition.

Established, familiar routines allow children to participate with confidence and without resistance.

So when you are tempted to dismiss the humdrum sameness of routine, see it from your child's point of view: "This is the way we always do it."

Let's move on from this first principle and consider the second of the three R's: responsibility.

When parents are asked what characteristics they hope to see in their children twenty years from now, they almost always include the idea of being responsible people.

So, what do we do to instill this trait?

One answer is that we give young children responsibilities so that they can experience for themselves how to be accountable for a required activity. Actually, real work is extremely appealing to children who enjoy participating along with adults.

Too often, in the hectic pace of today's families, it seems quicker for adults to just do the jobs themselves. And let's face it: young children's standards of cleanliness may not be up to our own. (Basic principle: acceptance of what they can do now.)

But look at what is being lost by not involving the children. Preschool teachers complain that children are not used to cleaning up after themselves or handling other responsibilities as parents are doing it all for them.

The most unfortunate aspect to this is that children are not getting the opportunity to see themselves as competent or as contributing members of the community they live in.

When family patterns have been long established where Mom or Dad do it all, it is so much harder to get children involved when they are older and have other interests

Responsibility also means being responsible for one's actions. Two guidance strategies help young children learn this important idea.

One is the use of contingencies: making a desirable result dependent on completion of a task for which the child is responsible. "When you have picked up your toys, then we can blow bubbles outside."

The responsibility for work first is clearly given to the child, and there is no ambiguity about this expectation.

Logical consequences, as named by psychologist Rudolph Dreikurs, also help children learn to take responsibility for their actions.

Devised by the adult, who supports the child in following through, a logical consequence is a necessary result of the child's action.

If you have made a mess, spilling milk for example, then here's the sponge to wipe it up.

If you have hurt your little brother and made him cry, let's think of something you can do to help him feel better.

By taking direct action, children learn the important idea that they alone are responsible for their own actions and the results.

This is an important concept that is part of the slow process of developing self-control.

Logical consequences teach without punishing because they are directly related to the child's actions.

It might not seem like much in the grand

continued on page 413

scheme of things, but being responsible for setting the table and for wiping up spills are some of the small steps that go toward helping develop that characteristic of responsibility. And without it, neither you nor your child will ever be comfortable with the idea of his/her leaving home.

Now we're ready to think about the power of reinforcement.

First, a question: How do you feel when someone notices that you cooked an especially good meal, or did a great job on the last report you had to write?

It probably gives you a good feeling, as well as increases your feeling of competence.

Such attention is known as reinforcement, and studies show that reinforcement strengthens behavior as well as increasing the probability that the behavior will recur—more good meals for your family or effective reports for your boss.

Using this same principle with children's behavior, it makes sense to "catch children being good", to pay attention to desirable behaviors that we want to see repeated.

Yet many times we pass up opportunities to do so. Often when children are behaving well, we just go about our business, glad of the positive actions that free us from having to step in to stop or change less desirable behavior.

So when Sarah is playing nicely with her little brother while you prepare dinner, you're so happy for the peaceful time that you just proceed on.

What's happening here? In fact, Sarah's positive behavior is being ignored rather than reinforced. Learning theorists tell us that the fastest way to see a behavior disappear is to consistently give it no reinforcement.

A much more effective action would be to say: "Gee, Sarah, I really appreciate your playing with Bryan while I'm fixing dinner. It is helpful to me."

Sarah's positive behavior has not gone un-

noticed, and is more likely to be repeated as she now thinks of herself as a helpful person. (Notice also that the reinforcement is specific and sincere, not the vague "Good job" that has become part of parents' vocabulary.)

There is something else to consider about reinforcement. It is also possible, unintentionally, to reinforce negative behaviors, the kind that we would rather not see again, but certainly will if they are reinforced.

So the child who receives repeated attention for hitting his brother is more likely to continue hitting. Hard to believe, but negative attention is also a reinforcer.

More effective parenting behavior is a

quick stopping of the negative behavior, and redirection to a more positive action, which can then receive positive reinforcement.

Reinforcement is a powerful tool that can work for parents with long-term effects.

Children see themselves more positively, and act according to that self-concept. Parents too feel more successful.

It may require changing a mindset, especially when we have become accustomed to noticing behavior that is negative.

An interesting observation is that life becomes more pleasant for everyone involved when parents spend more time "catching children being good."■

Checklist for Helping Brain Development

There is increasing evidence that a young child's environment plays an important part in brain development.

Providing a child with appropriate developmental activities and experiences—such as the ones we suggest in *Growing Child*—can lead to an increase in brain cell connections.

By so doing, the child is not only using existing brain cells but these increased connections can actually reshape the brain and enhance the brain's power to learn and remember new material.

Here is a short checklist to serve as a reminder of what parents can do for their child's brain development.

• Provide opportunities for your child to explore and gather information both in your home and outside the home.

• Give your child many opportunities

to develop new skills, such as sorting, sequencing, comparing, and discovering relationships, such as cause and effect.

• If your child doesn't know how to get started on a new task, you can provide some guided rehearsal, but have him become actively involved as soon as possible.

He will learn better as an active participant than as a passive observer.

• Don't push if your child's behavior indicates that a task is too difficult. Back off to a simpler task at which your child can experience success.

• Avoid disapproval, mockery or teasing, if your child makes a mistake.

• Talk to your child in simple language to explain new words and concepts.

• Give lots of praise and encouragement for good effort and celebrate new accomplishments.■

Dealing With Anger

Rules and threats parents make when they are angry usually prove very hard for either the parents or the child to live with.

Parents who are angry sometimes shoot from the hip and say things like: "Just for that you can't go out and play for a month," or "That does it. I'm never going to talk to you again."

When things like that are said, children are often confused and parents are sorry they said them. The whole process ends up doing nothing to improve or change the child's behavior.

None of this means that parents can't ever get angry. Even the best parents get angry at times and say and do hasty things.

Children can often be irritating, and they sometimes seem to be provoking their parents deliberately.

Such behavior would try the patience of a saint. But it is best if the parent's anger can be aimed at the particular act or behavior of the moment rather than at the child as a whole.

That will make it clearer to the child exactly what it is that has made the parents angry and disapproving.

It is also much better if the anger is expressed in words rather than by hitting.

Although parents may occasionally feel like hitting their children they must realize that spanking is not a good way of helping children to learn what is right and wrong.

It may relieve the parent's anger, but it doesn't really tell the child what the problem behavior is.

When parents hit children, they are in danger of inflicting real harm on the child. Getting and acting out of control is no way for parents to help children learn to control themselves.

Child abuse, the doing of serious, often permanent, violent damage to children by their parents or other caregivers is being increasingly recognized as a major concern.

The problem is that much of the damage is done by parents who get in a terrible rage.

They convince themselves that all they are doing is helping to discipline their children to make them better behaved.

People who get violent with their children were often themselves beaten as children.

It is imperative, then, if we hope to cut down on the amount of violence in future generations, that we reduce the amount of physical punishment inflicted on children now.

In fact, if we were to make a rule about it, it would be safer and better NEVER to hit children at all.

What is really needed at such times is a cooling off period for both parent and child.

The parent may need time to withdraw to a quiet place to think things over.

Sending children to their rooms will provide both parent and child with an opportunity to calm down before deciding on any further action to be taken. ∎

(Excerpted and revised from "Your Child From One to Six," Richard H. Granger, MD, HEW publication.)

Growing Child™

P. O. Box 2505 • W Lafayette, IN 47996
(800) 927-7289
www.GrowingChild.com
© 2012 Growing Child, Inc.

Contributing Authors
Phil Bach, O.D., Ph.D.
Miriam Bender, Ph.D.
Joseph Braga, Ed.D.
Laurie Braga, Ph.D.
George Early, Ph.D.
Carol R. Gestwicki, M.S.
Liam Grimley, Ph.D.
Robert Hannemann, M.D., F.A.A.P.
Sylvia Kottler, M.S.
Bill Peterson, Ph.D.

Visual-motor Coordination

These are some ways in which you can help to develop your child's visual-motor coordination skills:

1. Encourage your child to experiment, scribble, and draw with a variety of media (crayons, fingerpaint, clay, play dough, for example).

These media allow free movements without expecting or requiring a specific end product.

2. Get your child to cut and paste with different colored paper, yarn, pictures, and other suitable items.

3. Provide opportunities for your child to play card games which involve matching letters, numbers, pictures, and shapes.

4. Encourage your child to engage in creative play, building with blocks, Lego™, Tinker Toys™, or Lincoln Logs™, for example.

All of these activities are fun for a child. At the same time, they help your child develop better visual-motor coordination skills which are important for later school learning.∎

Growing Child

Developing Responsibility in Your Child

Your child is in another transitional stage of his life.

Though still a young child, he's no longer as dependent on you as he was even a year ago.

Going to school widens his world even more. He's beginning to be concerned about the opinions and expectations of other children.

In the next year or so, you'll notice dramatic changes in the way he thinks as well as the kinds of things he thinks about.

You'll see this in the way he uses language and in the kinds of activities to which he's drawn.

In addition he's undergoing physical changes that make him begin to look more grown up.

This period of transition from preschooler to school age child requires the development of new responsibilities.

These range from such things as learning to get ready in time for school every day to learning to take care of his possessions away from home.

They include learning to take responsibility for the ways in which his actions affect other children and adults with whom he will spend time away from home.

They also include learning to meet new sets of expectations associated with school, such as taking responsibility to finish assignments on his own, getting them in on time, and putting forth his best effort.

You won't be able to be with your child to help him understand and carry out the varied responsibilities expected of him at school and in other activities in which he will engage on his own.

How can you feel a sense of confidence that he'll be able to assume these responsibilities successfully?

How can you prepare him now so that you can have confidence in his ability to take responsibility for himself when you are not with him?

Following are some guidelines to explain how you can help your child become increasingly more responsible.

1. Encourage your child to do things for himself. Be clear about the things you expect him to do, such as putting his laundry in the hamper, taking out the trash, being at the table ready to eat on time without your having to keep reminding him, and so on.

Let him know what will happen if he doesn't follow through on his responsi-

bilities. For example, he will not be allowed to go out and play when his room is a mess. And make sure you follow through with whatever you've told him he can expect.

Teach him how to do things around the house that he doesn't know how to do. Break the tasks into small, easy-to-follow steps, and give him a chance to practice until he can do them well.

Resist the impulse to take over and do things for him even though you know you can do them better and more easily yourself.

No doubt you can. But it's worth the investment of your time and the temporary acceptance of a less than perfect job to enable him to learn.

When you do things for him, you deprive him of the opportunity to learn for himself.

It's especially important that you not deprive your child of the opportunity to learn certain tasks because of his gender.

It's simply not fair to a son (or his future wife) to let him grow up unable to do such simple things for himself as make his bed, vacuum a rug, clean his room, wash dishes, and cook.

And it's not fair to a daughter to let her grow up unable to make simple repairs around the house, use tools to build things, hang a picture, and the like.

If your children see that you and your spouse both are able to take care of various household responsibilities, this

continued on page 416

continued from page 415

will also help them be more interested and willing to learn to do the same.

If you are a single parent, it's important to you as well as to your child that you teach him to help you with the full range of household responsibilities.

2. Let your child experience the natural consequences of his actions. If he deliberately or carelessly breaks a toy, he has to do without that toy. That's a natural consequence.

No doubt you tried to warn him of this when he was a toddler, but it may have taken the actual experience for the message to sink in. So it is with many things.

For example, if he spends his weekly allowance the minute he gets it and then finds he doesn't have enough to get something he wants later in the week, this experience will teach him—in time—to think more seriously about how, where, and when to spend his money.

But if you routinely advance him money on next week's allowance, he won't learn the lesson because you're destroying the natural consequences of his actions.

If he's going to miss an outing he's looked forward to because he insists on seeing the end of a television program, let him know that, but don't take responsibility for his actions.

If you were to keep warning him and finally drag him away from the TV, you'd be denying him the lesson he would learn from experiencing the natural consequence of his own choice.

3. Help your child learn to accept responsibility for his feelings and actions. In a previous issue we talked about the importance of language in helping a child learn that his thoughts, feelings, and actions are in his control and not caused by others.

For example, if you say "You make me angry when you do that," you communicate a different message than if you say "I get angry when you do that."

The first blames him for your feelings,

whereas the second says more accurately what you really mean: when he behaves in a certain way, you get angry.

By clarifying your language, you let him know that he's not responsible for your feelings, but he is responsible for his actions.

You also need to practice the technique of "responsive listening." This involves your listening to what he says (in words or actions) and saying back what you think he means.

Your feedback gives him a chance to clarify his thoughts and feelings and can help him learn to accept responsibility for them rather than blaming others.

For example, suppose he comes to you, angrily crying, "Nancy made me break my new toy!" You might ask, "Did Nancy break your toy?"

Through this kind of communication, you'd probably slowly unravel the real story and perhaps get him to admit that it wasn't really Nancy's fault that he broke his toy.

If you tried to convince him that it was his own fault, he'd feel misunderstood and would end up defending his position even if he knew he was wrong.

The way you respond to your child when he's done something wrong can help him learn to accept responsibility for his actions rather than trying to avoid blame or

look for excuses.

On the other hand if you ask him, "Why on earth did you do such a thing?" you communicate the message that you expect him to come up with an acceptable excuse for his behavior.

In fact, there probably isn't a good reason. It's better that he simply acknowledge that he made a mistake and that he'll try to learn from it, than have him make up some excuse.

In general, the more understanding and accepting you are when he does something wrong, the better he'll be able to learn from his mistakes.

If he doesn't feel frightened of your anger or disappointment, he won't feel he has to defend himself.

Thus, he'll be able to accept responsibility for having made a mistake and use the experience to learn not to repeat it.

4. Allow your child the luxury of making some mistakes. Sometimes you know that your child is following a course of action that may lead to failure and disappointment.

It's hard at these times to stand back and let him follow his own course anyway. But, unless what he's doing is dangerous to himself or to others, it's usually better not to interfere.

When you try to protect him from the experience of failing, you communicate a lack of faith in his ability to handle it.

He'll learn to cope with failure and disappointment by finding out through experience that he can live through it.

Making mistakes and falling short of one's hopes and expectations is part of life. With your support and lack of interference, he can learn valuable lessons from his own mistakes.

5. Help your child learn to take responsibility for his successes as well as his failures. If he doesn't succeed at something he tries, be sympathetic, but don't make excuses for

continued on page 417

continued from page 416

him or try to make up for his disappointment.

For example, suppose he's just found out that he did not win a prize in an art contest for a picture on which he worked very hard.

You might be tempted to tell him that the judges don't know what they're doing because you're sure his was the best picture. Or, that the contest wasn't really very important anyway.

You'd help him better by letting him express his disappointment. Let him decide that he thinks his picture is very good, and that's what's really important.

If he does well at something to which he set his energies, encourage him to feel and express pride in his success.

Even some adults are so busy bemoaning their failures and/or striving toward greater and greater recognition of success by others that they never take the time to appreciate their own real accomplishments.

You can help your child enjoy his successes. Pay more attention to them than to his mistakes and failings.

Share his enthusiasm for the things which give him pride, however small. And take pride yourself in the things which you feel you've done well.

Your child needs to learn to trust his own judgment of whether or not he's been successful by his own standards.

Such self-evaluative skills are essential to creativity and effectiveness—in his future work and in his personal life.

Unless he can rely on his own judgment, he'll always be dependent on others to tell him what value he has.

Allow him to be the judge of his own success and failure. Teach him by your example to accept success with pleasure.

Use mistakes as an opportunity to learn. In this way he can learn to accept responsibility for the outcome of his efforts.

A final note: Remember that in this period of transition, your child will swing from moments of behaving very grown up and responsible to moments of acting as if he can't do anything for himself.

This is just a part of his stage of development. Part of him is still a small child and part of him is growing up very quickly.

Until he masters his new responsibilities, he'll have his moments of wishing he were little again so someone else would take care of him.

Like a pendulum he'll swing back and forth. But with your patience and understanding, he'll find his point of balance.■

The Three-legged Stool of Self-esteem

One of the most important outcomes and rewards of good parenting is the emergence of a strong, high sense of self-esteem in the child.

Children with high self-esteem evaluate themselves positively. They are satisfied with who they are.

Those with low self-esteem, on the contrary, perceive a discrepancy between who they are and who they would like to be.

There are many benefits related to having high self-esteem. Research studies indicate that children who evaluate themselves positively (1) relate better with their parents, (2) have more friends, (3) get better grades in school, and (4) are less likely to become depressed than children with low self-esteem.

A child develops positive self-esteem as a result of her parents helping her build what we may call the "three-legged stool" of *competence, responsibility, and appreciation.*

Competence refers to the child's ability to develop new skills and abilities so that she takes pride in being able to do things on her own. *Responsibiity* relates to the child's growing sense of independence as well as personal ownership of actions and mistakes. *Appreciation* refers to the child's need to be loved and valued by others.

1. *The first leg: feeling competent.* List three ways in which you have recently recognized some of your child's unique developing skills and abilities.

(i) _____

(ii) _____

(iii) _____

2. *The second leg: feeling responsible.* List three recent occasions on which you gave positive recognition to your child's growing sense of autonomy and responsibility.

(i) _____

(ii) _____

(iii) _____

3. *The third leg: feeling appreciated.* List three ways in which you have openly communicated to your child recently that she is loved and appreciated by you.

(i) _____

(ii) _____

(iii) _____

Children's understanding of themselves is highly dependent on the quality of their interactions with their parents, especially during the early developmental years. By helping a child build the "three-legged stool" of competence, responsibility, and appreciation, they are helping her develop more positive self-esteem.■

Tests and Test Scores

Of the many experiences a child has in school, one that frequently raises parents' anxieties is when their child has to take a test.

Parents need to remember that the administration of tests is simply a standard practice included within the school experience.

Part of the confusion results from the fact that parents are sometimes not given an adequate explanation of the test scores.

The scores are not intended to be a secret code known only to teachers or other school personnel. When test scores are explained properly, understanding their meaning is relatively straightforward.

Teacher-made tests given throughout the school year are most familiar to parents since they can remember taking them.

It is formal group tests of readiness, achievement, or intelligence that are sometimes more difficult for parents to understand. These tests are given to groups of children, sometimes to an entire class or grade.

Test results are used by the school or on a statewide basis for two purposes.

One is to check individual progress to determine the most satisfactory educational program for the child.

The other is to look at scores of an entire group to see how the group is performing based on the school's long-term educational requirements.

The No Child Left Behind legislation mandates regular testing for schools and school systems.

Achievement tests indicate the child's current performance ability in basic school subjects like arithmetic, reading, or spelling.

Results of these tests may be stated by scores indicating grade level ability—such as 1.2, which indicates the child performed like the typical child in the second month of the first grade year.

Grade equivalents are many times misunderstood, however, since the ranking means only that on that test the child performed at a specific level, not that she can do all the work for that grade level.

The test score may also be expressed as a percentile—such as 90, indicating that only 10 percent of the children in this child's age group scored higher.

Or the score may be a stanine, which divides all scores into nine levels with one being the lowest and nine being the highest.

A percentile of 50, or a stanine of five represent average performance for a child that age.

Some tests use other kinds of scores and parents should make sure the teacher explains any test score that is unclear.

Intelligence tests—sometimes called aptitude or cognitive ability tests—attempt to evaluate the child's ability to learn.

They are, therefore, different from achievement tests which assess what the child has learned thus far.

Results of intelligence tests are used to estimate the child's potential for later achievement.

Questions on an intelligence test cover a range of items the typical child learns as she grows.

Thus, items are quite broad and diverse and may include such things as vocabulary, perceptual skills, language abilities, coordination skills, problem solving abilities, and social awareness of the world the child lives in.

Results on all these items are pooled to give one or two scores indicating the child's general learning potential.

Results of the test will be an intelligence quotient or IQ which is a way of comparing a child to others of that age.

An IQ is simply a convenient shorthand for comparing a child's performance on

the test to her age group.

If the child performs like an average child of the same age, her IQ will be 100.

If this child's performance was like children older than her chronological age, her IQ would be higher, and if her performance was like younger children, the IQ would be lower.

Using this shorthand form of comparing one child to others, an IQ between 90 and 110 would be considered "normal," indicating the child has the skills expected of a child that age.

Parents must remember that tests are not perfect. Results are fairly accurate, but for an individual child, they may not represent the child's actual abilities.

In looking at the child's test scores, both parents and teacher need to evaluate whether scores are consistent with their own observations of the child.

If not, current observations may more accurately reflect the child's abilities, or additional individual testing may be called for.

It should be remembered that test items are designed to represent items known to the typical child.

continued on page 419

Dealing with Aggressive Behavior

Some children, as they get older, will react to frustration by fighting, hitting other children or adults, provoking fights by teasing and calling names or by using bad language.

This is the way some children show or express their feelings.

Whether they continue to use aggression as a way of settling problems or taking out their disappointments depends very much on how the parents handle it.

Obviously, hitting children is not a good way to set an example to stop them from hitting others. A good rule is: Hitting is not allowed.

Instead it is most important for you to set firm limits and indicate your disapproval of that sort of aggressive behavior without getting violent about it yourself.

Children's behavior most often reflects what parents do rather than what they say.

Usually when children can't control their tendency to fight, it is because something at home is going badly.

Parents whose child is always fighting will do well to look at the way in which they are treating the child and each other.

Children also imitate each other's behavior, and some children learn bad habits from other children. But they imitate their parents even more.

If they hear shouting and see fighting at home they will tend to do the same thing in their play and other activities.

The child who is always fighting and bullying others is usually feared and disliked by other children and adults.

He finds himself more and more left out by other children which makes him angrier and even more ready to fight.

Children have to learn other ways of dealing with difficult situations. Parents can help them by setting a good example in controlling aggressive behavior.

The child who is always a victim—always being bullied or picked on by other children—is probably repeating behavior learned at home.

This is often a child whose parents are never satisfied with him and are always belittling him.

In the same way the child who is always being beaten at home may learn no other way of relating to people but to be beaten by them or, in turn, beating on them.

Both kinds of children have a very poor opinion of themselves. They can seldom handle problems in a calm, strong way because they have no confidence in themselves.

Instead they either become victims or they strike out in rage from time to time at their frustration in always being the victim.

In either case they seldom get what they want. Children like this find it difficult as they grow up to do well in school, at work, in marriage or in any other important aspects of their lives.

Parents who want to avoid having their child grow up in such a way must watch their own behavior.

For parents who have always been shouters, name callers and hitters, this may be difficult to do.

Some parents don't even recognize that they are that kind of person until they see their child behaving in those ways.

No matter how difficult it seems, the effort to change this pattern is worthwhile. It can help spare children a lifetime of frustration and difficulty.

If you find you are unable to prevent or to control either your own or your child's aggressive behavior, it is time to get some professional help.

(Excerpted from "Your Child From One to Six," Richard H. Granger, MD. HEW publication).■

continued from page 418

Individual children simply may not have had experiences common to others, so that on a particular test, results would not really represent the child.

Some flaws in testing are fairly well known, such as: the child may not understand the directions or the child may not feel well on the particular day of the test or may feel excessive pressure when taking the test. These are things that can make the score on one test inaccurate.

The manner in which items are presented should also be considered. For example,

one bright fourth-grader who took a group test had an IQ score of 85. Two weeks later, on an individually-administered test, her IQ score was 115.

At first sight, this is a startling discrepancy.

Why the difference? On the group test she had to read some items and on the other test she did not.

This child had a serious reading problem, so the large difference between the scores was understandable. Every test score needs to be interpreted very carefully.

By law it is required that any records the school has on a child must be available to the child's parents.

If a child is given an IQ test at school, that information must be shared with the parent. The parents should be helped to interpret and understand the test scores.

Schools cannot give this information to anyone outside the school without the parent's written consent. And, if the school is asked by the parent to give test results to someone else, they must do that.■

Logical Thinking

Watching your child organize groups will provide you with much insight into how the child is thinking. There are two levels of young children's decision making:

A. A Perceptual Approach

The child matches chips to a model so that there are the same number in each row. And the child, after making a one-to-one match, recognizes equivalence—for the moment.

When the chips in one group are pushed together

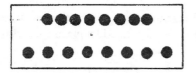

the child may declare that there are now more in one group simply because the spatial arrangement has been changed! The child is deceived by her visual perception.

B. A Logical Approach

The child selects one chip at a time alternately from each row until the supply is exhausted.

At this level the spatial correspondence is irrelevant and the child can't be fooled by the seemingly different quantity.

The child has resolved the problem with logic—no chips have been added, none has been taken away; therefore, the quantity remains the same, even though the configuration is different.

The logical approach may be observed in first graders while preschoolers are said to be "perception bound."

Children who have not had sufficient challenging experiences because they are "told" what to do will not generally arrive at the logical stage as early as their more independent and thinking peers.

What can parents and teachers do to help children develop logical thinking? There are three easy ways.

(1) The use of practical everyday division of objects.

It can be easily done at snack or mealtime. The child is offered a chance to divide the treats among the family.

In such a division problem, she does not know in advance the number of treats each individual will receive.

The task requires the child to take a larger set and divide it into equal subsets.

Contrast this to a distribution problem. Here a given number of treats is known in advance and the child knows how many treats are to be given to each person. The child need only take a small subset from a larger set.

(2) The collection of a broad variety of objects is a very natural way of learning about the additive nature of numbers.

Collecting real or play bus tokens, lunch money passes, milk money receipts, or permission slips, are good tasks from school.

Collecting laundry, tableware and soiled napkins are practical and meaningful tasks for home.

Questions can be asked such as "Do we have all the soiled napkins from everyone at the table?" "How many do we still need to collect?"

"Did everyone remember to put their dirty shirts in this laundry basket?" "How many people forgot?"

(3) Homemade card games.

Materials: 10 file cards which are cut in half; decals—animals, birds, flags, etc., or sketches made by you.

Procedures: Arrange the decals on the cards, 4 cards each with the identical pattern.

(The pattern should contain no more than 5 decals or sketches in the first deck of cards.) Example:

The game can be played by any rules you devise. One common game is the division of all cards equally.

Each player turns up the top card from his pile. The player whose card has the most decals takes both cards.

The winner is the player who ends up with the most cards.

There will be conflicts about who has more. Here is the opportunity to ask for opinions rather than providing the authoritative answer.■

P. O. Box 2505 • W Lafayette, IN 47996
(800) 927-7289
www.GrowingChild.com
© 2012 Growing Child, Inc.

Contributing Authors

Phil Bach, O.D., Ph.D.
Miriam Bender, Ph.D.
Joseph Braga, Ed.D.
Laurie Braga, Ph.D.
George Early, Ph.D.
Carol R. Gestwicki, M.S.
Liam Grimley, Ph.D.
Robert Hannemann, M.D., F.A.A.P.
Sylvia Kottler, M.S.
Bill Peterson, Ph.D.

The Importance of Friendship

When children are of school-going age, the ability to make friends becomes a very important aspect of their lives.

The starting point for friendship among school-age children is usually a shared interest or hobby.

Some children will even develop a specific interest in order to establish and maintain friendship with someone whom they like or admire.

As children grow older, they begin to share not only interests and hobbies but also values and outlook on life.

It is important, therefore, for parents to be aware of the influence which friends may have on their child.

Parents of a five- or six-year-old child are in a favorable position to encourage friendships that are beneficial to their child.

For example, they can invite such children more frequently to their home and can establish and maintain contact with their parents.

At the same time, parents can discourage the friendships that appear to have a detrimental effect on their child's behavior.

Skills children need to make friends

There are a number of ways in which parents can help a child more easily develop friendships. Here are some skills that children need in order to make friends:

• Observe and learn from the behavior of children who are well-liked by others.

• Become a good listener.

• Maintain eye contact with the person with whom you are interacting.

• Give praise or compliments to others when appropriate.

• Use self control.

• Express anger or displeasure verbally rather than physically.

• Learn to compromise and negotiate.

• Develop a good sense of humor.

• Accept the consequences of one's own actions.

• Become more aware of how others may be feeling.

• Make "we" statements rather than "I" statements ("We did well," rather than "I was terrific.").

The benefits of childhood friendships

Besides the most obvious benefit of childhood friendships—namely, providing a child with companionship—there are several other benefits that can be derived:

• Friendship can help stimulate a young child's cognitive development. Friends constantly share information and learn from one another.

• Friends often combine their knowledge and skills in cooperative learning. What one child doesn't understand, the other can explain—sometimes being more effective as a tutor than any adult!

• Friendship often provides a safe and secure base from which to explore new areas of knowledge.

What might have been a frightening or burdensome task if performed alone can, in the company of a friend, become an exciting, shared adventure.

• Friendship can also provide a stimulus to expand one's social interactions and experiences, knowing that one can fall back, if necessary, on the companionship of one's friend.

• Friendship is also a means by which values are shared and strengthened.

• In childhood friendships, children learn to interact with their own equals.

This type of interaction is different from family relationships.

In a family, children learn to relate to those who are either above or below them in age and status.

But, in school, they must learn to relate to one another as equal partners. This is the preparation they need for the friendships they will develop in later life.

• Childhood friendships are also related

continued on page 422

to later life adjustment. Research studies indicate that the single best childhood predictor of adjustment in adulthood is not academic or athletic success in school but rather the ability to get along with one's peer group.

• Friendship can also help children deal with stressful situations, such as school difficulties, illness, death, divorce, or other family problems.

• Most of all, childhood friendships provide an invaluable source for fun, happiness, and enjoyment of life.

Problems some children face

If your child has difficulty making friends, it's important to discern possible causes.

Does she know how to approach and mingle with a group of children who are having a good time?

When she is with other children, does she appear to be lonely or shy or overly aggressive?

To make friends, a child must know how to approach other children without being either too pushy or too shy. She must become attuned to the feelings of others and learn to interpret their body language.

A good way to learn these skills is simply to watch the screen on a TV set with the sound turned off.

Ask your child how she thinks the different people on the TV screen may be feeling as judged by the expressions on their faces and other body language indicators

("Does that girl look like she feels happy or sad? Why do you think she is feeling that way?").

The better your child is able to interpret the body language of others, the more likely she will get along with others and be accepted by them.

A lonely or introverted child will usually experience difficulty making friends. In general, the lonelier she is the more she will crave friendship.

Unfortunately, the more she expresses her craving for friendship, the more other children will withdraw from her, not wanting someone to cling to them in a dependent manner.

If you find that your child is lonely or shy, look for a child with whom she can get along.

Invite that child to your home, making sure to have some fun activities planned, such as a visit to an ice cream parlor or a trip to the zoo.

Children enjoy one another's company much more when they are having a good time together.

If you discover, on the contrary, that your child's problem is overly aggressive behavior, you can discourage her from playing with children who exhibit similar behavior and then help her find more suitable non-aggressive companions.

In summary, childhood friendships are important not just because of companionship but also because of the many other benefits—intellectual, social, and emotional—which they provide.

The child who can make friends becomes more competent in each of these areas.

The benefits are also cyclical because, as a child becomes more competent, she will be more admired by others and will, in turn, more easily establish friendships.■

Cultural Differences

Parents are sometimes amazed and horrified at the hurtful remarks young children make to each other ("You whites are dumb." "You blacks are stupid." "We don't like you because you're just a girl." "You boys are all mean." "We don't want to play with you 'cause you're Jewish.").

These hurtful remarks, which can devastate a child's sense of self-esteem, are frequently based on cultural differences.

Between any two people, there may be cultural differences in terms of gender, race, age, religion, socioeconomic status, or other variables.

As used by sociologists, the word "culture" refers in this context to the influence of various groups on an individual's way of perceiving, thinking, believing, feeling, and behaving.

Research studies indicate that children become progressively more aware of cultural differences between two and seven years of age.

Children as young as three years of age were found to identify with other children of the same race.

continued on page 423

continued from page 422

Not surprisingly, minority children were found to be more sensitive to racial cues—and their implications—than children of the majority or dominant group.

As a young child forms concepts of cultural differences, it is important to begin at as early an age as possible to teach respect and appreciation for these differences.

Children who develop a healthy attitude toward cultural differences are more likely to grow up well adjusted to the pluralistic world in which we live.

Due to modern means of communication and transportation, today's world has been aptly described as a "global village."

With greater interdependence among people of all nations, understanding and appreciation of cultural differences is now more important than ever before.

In the United States, cultural diversity has long been perceived as a defining characteristic of our society.

The motto on our coins, "e pluribus unum," ("from many people, one nation"), proclaims our national pride in that diversity. Yet problems of prejudice and discrimination remain.

Prejudice is defined as having an unjustified negative attitude toward an entire group of people. It is characterized by preconceived beliefs and opinions that are unreasonable, ill-informed, and unjust.

Discrimination consists of negative behavior toward others that deprives them of their basic human rights.

Some studies indicate that, in spite of an overall improvement in race relations among adults in our society, the level of prejudice among young children, ages four to seven, remains high.

An understanding of child development may help explain why young children are sometimes more prejudiced than their parents.

During the preschool years, as children seek to mentally organize their experiences

Many stereotypes can persist into later years unless children are helped by adults to become less prejudiced and more tolerant toward those who are different from themselves.

to make meaning out of the world around them, they learn to categorize.

Categorization implies developing increased awareness of similarities and differences.

At first, the categories they create can lead to over-generalizations. ("Grandpa has gray hair, so all men with gray hair must be grandpas.")

Overgeneralization, however, can easily lead to unjustified and prejudiced stereotypes. ("Girls can't do math." "All boys are hyperactive.")

Many of these stereotypes can persist into later years unless children are helped by adults to become less prejudiced and more tolerant toward those who are different from themselves.

It's important to help young children understand that cultural differences—such as race, ethnic background, gender, or religion—are something to be acknowledged, respected, and appreciated, rather than rejected or despised.

Being able to see beyond labels ("black," "white," "boy," "girl")—to the unique person inside those labels—will help children interact in a more warm and friendly way with people who are different from them.

By talking with your child about cultural differences during the early, formative years, you are laying a solid foundation on which dialogue and interaction can build in later years.

For example, if your five-year-old asks, "Why is Jimmy's skin black (white)?", you might answer, "Because Jimmy's parents are black/white."

With an older child, a parent might give a more informative answer. "We all have a special chemical in our skin called melanin. The more melanin a person has, the darker the skin will be."

In discussing cultural differences with their child, parents may find that they have to confront and challenge some of their own stereotypes and prejudices with which they may have grown up and have taken for granted.

For example, some people may believe that no woman ever will be or ever should become President of the United States of America.

Parents who have been victims of discrimination—as members of a minority group, for example—may still harbor feelings of hatred and rage.

It is unwise for them to transmit these negative feelings—however justified they may feel—to their children.

Hatred and rage convey the message that conditions are hopeless and irreversible, without any positive outcome for which to work.

Such feelings ultimately result in lowering a child's self-esteem.

There are more positive ways of dealing with cultural differences that we will address in the next article, "Teaching Tolerance and Respect."■

Teaching Tolerance and Respect

Children who learn to appreciate cultural differences are more likely to grow up well-adjusted to the multicultural world in which they live.

Here are some practical ways in which parents can teach tolerance and respect for cultural differences:

• **Be prepared.** It is wise for parents to anticipate questions their child may ask about differences. ("Why is that girl in a wheelchair?")

If parents don't know the answer, they should say so. An embarrassed silence can communicate a negative attitude about that person.

Furthermore, avoiding children's questions deprives them of information about life which they need.

Being uninformed or poorly informed about the realities of life only makes a child vulnerable to ridicule by others.

• **When a child has been hurt because of a remark made by someone else, it is wise for parents to intervene as early as possible.**

Since it is virtually impossible to shield a child completely from hurtful remarks ("You can't play with us 'cause you're Polish.") it's a good idea to teach the child how to cope with such situations.

For example, it might be pointed out that when someone makes a prejudiced remark, it is, in reality, the person making such a remark who has a problem, rather than the person about whom the remark was made!

• **Parents shouldn't let a prejudiced remark by their own child go unnoticed.**

The child may simply be repeating something heard earlier in the day. Now is not the time to scold or lecture, however.

Such methods have been found to be ineffective in teaching tolerance and respect.

Rather it is best to try to teach a child the importance of understanding and tolerance toward others, especially toward those

who are different from oneself.

A young child should be made aware that, while it is normal to take pride in one's own cultural characteristics, this does not give anyone the right to mistreat or hurt another human being.

• **In discussing cultural differences with a child, it is important to talk as simply and honestly as possible.**

The realities of prejudice and discrimination should be frankly pointed out. Possible ways to overcome those problems—for example, through a better understanding of other people—should also be discussed.

A young child will not learn prejudice in a family where parents discuss cultural diversity in a truthful, open, and honest manner.

• **Parents can encourage the use of non-sexist language.**

For example, saying "firefighter" instead of "fireman," "police officer" instead of "policeman," is not only less discriminatory but more accurately reflects the realities of today's society.

• **Some parents may say that even though they are doing their best to**

teach their child to be more tolerant, they feel helpless in trying to counteract outside influences, such as television programs, magazines, or books.

For example, when the doctors in a story are all portrayed as men and the nurses are all women, or when the part of a criminal is usually played by a person of color, this can convey a stereotyped and prejudiced message.

Learning to detect such subtle, biased messages can be a most valuable educational experience.

• **Parents can carefully select TV programs, CDs and movies which provide good role models for dealing positively with cultural differences.**

In a study of children who watched Sesame Street, for example, it was found that when they regularly observed various ethnic groups portrayed in a positive manner, they interacted later with children from these same ethnic groups in a similar positive manner.

• **An excellent way to educate a young child about cultural differences is to obtain from the public library books, CDs, and other materials which deal with different countries and their customs.**

It's a good idea for parents to prepare a set of questions to later discuss with their child.

• **Visiting ethnic fairs and festivals is yet another way to expand a child's mind.**

Seeing the types of dress or tasting the foods used in other cultures can be a broadening intellectual experience for children as well as for adults.

• **Parents could help organize an ethnic festival in their child's school.**

By inviting people from other countries to display their cultural artifacts, they not only make the different ethnic groups feel more at home, but they also enrich their

continued on page 425

continued from page 424

Learning To Read

own cultural environment.

• **Parents might also, if possible, invite children from other countries to visit their home.**

If these children have only recently left their own countries, parents might coach their child beforehand regarding possible questions to ask. ("What are some of the things you find different in this country? What do you like best about your own country?")

In this way, young children not only learn about other cultures, but also become more aware of their own self-identity; how their own cultural background and experiences have influenced their ways of thinking, feeling, and behaving.

• **Some families have enjoyed hosting a student from another country in their home.**

Many families have derived great benefit from this type of experience of cultural diversity.

• **In teaching tolerance and respect, it is good to remind ourselves that a young child is generally more attuned to what parents do than to what they say.**

A parent's behavior often communicates subtle, unspoken messages which can have a profound influence on a young child's mind.

On the positive side, the good example of parents can teach and empower a child to think and behave in a similar, positive manner.

• **Teaching children to view cultural differences in a positive manner can have far-reaching consequences.**

The goal of peace—peace in our neighborhoods, peace in our cities, peace in our nation, peace in our world—is a challenge that faces each new generation.

Teaching children tolerance and respect for cultural differences can be an important step toward that lofty goal.■

All parents would like their children to become good readers. Yet parents are sometimes not too sure what they can do to help.

Some parents, in their desire to develop their child's literacy skills, may push too hard too early.

Pushing a child who isn't yet ready to read is usually counterproductive.

The parent becomes more and more frustrated, while the child begins to associate learning to read with anxiety and failure.

On the other hand, other parents are so confused and intimidated by conflicting theories regarding the so-called "one right way" to teach reading that they decide to leave it entirely to the teacher and the school.

In so doing, they unfortunately deprive their child of the unique learning environment which only the home can provide.

Is my child ready for reading? In determining reading readiness, it is essential to take one's cue from the individual child. The child's age alone is not an adequate indicator.

Some children who are not yet ready to begin reading will be content to listen to a story being read or just look at the pictures.

The child who is ready will want you to identify words in her favorite books.

When your child starts pushing you, rather than the other way around, it's a good indicator that she is probably ready for reading.

How to foster a love of reading in the home: One of the best ways for parents to foster a love of reading in *all* children is by reading stories aloud.

Even after children have learned to read, they still enjoy having a story read to them. This should always be a fun activity—such as at bedtime—for both parent

and child. Even in the daytime, a reading period should be limited to no more than 30 minutes at a time. As soon as the child shows signs of restlessness, it is best to stop and resume the reading at a later time.

Here are some suggestions that will help to make reading to your child at home more beneficial and enjoyable:

• Let your child have input—such as a particular interest or favorite author—in choosing the books to be read.

• Look over the material before reading it to your child. Choose a comfortable and relaxed setting

• Let your child know the importance of this reading time together by eliminating distractions or interruptions, such as telephone or television.

• Read the book in a lively and animated manner, using a different tone of voice for the different characters in the story.

• Remember that language games like rhyming and singing songs, also provide practice and a different format.

• Look frequently into your child's eyes to maintain active interaction.

• Pause periodically to discuss what is happening in the story or to raise some

continued on page 426

continued from page 425

Me First!

questions. ("Is the little dog afraid? What do you think she should do next?")

• Discontinue reading—until some later time—if your child appears bored or restless.

Other ways to stimulate your child's interest in reading:

• Some parents put identifying labels on objects in the child's room: bed, door, drawer, chair.

• Parents can also point out words on vegetable cans, cereal boxes, T-shirts, signs and billboards.

The more a child becomes aware of the written word in everyday living, the more interested she will become in learning to read.

Using the public library: Parents can also make use of the children's section at the local public library. This is a very good way to learn about an individual child's special interests.

Once a child shows an interest in a special topic, or in books by a particular author, the librarian can usually find more books related to those interests.

Many public libraries organize children's story hours and other programs to stimulate children's interest in reading.

Connecting reading with writing: It is also a good practice to connect reading with writing.

Have your child develop a story which you can write down. When you read it back to her, point to each word as you say it.

After reading her own story to her a number of times, invite her to read it with you, helping her with the words she doesn't recognize.

It is best, at this stage, to ignore any errors she makes as this will only inhibit her desire to learn.

You can also encourage your child to dictate a letter to a favorite aunt or uncle. As she expresses her thoughts, she can see you writing words on paper so that she learns the connection between ideas and written words.

In this way, she learns how to construct meaning with language.

She also sees you begin the letter in the top left-hand corner, moving from left to right and from top to bottom of the page—all of which adults may take for granted, but a young child must learn in order to become a reader.

Good example: One of the most effective ways for parents to foster a love of reading in their child is by being good role models of the joy of reading in the home.

If your child sees that reading is one of your own favorite activities, she will be more eager to experience and enjoy the fun in becoming a good reader.

Summary: Learning to read can be an exciting and rewarding experience, not just for the child, but also for the parents.

As children learn to read, they need the encouragement, support, and good example of their parents and other adults.■

P. O. Box 2505 • W Lafayette, IN 47996
(800) 927-7289
www.GrowingChild.com
© 2012 Growing Child, Inc.

Contributing Authors

Phil Bach, O.D., Ph.D.
Miriam Bender, Ph.D.
Joseph Braga, Ed.D.
Laurie Braga, Ph.D.
George Early, Ph.D.
Carol R. Gestwicki, M.S.
Liam Grimley, Ph.D.
Robert Hannemann, M.D., F.A.A.P.
Sylvia Kottler, M.S.
Bill Peterson, Ph.D.

Some six-year-olds want to be first in everything. Therefore, younger brothers or sisters who require care and attention often threaten the child's feeling of 'firstness.'

The older child may appear at times to be consumed by "Me first!" For example, her whole day may be spoiled if a younger sibling gets to the breakfast table before she does.

Often she will be quite attentive in noticing who gets the 'best' seat in the car, or whose favorite dessert is served.

It is also true that she can be most jealous of the very sibling of whom she is most proud.

She is also jealous of any attention or gift given to a younger sibling by a guest. She can be reassured of her position with some simple attention—an "I love you" smile or an arm around the shoulder hug.

The lecture approach ("You mustn't be jealous, that's not nice!") only aggravates the situation.

At this stage her intense awareness exceeds her ability to manage self and event, and she is terribly vulnerable.

If her needs are met now, she can more easily discard her egocentric demands later.

Take heart. At least six-year-olds get along fairly well with older siblings—as long as they don't treat her "like a little kid!"■

Growing Child

Getting Ready for First Grade

Preparation for first grade should not be left until the last minute.

The more gradually a child is prepared for this transition in his life, the more successful will be his adjustment to school.

Here are some ways in which parents can begin to help their child get ready for first grade:

1. Make preparation for school a part of your child's life.

Whenever you can find an opportunity—such as when you see a school bus filled with children—talk to your child about what he can expect when he goes into first grade.

Be realistic and honest. Try not to oversell either its good points or its bad points.

If he has older brothers or sisters, let him hear you ask them about what they did each day in school.

Tell him what you already know about what he will be doing in first grade.

Above all, help him by your attitude to look forward to going to school rather than being afraid or nervous about it.

2. Give your child an opportunity to talk about his feelings.

Even when you get your child ready in a positive manner for school, it still involves a major transition in his life (see box).

It is wise to give him an opportunity to express his feelings, especially if he has

feelings of hesitation and uncertainty. Let him know that "It's okay to have those feelings."

Don't try to contradict or talk him out of those feelings in your efforts to view this new experience positively.

Role-playing is an effective way to help a child deal with feelings. You and your child can take turns playing teacher and pupil.

You can enlist some stuffed animals as the other "children" in the classroom. Let him tell you how each one of the stuffed animals is feeling about being in school.

In a very natural way, you can ask your child if he sometimes has feelings like that about going to school.

3. Help your child learn the skills

he will need in order to be ready for school learning.

In recent months, we have provided articles in *Growing Child* that dealt with getting ready for reading, writing, and mathematics. Look for opportunities for him to use those skills in his everyday life.

If possible, talk with the teacher he will have. Find out what some of the expectations will be for the beginning of the school year.

Ask the teacher to share with you some ideas about what you can do at home to help your child get ready for first grade.

4. Some other things you can do to help. As soon as your child has been

continued on page 428

An Important Transition

It may seem like a long time before your child will be entering first grade. This will be an important transition in your child's life.

By preparing well in advance for that event, the adjustment to school will be made easier. Let's consider some of the challenges that face a child entering first grade:

• Spending a large part of the day in a setting that is unfamiliar.

• Establishing new relationships with adults who will be in positions of authority.

• Sharing the attention of these adults with many other children.

• Getting along with other children, none of whom he may have known previously.

• Adjusting to a more structured daily routine.

• Getting to know the rules for what is considered acceptable/unacceptable behavior.

• Acquiring new knowledge and new skills.

• Becoming more self-reliant and responsible.■

continued from page 427

assigned to a classroom, make arrangements, if possible, for him to meet with his teacher.

If this can be arranged before the end of a school year, he will have the advantage of seeing first-grade students in action.

Otherwise, the visit to meet his future first grade teacher can be arranged during the summer months.

If you can find out what other children from your neighborhood will be in his classroom, invite some of them to your home before school begins.

Let them play games, such as "riding together" on an imaginary "school bus."

On the first day of school, you may decide to car pool with other parents, so that your child won't be alone on his new adventure.

5. Be understanding and supportive when school begins.

For some children, the first days of school are a positive and exciting experience. For others, the transition may be more difficult.

For the child who is having problems adjusting, parents need to do two things:

(1) Be as understanding and supportive as you can.

(2) Be firm with him about the fact that he does have to go to school. Letting him stay home, unless he is truly sick, will only make the problem worse.

Be on guard for "before-school-sickness." Some children act as though they are very sick—until they're told they don't have to go to school. Suddenly, their parents

discover they are no longer sick!

Don't be too alarmed if your child's behavior changes somewhat during the first days of school. For example, he may want you to cuddle him more, or he may wet his bed at night. Also, he will probably show signs of fatigue, which is to be expected.

These are just signs that he is having some difficulty in adapting to the changes in his life.

They are indicators that he is experiencing anxiety, which is a natural reaction. For that reason, it would be wise to let up somewhat on any demands or pressures at home.

With your understanding, encouragement and support, he will learn to look forward to going to school each day with eager anticipation.■

Nine Practical Points for Parents

• **Read to children at an early age.** By providing quality reading materials in the home and encouraging regular library visits, you will establish that reading is fun and also essential, not only in the classroom but to life in general.

Be a good role model and read more yourself!

• **Arrange for the sharing of duties in the home and see to it that such duties are performed.** Being responsible for chores encourages self-discipline and having a regular job makes your child feel needed and a part of the family.

These are important contributions to positive self-esteem.

• **Show by example** that a consideration for others and a commitment to family and community are vital to individual growth and self-satisfaction.

• **Speak well of education** and praise its importance.

• **Help your child with homework at the end of a school day** by providing a place to study and a quiet atmosphere.

Rejoice in your child's successes yet be alert to recognize personal social problems that may affect the school experience.

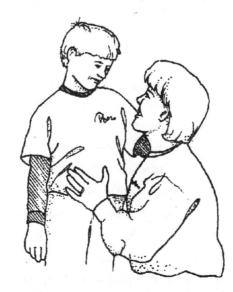

• **Carefully watch and monitor** the cultural influences in the home, including the viewing of television, CDs, use of the internet and electronic devices.

Children can be shown how to discriminate between the good and the gaudy and cheap.

A good way to teach this is to watch television (movies, games, other programs) with your children. Discuss the ideas and situations which are presented from a realistic point of view.

• **Take an active part** in ongoing communication with the teacher and the school. Keep abreast of your child's progress in school.

• **Share at least one meal per day** together as a family. Discuss homework, ideas, and happenings from your day.

• **Cultivate and encourage a sense of humor.** The ability to laugh at oneself indicates a sense of maturity.■

Becoming a Good Reader

It is important for every child to become a good reader. Reading ability is the gateway to success in school.

Helping a child become a good reader involves both the school and the home. But the roles of the teacher and the parent are quite different and distinct.

In many ways, the role of the parent is more fundamental than that of the teacher. While the teacher will teach the "mechanics" of reading—spelling, grammar, punctuation—in the classroom, the parent's primary role is to create in the child an *enthusiasm* to want to read.

The child who comes to school motivated to learn is the one who will benefit the most from classroom instruction.

On the other hand, school reading lessons will not likely be successful unless the child comes to school with a positive attitude toward reading.

How does a child develop an enthusiastic attitude toward reading and learning?

Experts in reading education have found that there are many ways in which parents can help their child develop a love of reading, including:

(1) Being a good role model; (2) using the daily newspaper; (3) making television an ally of reading; and (4) capitalizing on experiences in the child's environment.

(1) Being a good role model. How much importance do you give to reading in your own life?

Do you set aside a certain time of the day—with the television turned off—during which all members of the family read?

From the behavior of parents, children develop priorities in their lives. They learn that reading isn't just for school learning: It's an enjoyable way not only to acquire new knowledge, but also to relax.

They also learn that lifelong learning can be filled with enjoyment.

(2) Using the daily newspaper.

Parents can help their children develop an enthusiastic attitude toward read and learning by being a good role model. Children get the message that reading reading books, newsletters, and newspapers is something interesting and rewarding to do when they see their parents and other adults reading.

Children need to learn that, besides books and magazines, there are many other sources of interesting reading material.

The daily newspaper, for example, provides an inexpensive way to stimulate a child's interest in reading.

Newspapers help a child realize that reading is connected to real life events. Reading helps broaden her awareness and understanding of his environment.

Many newspapers publish a special section for children at least once a week.

Newspapers also usually have cartoons that not only provide material for reading but also help a child develop a sense of humor.

If your child enjoys sports, a picture in the newspaper may attract her attention.

You can then read with her the caption under the picture or an account of some game that she has already enjoyed watching.

All of these experiences help to stimulate her desire to read by connecting reading with her own interests and experiences.

(3) Making television an ally of reading.

Much has been written about the negative effects of television on children's reading habits. It is true that time spent in front of the TV screen is time that could have been spent in reading.

Since an average youth in our society watches over 900 hours of television per year—and, by comparison, will have spent only 1200 hours per year in school—it seems wise to seek ways in which TV watching can be made an ally of reading.

One of the most effective ways to do that is to select TV programs which are designed specifically to have an educational impact on viewers.

Watch the show with your child and discuss with her what she has seen, so that TV watching will become an interactive process rather than a passive one.

In this way questions will arise for which answers can be sought in a dictionary, an encyclopedia, on the internet or from other reading material.

What makes TV-watching attractive to a child is that it can be not only informative but relaxing and fun as well.

Eventually she will discover that the same qualities can be found in an interesting book.

She will learn that, while reading, she has more time and opportunity to reflect on new and enjoyable experiences than while passively watching a more fast-paced TV program.

When a child's interest in a new subject is sparked by a TV program, parents can

continued on page 430

The Importance of Music

capitalize on that interest.

Learn about dinosaurs, for example—by finding appropriate books or articles related to that interest.

In this way television can become an ally of reading by stimulating interest in a topic that can later be studied in a book or other reading material.

(4) Capitalizing on experiences in the child's environment.

Reading experiences are not confined to books. They can be found all around us, such as in advertisements, road signs, and grocery store labels.

Every trip you take—to the bank, post office, or grocery store—can become an educational reading experience for your child.

The more a child realizes that reading is related to important everyday happenings, the more she will be motivated to become a better reader.

Whatever interests your child displays can be further explored in appropriate reading material. Your child will come to realize that almost everything she wants to know may be found in a book.

As books help to broaden her mind and expand her world, she will, in turn, be more and more motivated to improve her reading ability.

In summary, when helping a child become a good reader, the role of the teacher is different from that of the parent:

The teacher will take care of instruction and correction.

The parent's primary role is to foster and develop *a love of reading* in the home.

The teacher's role is then made easier and more effective when a child comes to school—with a love of reading—eager and enthusiastic to learn.■

There are many questions parents ask about music for a young child.

At what age should formal music lessons begin?

Are some musical instruments better suited to young children than others?

Are some methods more appropriate and successful?

What can be done in the home to enhance music readiness or improve a child's musical ability?

A musical environment in the home

Creating a musical environment in the home is one of the most important ways to enhance a child's music readiness.

Children, even at a very young age, take an interest in the different sounds they can produce.

Babies, for example, are fascinated with the sound of a rattle.

A toddler's drumming on pots and pans may not sound like real music, but to the child, exploring different sounds becomes a fascinating area of new discovery.

Bells, tambourines and maracas — which require no musical ability other than a basic sense of rhythm — are often a young child's favorite playthings.

What can parents do?

Parents can build on a child's fascination with sounds to develop music readiness.

For example, imitating the sounds of nature (wind blowing, dog barking, bird singing) makes a child more aware of different sounds and how they can be produced.

There are many kinds of musical activities which children and adults can enjoy together.

For example, most children will enjoy marching to the beat of music, such as "Yankee Doodle" or a Sousa march.

They also enjoy simple sing-along tunes, especially if they are accompanied by body movements.

For example:

• "The Hokey Pokey" (moving various parts of the body as indicated in the song)

• "Row, Row, Row Your Boat" (rocking back and forth to the beat of the music)

• "The Eensy Weensy Spider" (making a crawling motion with fingers to imitate a spider)

• "Ring Around The Rosey" (which can involve several people in a circle dance)

In all of these activities, it is wise to use the K-I-S-S (Keep It Short and Simple) approach because young children generally have a short attention span. It is also wise to provide lots of variety in the activities.

Parents can also expose a child to many different kinds of music in the home, such as classical, country, jazz and popular songs.

They can also take a child to a family-oriented concert which is geared toward young children.

When to begin music lessons?

The answer will depend on a number of different factors, including the characteristics of the child, the parent, the teacher and the method to be used.

In considering the characteristics of the child, it is important to take into consideration the child's overall level of maturity, as well as musical aptitude and interest.

The child must be mature enough to realize that music study involves work (that is, practice) as well as pleasure.

For some exceptional children, with outstanding musical ability, formal music lessons might begin as early as three or four years of age.

For the average child, however, some type of music- readiness program, such as "Kin-

continued on page 431

continued from page 430

dermusik" is usually more appropriate.

In assessing a young child's musical aptitude, three indicators are helpful:

(1) Overall interest in music as demonstrated, for example, by the child wanting to sound out a familiar melody on a piano or other instrument;

(2) a good sense of rhythm, and

(3) an ability to sing in tune.

Parent involvement and commitment are also important factors. The parent's commitment involves not only financial support but also time, effort and encouragement.

For example, children usually need transportation to and from music lessons, parental supervision for music practice, and encouragement when faced with new challenges.

The personality of the teacher can also be a key factor in the success or failure of music lessons.

During the early stages, a good teacher will focus more on the process— developing a love and appreciation of music— than on the end product of perfect performance.

The specific method which the teacher uses is also important. For children under seven years of age, many teachers recommend music-readiness programs.

More formal training is provided in programs such as the Suzuki method for violin and piano.

Other music teachers recommend methods which use pre-reading approaches to music study.

Still others prefer that children not begin music lessons until they are in the second or third grade, when they are better able to read, follow directions and work independently.

Ultimately, it is for the parents to decide when music lessons will begin, taking all of these factors into consideration.

Children can learn that music will provide them with lifelong pleasure. It can provide entertainment in place of boredom, as well as relaxation in time of stress, and will enable them to become morecreative and well-rounded human beings.

Which musical instrument to use?

In choosing an appropriate instrument for a beginning student, piano and violin are the ones most frequently recommended.

If parents do not already own an appropriate instrument, it may be wise to rent the instrument until the child's aptitude and interest can be determined.

Since violins, for example, come in different sizes, young children may quickly outgrow the one with which they began.

How long will it take my child to learn to play well?

Although parents would love to have an answer to this question, it is unfortunately not possible to make this type of prediction with any degree of accuracy.

It is safe to predict, however, that only a few children who begin music lessons will one day become professional musicians.

It is more important, therefore, for parents to consider the many benefits which *all* children — irrespective of level of ability — can derive from studying music.

Physical and mental benefits

Some musical instruments—such as percussion, for example—can help develop gross motor skills.

Other instruments—such as piano and violin, which require finger dexterity—help develop fine motor skills.

Music study also improves eye-hand coordination.

These skills can transfer to other areas of study, such as handwriting, artwork, word processing and computer skills.

Voice lessons can help strengthen vocal chords and improve breathing techniques.

They can also improve diction, with clear sounding of vowels and consonants.

All of these skills are needed for good public speaking, acting, and media communications.

The mental benefits are also many. Children develop better listening skills and can learn to focus attention by blocking out distractions.

They can improve their abstract thinking abilities. For example, they learn to translate symbols (musical notes) into reality (producing a melody).

Music study can also help in the development of different types of memory: aural, visual, tactile, and analytical.

All of these can transfer to other aspects of school-related learning, such as test-taking ability.

continued on page 432

More About Form Perception

continued from page 431

In a previous issue of *Growing Child,* we discussed the importance of form perception for school learning.

Form perception is involved, for example, in recognizing letters and numbers.

Here are some simple activities that will help your child improve form perception skills.

In the figure below, you may not, at first, recognize that it has two or more possible perceptual organizations.

If you focus on the dark aspect of the figure, you will see either a table with a broad base or a classical urn.

If you focus now on the white aspect of the figure, while ignoring the black aspect, you will detect two heads facing one another.

It is wise to expose a child to such ambiguities. A child who has difficulty dealing with ambiguities may perceive an upper case "B," and only "B," when in reality it is the numeral 13 which is on the paper.

Another activity involving ambiguous forms is the game of identifying silhouettes on a wall.

In a darkened room place a lamp behind you as you face a bare wall. By manipulating your hands and arms you can project different forms on the wall.

Those in the room can take turns guessing "What can it be?"

These activities will help your child not only to deal with ambiguous forms but perceive and integrate the elements of each form, all of which are important for school learning.

When recognizing letters, words, numbers, and graphics, a child must likewise keep in mind the different parts of the figure while processing the total form.■

P. O. Box 2505 • W Lafayette, IN 47996
(800) 927-7289
www.GrowingChild.com
© 2012 Growing Child, Inc.

Contributing Authors

Phil Bach, O.D., Ph.D.
Miriam Bender, Ph.D.
Joseph Braga, Ed.D.
Laurie Braga, Ph.D.
George Early, Ph.D.
Carol R. Gestwicki, M.S.
Liam Grimley, Ph.D.
Robert Hannemann, M.D., F.A.A.P.
Sylvia Kottler, M.S.
Bill Peterson, Ph.D.

Children can also improve in other aspects of mental functioning, such as the ability to understand and use spatial concepts (over/under, in/out, up/down) and temporal concepts (fast/slow, long/short, before/after).

Social and personal benefits

There are many social benefits which can be derived from involvement in musical activities.

These activities can become a way of meeting new people and dealing with new situations.

As social interactions are broadened, new friendships are formed through the common bond of music.

Great personal benefits can also be derived by the child. Good organizational skills are developed in music study.

For example, children have to learn to budget their time in order to fit music practice into their daily routines.

Children learn the importance of reviewing periodically what has already been learned in order to retain it.

At the same time, they learn not to waste time needlessly on what they have already mastered thoroughly.

Through dedication, commitment, and perseverance in music study, their mental discipline is also improved.

The development of musical ability can also improve a child's self-confidence and boost self-esteem and can provide opportunities for the development of leadership skills.

Most of all, children can learn that music will provide them with lifelong pleasure.

It can provide entertainment in place of boredom, as well as relaxation in time of stress, and will enable them to become more creative and well-rounded human beings.■

Growing Child

The Challenge of Parenthood

When we were children and on the receiving end of our parents' occasional slights and misunderstandings, most of us promised ourselves that we'd never treat our children that way.

We wouldn't be impatient. We wouldn't get angry. We wouldn't hurt their feelings.

We wouldn't make such a big deal of little things. We wouldn't pressure or push. We wouldn't criticize or ridicule.

It was hard for us to understand how our parents—who claimed to love us—could sometimes treat us in ways that made us feel bad. And we were sure we'd never do that to our children when we were grown up!

Now that we are parents, we find it isn't as easy as we thought when we were children.

We have different needs and attitudes than we did then, And our childhood relationship with our parents created habit patterns that influence the way we treat our own children now.

Thus, we may not always act toward our children as we'd like. This can cause guilt and anxiety which further interferes with our ability to be the parents we want to be.

Parenthood is a difficult and often unappreciated job. There are many pressures on you to be a good parent, but there are few supports to help you.

There are always plenty of people around to criticize and question how you treat your children. But there are few, if any,

to applaud and congratulate the good job you do.

If you work in an office or on an assembly line, you at least get paid for what you do, even if you don't find it very inspiring.

If you produce a fine piece of art, you might gain recognition for your creative effort. But if you make it possible for

your child to grow to be a kind, intelligent, responsible human being, it's unlikely anyone will give you a special medal for a job well done.

As you know, the reward is in the work itself ... the look of exhilaration on your child's face when she finally masters a challenging task ... the tender moments

continued on page 434

Six Years Old!

This issue marks not only a birthday—and an important one—for your child; it also marks the end of the **Growing Child** series. We're proud to have spent some time with your family and to have had the opportunity to inform, educate, encourage, and guide you in the most important job you'll ever have: raising your children.

On this six-year anniversary, we hope you'll write to us and share with us your thoughts and feelings about how **Growing Child** may have helped you, about how your family has grown and changed, about your goals and dreams for your children. Your comments and suggestions will help us evaluate our publication and make valuable changes and additions.

Most of all, we want to wish you the very best; we hope all your dreams come true; we hope your children will grow up to be beautiful, successful, content, and all those other good things. You know we've never been Cinderella-types, so we'll also add a more realistic note that says we hope your children will always be okay.

For you, Mom and Dad, here's wishing you good luck with: PTO, ballet lessons, piano lessons, Webelos, Brownies, Scouts, camping out, sleeping over, school plays, measles, cats, dogs, turtles, bicycles, 4-H, orthodontists, broken arms, baseball, softball, basketball, football, soccer, choir, band, boyfriends, girlfriends, prom night, and, of course, driver's ed.

It all lies ahead of you and your child. We hope that we have helped you give your child a better start during the all-important first six years of life.■

Nancy E. Kleckner, Editor   Dennis D. Dunn, Publisher

continued from page 433

when, out of the blue, she looks up and says, "I love you"...the sense of trust communicated when she comes to you with a problem.

These are the rewards that make all the frustrations, aggravations, discouragement, and sheer exhaustion seem worthwhile.

These are the rewards you get—not for being a perfect parent who never makes a mistake—but because you care, and your child knows that you care!

Your consistent support and caring gives her the confidence and the courage to be her own person ... and thus to be the source of great joy as well as the enormous challenge that she is for you.

The fact that you are reading this newsletter means you take your job as a parent seriously. You care about your child, and you want to do your best for her.

There are two key elements to your being successful in raising your child. One is that you enjoy your relationship with her.

The other is that you feel a sense of confidence in what you're doing. Neither of these is possible when you're feeling anxious and unsure of yourself.

Think about the areas of your relationship with your child that pose problems for you. Are they not related to issues which you're not quite sure how to handle and which cause you to feel overwhelmed and exasperated about being a parent?

Now think about the parts of your relationship that run very smoothly. Are these not areas in which you know exactly where you stand and feel confident in your stance? And, are you not also able to feel good about yourself and your child in these areas?

It is important that you be consistently supportive and encouraging. However, it's unrealistic to expect yourself to be constantly so.

Mistakes are inevitable. If you can accept

the fact that you won't always do the "right thing," then you can learn from your mistakes.

They offer valuable lessons about what doesn't work that can help you discover what does work. The pressure of feeling that you should be a "perfect" parent makes it very hard for you to relax and enjoy your child, and it certainly does not help you to be a better parent.

There is no one "right way" to raise your child. Some approaches get better results than others.

Some work well now but may have undesirable long-term consequences. Some are effective in one situation but not in another.

You can get ideas which may help guide you from a book or a television program or your neighbor or your mother-in-law. But it's the "on-the-job-training" you get from seeing what works best for you and your child that has to be your final teacher.

We at *Growing Child* have tried to offer suggestions and guidelines to help you decide for yourself how to approach parenting in a way that makes it possible for you to enjoy being a parent and feel

confidence in the job you're doing.

As people who care for children, we ask you to "be on the side of the child." Try as much as possible to put yourself in your child's shoes in your choices of how to deal with her.

On those days when your child gets bubble gum all over her hair and clothes, the baby cries all day because his gums hurt from teething, the mail brings nothing but bills and your spouse brings home all the problems from the office, it's a super-human feat just to stay sane, much less be kind, patient, understanding, fair, respectful, and encouraging!

Try not to make it any harder on yourself by feeling guilty if you treated your child in a way that wasn't considerate of her feelings.

She'll survive it. And she'll learn a valuable lesson about being concerned for the needs of others from your letting her know, honestly, that you're overwhelmed and don't need any additional problems from her.

Being a parent is a hard job, deserving of respect and admiration. You'll have some good days on which all your good intentions seem to spring miraculously into reality.

Other days, when everything seems to be going wrong, you may feel like giving up.

Most days you probably just make it through and wonder at the end where the time went.

You'll make mistakes and you'll have successes. It's all a part of life. Just try to learn from the former and enjoy the latter.

As long as you keep trying and continue to care—no matter what—it will all work out in the end. This stage of your child's development will be over much faster than you can imagine.

Try to enjoy it now while you're living it.■

School Bus Safety

Now that your child is old enough to go to school, it's important to think about school bus safety.

Even if you drive your child to and from school each day, there will likely be some occasions—such as a field trip—when your child will need to be aware of the importance of school bus safety. It could mean the difference between life and death.

Of the 22.5 million children who ride school buses every year, on average 30 are killed and close to 8,000 are injured in school bus related accidents.

It is particularly sad to report that, over the past ten years, five- and six-year-olds represented more than half of those killed. The saddest aspect is that most of these accidents were avoidable.

Studies of school bus accidents involving children provide some revealing information:

(1) Sixty-five to seventy percent of the fatalities that occurred outside the bus were caused when the bus ran over a student whom the bus driver could not see.

(2) The majority of these fatalities occurred when the child had to walk in front of the bus in order to cross the street.

(3) Accident reports indicated that children were sometimes run over by the right rear wheels of the bus when the driver made a right-hand turn without seeing a child who had remained by the side of the bus after alighting.

(4) In a study of school bus fatalities in one state, children in grades K-3 accounted for 87 percent of the deaths involving the child's own school bus.

School bus drivers sometimes report that they can be overwhelmed by the amount of misbehavior with which they must deal.

This is an area in which parents, school officials, and transportation personnel must work together to improve the safety of all children.

In addition to what may be taught at school and on the bus, here are some rules which parents can discuss with their child.

Before the bus arrives:

• Before leaving home make sure that anything being brought to school (homework, papers, lunch) is safely tucked inside the school bag.

Loose papers could cause a child to rush into traffic if they happened to blow away.

• Leave home each day at the same time.

• Arrive at the stop five minutes before the bus is due. Last minute rushing or having time on one's hands because of being too early can both contribute to accidents at the bus stop.

• Stay back at least 10 feet from the curb.

• Wait quietly for the bus to arrive.

• Do not play while at the school bus stop.

When the bus arrives:

• Wait until the bus comes to a complete stop before moving toward the entrance.

• Allow smaller children to get on the bus first.

• Keep one hand free to hold the handrail on the bus.

• Enter the bus in single file.

• Take your seat promptly and quietly.

While riding the bus:

• Remain in your seat whenever the bus is moving.

• Don't make unnecessary noise because the bus driver must be able to hear traffic sounds such as a car horn, ambulance, fire truck, or police siren.

• Listen carefully and follow instructions

that the bus driver gives.

• Keep your arms, hands, and head inside the bus at all times—even if the windows are open in warm weather.

• Never throw anything out of a bus window.

When getting off the bus:

• Walk in single file to the exit without rushing or pushing.

• After you get off the bus, immediately step back a few feet from the bus. Make sure the bus driver can see you.

• If you must cross the street, always cross at least 10 feet in front of the bus so the bus driver can see you.

• Never cross behind the bus.

• Always look both ways before crossing the street.

• Be aware that, although all drivers are supposed to stop when the school bus red light is flashing, some drivers may fail to do so.

• If you drop something on the ground (for example, if some of your papers blow away), don't bend down to pick them up unless you are absolutely certain it is safe to do so.■

A More Healthy Lifestyle

Many parents are rightly becoming concerned today about the health and physical fitness of their children.

Recent studies indicate that, among young children, eating disorders—such as obesity, bulimia, and anorexia nervosa—are on the increase.

Obesity is generally defined as actual weight that is 20 percent more than normal. Parents can consult with their physician regarding the growth chart norms for a child's age, height, and weight.

In interpreting growth charts, variations in the timing of a child's growth spurts should be carefully taken into consideration.

Obesity often has an early onset, by four or five years of age. It may result from a genetic predisposition, from overeating, or from a combination of both factors.

Studies have found that if one parent is obese, there is a 40 percent chance that the child will also be obese.

The likelihood increases to 80 percent if both parents are obese. This increase in risk is not, however, solely due to genetic predisposition. It is also due to the child learning bad eating habits from the parent.

It should be noted that obesity during childhood does not necessarily result in obesity in adulthood, but the likelihood increases when there is a history of obesity in the family.

Obesity can have many different effects on a child's later development. Girls who are obese tend to begin puberty earlier and boys who are obese have an earlier growth spurt in adolescence.

Many obese children feel insecure and have difficulty getting along with other children. They also frequently experience school difficulties.

Not only do these problems result from being obese, but they also set in motion a vicious cycle by which these same problems, in turn, often lead to more overeating and weight gain.

Besides obesity, other eating disorders, such as bulimia and anorexia nervosa, are also on the increase.

Bulimia involves binge eating, usually followed by induced vomiting or excessive use of laxatives. Bulimia is often accompanied by feelings of self-loathing, guilt, and depression.

Anorexia nervosa involves severe dietary restriction. The effects include frequent constipation, dehydration, and insomnia, as well as dry skin, brittle hair, and muscle atrophy. Normal growth and development are often impeded.

In a study of 300 children conducted by researchers at the Children's Hospital Medical Center in Cincinnati, 39 percent of third-grade girls and 29 percent of third-grade boys reported trying to lose weight because they were anxious to be thin.

It was found that children sometimes begin to diet because they hear their parents repeatedly talking about their own need to lose weight. These children do not realize that low calorie diets are not appropriate for them because they may need those calories for normal growth and development.

There are a number of factors which have contributed to the increase in eating disorders among young children in recent years, one of which is the amount of time children spend in sedentary pursuits, such as watching television, using computers, or playing video games.

These pursuits have replaced the more active types of experiences which children of previous generations enjoyed.

According to the American Academy of Pediatrics, fewer than 50 percent of all school children get enough exercise for healthy lung and heart development.

Here are some of the benefits your child will derive from having lots of physical exercise:

• **Large muscle development:** Developing a healthier and stronger body is the most obvious benefit of regular exercise.

• **Improved self-esteem:** Physical development affects how one perceives oneself and how one is perceived by others, especially one's peers.

• **Social interactions:** Physical activity provides many opportunities for participation in sports and other social play activities.

• **Release of energy:** Daily exercise provides a healthy outlet for excess energy and tension.

• **Sounder sleep:** Generally children who exercise regularly also sleep more soundly at night.

• **Better school performance:** Some recent studies indicate that regular exercise can enhance intellectual performance. It is possible that this may be due to improved flow of oxygen to the brain.

continued on page 437

continued from page 436

Now is a good time to make sure that your child is developing good eating habits and getting adequate daily exercise. Here are some recommendations:

1. Be a good role model for your child. Merely giving a child a lecture about the importance of diet and exercise may only do more harm than good.

Parents must be the ones who set a good example by their own eating habits and regular exercise schedule.

2. Curtail your child's sedentary pursuits, such as TV watching. Don't let your child become a "couch potato."

Too much time spent watching TV or playing video games is time taken away from other more beneficial developmental activities.

Remember that five-year-olds respond better to a fixed schedule ("It's 3 o'clock—you remember that's the time to turn off the TV and go outside to play.") than to one that is determined arbitrarily ("You've been watching far to much TV lately. Turn it off right now.").

3. Develop good eating habits. Set a regular time for meals. Provide your child with well-balanced, nutritious meals. If you are uncertain about your child's dietary needs, consult with your physician.

Make mealtime an enjoyable time for family sharing—and not the time to discuss family problems.

4. Make exercise a regular, fun-filled family activity. Avoid the "boot-camp" approach which, for your child, would turn exercise into an unpleasant chore.

Combine your exercise program with whatever will enhance its enjoyment— the outdoors, lively music, good humor.

Ultimately the whole family will reap the many benefits of a more healthy lifestyle.■

Developmental Milestones—6 Years

Physical
• Walks a straight line heel-to-toe both forward and backward.
• Hops on either foot more than 10 times.
• Climbs on outdoor jungle gym and play equipment.
• Kicks a soccer ball with a greater degree of accuracy.
• Rides a bicycle with ease.
• Catches a tennis ball using both hands.
• Dresses and undresses self, including manipulating buttons, zippers, and shoe laces.
• Uses knife, fork, and spoon to eat.
• Uses small scissors to cut out various shapes.
• Does simple household chores such as sweeping floor or steps.

Intellectual
• Frequently asks "why" questions.
• Has better attention span and concentration skills.
• Is better able to make comparisons of size and weight (for example, bigger/smaller, heavier/lighter).
• Knows own left hand from right hand.
• Pretend play now involves more real life, rather than fantasy, situations (for example, school, church, grocery store).
• Enjoys puzzles and games that require matching items.

Language
• Speaks more clearly and fluently but may still have difficulty with "th" and "s" sounds.
• Knows correct rules of grammar but doesn't always apply them (for example, still says "Me and Chris went together").
• Enjoys carrying on a telephone conversation with some relatives or friends.
• More frequently uses polite expressions, such as "please" and "thank you."
• Likes to repeat simple nursery rhymes.
• Will construct a story from pictures in a book.
• Frequently asks the meaning of new words.

Social-emotional
• Enjoys playing competitive sports as well as board games which have simple rules.
• Selects own playmates, usually of same gender.
• Understands ownership and property rights of others but may still behave in egocentric manner.
• Can identify emotions such as anger or fear and can now express anger verbally rather than physically.
• Is protective of a younger sibling.
• Enjoys attention from peers.
• Likes to please parents.

These milestones are guidelines only. All children do not develop at the same speed, nor do they spend the same amount of time at each stage of their development. Usually a child is ahead in some areas, behind in others, and "typical" in still other areas. The concept of the "typical" child describes the general characteristics of children at a given age.

Influences on Children's Lives

There are many influences on a young child's life. It is important to give some thought to some of the most important ones.

1. Because you have such an important influence on your child, it is vital that you know, understand and accept yourself.

You can develop self-understanding by asking yourself questions like: "What makes me react or feel the way I do?" "What things make me happy?" "How do I react to other people?"

Self-acceptance requires a realistic view of what you can and cannot do. Perhaps you've had an important goal that you now know you can never reach.

If you can accept that fact, you can face other people, including your child, with respect for yourself and without the feeling that your child must do what you never could.

2. Understand your influence on your child. Have you ever noticed your child's reaction to your happiness or sadness? Your anger?

Children tend to display the same mood or disposition you feel. In fact, they may learn your behavior by imitating what you do or how you react to things.

3. Understand children in general. A knowledge and understanding of child development helps you to have standards with which to understand your own child.

For example, you cannot determine whether your child is developing at a normal rate unless you know what can be expected of a child his age.

4. Understand the uniqueness of your own child. He has specific desires, interests, and abilities as well as problems and difficulties.

5. Be aware of sibling influence. Brothers and sisters often play a big part in influencing a child. They may be companions while playing but rivals for your attention and love.

The interaction and sharing between brothers and sisters is an important aspect of the learning process. Such relationships help your child develop basic attitudes toward himself and other people.

6. Consider environmental influences. People outside the home also have an important influence on children.

Teachers, relatives, and children in your neighborhood can help your child learn how to get along with others. Of course, television, radio, and computers, present opportunities for your child to see and hear many types of behavior.

The physical, mental, and social development of a child are all affected by the environment in which he lives. A home that provides a child with such things as educational toys and interesting music helps to stimulate his development.

Your interrelationships as husband and wife, brother and sister, parents and children strongly influence the types of relationships your child will seek outside the home.■

P. O. Box 2505 • W Lafayette, IN 47996
(800) 927-7289
www.GrowingChild.com
© 2012 Growing Child, Inc.

Contributing Authors
Phil Bach, O.D., Ph.D.
Miriam Bender, Ph.D.
Joseph Braga, Ed.D.
Laurie Braga, Ph.D.
George Early, Ph.D.
Carol R. Gestwicki, M.S.
Liam Grimley, Ph.D.
Robert Hannemann, M.D., F.A.A.P.
Sylvia Kottler, M.S.
Bill Peterson, Ph.D.

Growing Healthy, Happy Children

To grow healthy and strong, children should have good food, plenty of sleep, exercise and fresh air.

Children have emotional needs, too. To be both healthy and happy, every child needs to have:

• A set of moral standards to live by —to know the difference between right and wrong.

• A belief in the human values —kindness, courage, honesty, generosity, and justice —beliefs boys and girls learn from those around them.

• Friendly help in learning how to behave toward persons and things in his or her world.

This can mean something as simple as how to treat a neighbor with kindness or how to care for a cherished pet.

• Grown-ups around them who show them by example how to get along with others.

All children need to know:

• That their parents have confidence in them and their ability to do things for themselves and by themselves.

• That there are limits to what children are permitted to do and that their parents will hold them to these limits.

• That although it is all right to feel jealous or angry, children will not be allowed to hurt themselves or others when they have these feelings.■

from Growing Child valuable information to help parents of school age children!

The **Growing Child** newsletter has helped thousands of parents better understand and relate to their pre-school children. But parents' questions don't end when a child starts school. So, **Growing Child** offers **Growing Up**, a series of newsletters for parents of children from kindergarten through grade 12. (See samples on backside.) **Growing Up is designed to be reproduced.**

Growing Up helps parents understand what their child may be experiencing in terms of academic, physical and behavioral development at a particular point in the child's life. It shows parents what's "normal" for their child at a specific age, how to respond to behavior changes and what to expect next.

Order your copy today!
Visit www.GrowingChild.com • 800-927-7289

Each copy of Growing Up is packed with useful information for children and their families.

Grades K-3   **$12.95***

- Help with learning problems
- Talking back and tattling
- Social poise and good manners
- Homework and study skills
- Physical development

Grades 4-6   **$12.95***

- Developing good reading skills
- Learning responsibility
- Dealing with temper tantrums
- Discipline and punishment
- Developing good study habits

Grades 7-9   **$12.95***

- Dating and companionship
- Coping with lying and stealing
- Sexual development and curiosity
- Keys to successful test-taking
- Preventing juvenile delinquency

Grades 10-12   **$12.95***

- Avoiding drug and alcohol abuse
- Career planning
- Budgeting and money management
- The difference between love/sex
- Taking responsibility

* A charge of $2.50 for shipping and handling is added to each order regardless of the number of books ordered. This fee is $5.00 for shipments to Canadian addresses.

Special note to teachers: Growing Up newsletter may be copied and shared with your students' parents.

Samples of GROWING UP by Grade
(Actual size of each issue is 8-1/2" x 11")

Growing Up

Grade 2 October Part 3

"Real writing"
Paper and pencil work, although of strong interest, still creates problems at this age. The student worries—ahead of time—if she will be able to finish her work in the allotted time.

She knows, because she is such a pessimist, that she will "stay in" at recess if her paper is incomplete. So her grip on the pencil becomes tighter, leads break, pencils grow shorter, careless errors become greater in number, and the eraser flies back and forth.

Some children, overloaded with normal-for-them anxiety and ruminating about finishing on time, will reverse letters when printing. When they learn "cursive writing," letter reversals will become much less frequent.

Playground politics for acceptance
The second grader really enjoys the playground and in anticipation almost "explodes" from her room to the outside.

Your child also really wants acceptance as part of the group on the playground. She wants to be chosen—and to choose—and is often concerned that the other children, or even the teacher, may not like her.

She wants to be able to perform the currently popular playground feats. If she is a top performer, she does not like to be singled out for praise. If she makes an error, she does not like to be singled out for criticism.

She likes praise of the entire group. This spurs her on to work for greater skill for "her" side.

By the way, at this age "the group" is slow to include a new member and may even make fun of newcomers.

Anxiety and accidents
The student has few or no toileting accidents this year. The school schedule provides toileting opportunities throughout the day. It is usually on the way home that any accidents occur. But now she can consciously "wait" until she gets home. A few very active boys may not have as long a retention span.

If accidents do occur, look for a cause. She may be coming down with something or some event may have caused a somber child more than the normal amount of anxiety.

If illness is the cause, you will know soon enough. If it's not illness, then use your eyes and ears to pick up clues. Your child will not broach the subject. She has already accepted the blame for whatever happened, whether right or wrong.

She will get over being so anxious next year. This year, however, you can help by demonstrating in your own behavior what is worth worrying about and what only merits a remark like, "That's the way the cookie crumbles."

If your worry-wort child tells you she is being excluded, explain that groups often behave this way, and that she will be included when the group gets used to her being around and sees that she knows good ways to play. Tell her it's better if she doesn't show hurt or hostility over it.

"Busy minds are happy minds."
—Dennis D. Dunn—

Growing Up

Grade 3 January Part 2

What's behind all those tears
The third grader does not have crying "jags." She *bursts* into tears like a rain shower. This is typical: a sudden expression of feelings, all wide-open, her vulnerable areas exposed. She does this especially when physically tired. But there appear to be other reasons as well:
- Disappointment over being denied some "thing" she wanted.
- Hurt feelings over being criticized by a peer—and especially by her mother.
- Guilt over something she did which she knew she should not have done

She cries less from "inner confusion" than she did when she was younger. She now has a specific reason for crying. Right in the middle of a sad, dramatic episode in a story or a movie she can suddenly burst into tears. But these outbursts *are* like warm, summer showers. No thunder. No lightening.

School check
If your child's teacher has not already arranged a conference with you, then you will want to do so soon. The third grade curriculum represents a big leap forward. There has been an increase in both the volume of work and the complexity.

From homework time and report cards, you have an idea of strengths and weaknesses. Do you need to help? The teacher will welcome your interest.

Don't forget to inquire about your child's personal and social adjustment. This facet of her development may be in the long run more important than grades.

A star is born!
You have a STAR, an actor in the family this year. A third grader can lose herself in her very real ability to dramatize. Last year when she observed everything about herself and everyone and spent longer, quiet times alone, she was laying a strong foundation for bringing forth those observations now. She's daring and open this year, and she's dramatic!

She readily becomes a character in the current book she is reading. She can imitate the voice and gestures of TV characters—and does it well. Her "pretend-cry" may be so realistic as to fool even you. And, her ability improves noticeably with audience response!

Girls' dramatizing is more verbal and less active than boys'. Girls like to dress-up, plan, and act out "skits". Paper-dolls also serve as the medium for expressing the dramatic urge. Listen carefully while your child plays, and you'll hear bits and pieces of "re-run" conversations from a "soap-opera" mixed in with what she overhears at home.

"Tears are the safety valve of the heart when too much pressure is laid on it."
—Albert Smith—

Testimonials:

"In a few short sentences, Growing Up answered so many questions I have been having about my child's behavior." Shirley R.

"When I became a fourth through sixth grade counselor two years ago, I continued the practice of distributing copies of Growing Up on a monthly basis. I have enjoyed reading these and have had many favorable responses from both students and parents." Paula D.

"Growing Up is great! A lot of parents just don't have this knowledge and seeing a newsletter with comments which relate to their child could make a world of difference in their parent/child relationship." Linda T

"I like the simple, easy-to-read format of Growing Up." Mary Ann H.